LEADING AND MANAGING IN THE EARLY YEARS

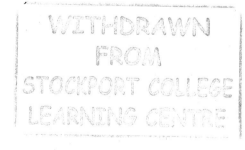

Education at SAGE

SAGE is a leading international publisher of journals, books, and electronic media for academic, educational, and professional markets.

Our education publishing includes:

- accessible and comprehensive texts for aspiring education professionals and practitioners looking to further their careers through continuing professional development

- inspirational advice and guidance for the classroom

- authoritative state of the art reference from the leading authors in the field

Find out more at: **www.sagepub.co.uk/education**

SECOND EDITION

LEADING AND MANAGING IN THE EARLY YEARS

CAROL AUBREY

Los Angeles | London | New Delhi
Singapore | Washington DC

SAGE Publications Ltd
1 Oliver's Yard
55 City Road
London EC1Y 1SP

SAGE Publications Inc.
2455 Teller Road
Thousand Oaks, California 91320

SAGE Publications India Pvt Ltd
B 1/I 1 Mohan Cooperative Industrial Area
Mathura Road
New Delhi 110 044

SAGE Publications Asia-Pacific Pte Ltd
3 Church Street
#10–04 Samsung Hub
Singapore 049483

Library of Congress Control Number: 2010939558

British Library Cataloguing in Publication data
A catalogue record for this book is available from the British
Library

ISBN 978-1-84920-754-6
ISBN 978-1-84920-755-3 (pbk)

Typeset by Dorwyn, Wells, Somerset
Printed in Great Britain by MPG Books Group, Bodmin, Cornwall
Printed on paper from sustainable resources

MIX
Paper from
responsible sources
FSC
www.fsc.org   FSC® C018575

CONTENTS

ABOUT THE AUTHOR

Carol Aubrey is Emeritus Professor of Early Childhood in the Institute of Education at the University of Warwick. She trained as a primary school teacher and then as an educational psychologist. Later, she spent a number of years in primary teacher education with a particular focus on the early years, first at University College Cardiff and then at the University of Durham where she directed the Postgraduate Certificate of Education (Primary) and for a time was Deputy Director of the School. Thereafter, from 2001, she worked at Canterbury Christ Church University where she led the Centre for International Studies in Early Childhood (CISEC). Her research interests lie in the area of the policy to practice context of early childhood care and education in national and international contexts, early learning and development, with a particular interest in early mathematics and inclusion/special educational needs. She has been convener of the British Educational Research Association (BERA) Special Interest Group for Early Childhood Care and Education and a member of the BERA Executive Council from 2004 to 2007. She was UK editor for *Journal of Early Childhood Research* from 2003–2009.

ACKNOWLEDGEMENTS

Special thanks go to the early years leaders who made this book possible: Latif Ahmed, Debbie Castle, Jill Coates, Baljit Gill, Helen Hurst, Elena Johnston, Sian Lawrence, Hilary Lorimer, Dawn Seth and Sue Webster. Also thanks go to Anne Nelson, former Chief Executive British Association for Early Childhood Education (Early Education), whose wisdom was invaluable at the time the project was originally conceived, as it proceeded and when it reached its close.

Thanks also go to our leaders who allowed us to use their photographs within this book, specifically: Debbie Castle, Jill Coates, Baljit Gill, Helen Hurst, Sian Lawrence, Hilary Lorimer and Sue Webster. Special thanks go to Karen Pearson, Teresa Kerr and Mala Razak who agreed to share some themes from their Master's practitioner research projects.

Most of the leadership research that underpinned this book took place throughout the year of 2005. The University of Warwick research team consisted of Professor Carol Aubrey as principal investigator, Professor Alma Harris, Professor Daniel Muijs (University of Manchester) and Mrs Mary Briggs as co-investigators, and Dr Sarah Dahl, Mrs Lucy Clarke and Dr Sulochini Pather as researchers. Dr Ray Godfrey, Canterbury Christ Church University, was responsible for analysing the survey data (Chapter 2). Research on multi-agency working was carried out by Carol Aubrey, Sarah Dahl and Lucy Clarke over the period 2003 to 2006. Sarah Dahl and Lucy Clarke were responsible for analysing survey and interview data (Chapter 7). The book draws upon two specific sources: a British Educational Research Association (BERA) symposium paper (Aubrey et al., 2006) and a research report (Dahl and Aubrey, 2005).

FOREWORD

The investigation that forms the backdrop to this book emerged from a preliminary leadership seminar hosted by the University of Warwick with local early childhood leaders. It began at a time when early childhood and leadership had never been higher on the English national agenda. The range of leaders we worked with were responding to this agenda in a variety of settings in their local contexts. Their settings were all unique but firmly embedded in the development of children's centres, integrated services and extended schools.

The leaders in the study took the opportunity to reflect upon their leadership practice. They reviewed the challenges of an external change agenda that was running at a faster pace than internal organizational change. The activity of videoing 'A day in the life' had simple beginnings but proved to have a powerful impact on the leaders. Their own self-evaluation and the dialogue with interviewers and peer professionals provided them with opportunities to reflect on their successes and to identify areas for development. It was very apparent that the opportunity to reflect on and self-evaluate in a supportive climate is not available to many leaders. Where successful mentoring was provided within the organization or externally, leaders were in a more powerful position to move forward and respond to the demanding challenges of their roles.

Through the continuing support of the University of Warwick we are able to share the outcomes of the study with a wider group. We offer it as a means of support and challenge to our current early childhood leaders and to those who aspire to succeed them. As one who no longer works on a day-to-day basis with children, I would like to express my admiration for our early childhood leaders who have overseen and implemented *the revolution*. Our youngest children deserve the best leaders to prepare them for the challenges they will face as they move forward into adulthood.

Anne Nelson
Formerly Chief Executive of the British Association for Early Childhood
Education (Early Education)

INTRODUCTION TO THE SECOND EDITION

It may seem strange to be revisiting definitions of leadership, management and administration when a book focused on leading and managing reaches its second edition. Nevertheless, as Handy (1999) pointed out, organizations are micro-societies and those who lead them have to understand the needs and motivations of people who work in them. At the same time, those who lead do so with the tacit agreement of those who follow, and this raises issues of power, influence and the working of groups.

Ten years ago Handy (1999: 96) was suggesting that leadership as a topic had a 'rather dated air about it' as he revisited trait theories (that relate to characteristics of the leader), style theories (that normally operate on the authoritarian–democratic dimension) and contingency theories (that take account of other variables in the leadership situation, in particular the task, work group and position of the leader within that group) that, in the final analysis, he regarded as failing to explain sufficiently the difference between effective and ineffective leadership. He proposed an extension of the contingency theory called 'best fit approach' that took account of the style preference of leader and followers, and the demands of the task that might range from tight or structured to flexible and supportive that 'fitted' the environment or organizational setting. This clearly locates leadership within a set of dynamic and reciprocal relationships and requires a core set of practices or activities. Hence, as noted by Rodd (1996: 126) a typology of an early childhood leader will include qualities, skills, roles and responsibilities. Ebbeck and Waniganayake (2000) proposed that each of these areas could be applied to administration, management and leadership.

Nivala (2002), however, has suggested that there is no overall agreement as to how notions of early childhood leadership, management and administration should be defined. Different theories have advanced, different values espoused, different practices have emerged and discourses have been generated in order to articulate these. Indeed, roles and responsibilities of early years professionals have been redefined and explored afresh by many different writers, and since the first edition of this book was published there has been a crop of new explorations of early childhood leadership, for example, Jones and Pound

(2008); Moyles (2006); Siraj-Blatchford and Manni (2006) and a third edition of Rodd (2006).

What stands out as most salient to changes in early childhood leadership in the twenty-first century, however, are the effects of globalization. On the one hand, there is an increasing diversity of young children and their families through migration, change and breakdown in traditional family structures, adverse effects of poverty and disadvantage, who comprise the client groups. On the other hand, there are continual changes to organized work that is becoming less stable and less fixed, with virtual collaborative teams and knowledge communities linked electronically to the means of production and global markets. Inevitably in these conditions traditional views of leadership and management give way to a distributive leadership model (Waniganayake, 2000) in which children's centres may be virtual, with professional knowledge at the centre that is shared and made explicit, and leadership located at the confluence of multiple spheres of activity.

Carol Aubrey

GLOSSARY

Children's centres provide multi-agency services that are intended to be flexible and meet the needs of young children and their families. The core offer includes integrated early learning, care, family support, health services, and outreach services to employment advice. Children's centres offer interesting models of multi-agency and partnership working. At the heart of this is high-quality learning and full daycare for children from birth.

Daycare for birth to 1-year-olds is provided for approximately 20 per cent of children, predominantly in licensed private day nurseries and with childminders. Most 1- to 3-year-olds are also in childcare provision in private day nurseries. State-funded nursery schools and reception classes are required to have children in the care of a qualified teacher. In childcare settings, staff qualifications vary, with 50 per cent in day nurseries having Level 3 qualification or above, 20 per cent with higher education qualification and 20 per cent with no qualification. Sixteen per cent of childminders are qualified to Level 3 or above (OECD, 2006), although a Childcare and Early Years Providers survey (DCSF, 2008b) revealed that this had risen to 36 per cent. Too few childcare staff have appropriate training however and high staff turnover can be a threat to children's consistent care.

Early excellence centres were set up in 1997 to develop models of good practice in integrating services for young children and families. They offer high-quality practice in 'one-stop-shop' integrated education and daycare for young children and services for parents, carers, families and the wider community both directly and in co-operation with other providers.

Extended schools set out a core offer of services that all schools were expected to provide for children to access by 2010. This includes a variety of support such as homework clubs, high-quality childcare on the school site from 8.00 a.m. to 6.00 p.m. all the year round, parenting programmes and access to a wide range of specialist support services such as speech therapy or intensive behaviour support, as well as adult learning and recreational facilities for the wider community.

Foundation stage units are intended for nursery and reception-aged children (5-year-olds in the first year of formal schooling) where practitioners work on

what has been a distinctive 'early years foundation stage' phase (for birth to 5-year-olds) to an agreed pedagogical approach. Nursery- and reception-aged groups combine to form an integrated teaching and learning provision across the foundation stage age range.

Integrated centre is a generic term that refers to local facilities delivering integrated early education and childcare for children under 5 years along with parent and family support services, health services, links to job opportunities and a base for childminders. It refers to settings such as early excellence centres, family centres, and voluntary and private provision, all of which now form the basis for Sure Start children's centre developments.

Neighbourhood nurseries were introduced in 2001 to narrow the gap in childcare provision between the most and least disadvantaged areas of the country. The aim was to create new high-quality, accessible and affordable, full daycare places for children under 5 in the poorest areas of England that previously had little or no daycare.

Nurseries may be of various kinds. Some nurseries are run by voluntary or community groups. Others are run by employers or local authorities. They provide full daycare, education and play for children up to 5 years and may be open from 8.00 a.m. until 6.00 p.m. There are also nursery and reception classes attached to or within primary schools (see foundation stage units above). Nurseries aim to provide the best possible start to children's education by providing a broad and balanced early years foundation stage curriculum that lays the foundation for reaching their potential when they reach statutory school age.

Sure Start local programmes were first announced in 1998. Their location was in areas of deprivation but they were not confined to poor families. They expanded on an annual basis from 2000, and in 2004 it was announced that in order to 'mainstream' the programme to all children, there would be 2,500 by 2008 and, a little later, 3,500 by 2010. The programmes brought together in a 'joined up' way, core programmes of child and maternal health, early education and play, and family support for under 4s. There was an emphasis on outreach to access 'hard-to-reach' families and autonomy for local projects to add extra services. They were locally administered by partnerships between the statutory agencies (local authorities and primary care trusts) and the voluntary and private sectors.

Note that all 3- and 4-year-olds are entitled to 15 hours of free early education for 38 weeks of the year from 2010. This applies until they reach compulsory school age (the term following their fifth birthday).

INTRODUCTION: THEORIZING LEADERSHIP IN EARLY CHILDHOOD

This chapter outlines the current national and international context to early childhood leadership. It introduces key concepts in the field in order to link early childhood leadership to broader theories in a changing world.

Background

Over the past few years there has been growing interest in concepts of leadership in early childhood (for example, Bloom et al., 1991; Hayden, 1996; Kagan and Bowman, 1997; Rodd, 1999). Initially these concepts often tended to focus on traits and characteristics, roles and responsibilities as well as specific leadership, management and administrative skills or behaviours. Indeed, debates have been conducted on the distinctions to be made between present-oriented management and future-oriented leadership (Bloom, 1997; Rodd, 1996). In many ways such studies represented very traditional approaches to leadership in the questions that they raised, for instance, about the extent to which leadership qualities and skills are innate or nurtured through training, associated with the person or the position (Waniganiyake et al., 2000). Historically, such approaches are located within organizational development theory, such as traits theories, style theories (for example, autocratic or democratic), contingency (or situational) theories and, more recently, the 'best fit' approach that takes account of leader, followers, task and environment (Handy, 1999).

As Blackmore (1989) has emphasized, however, organizational theorists have also characterized leadership by masculine traits of aggression, competition and independence. At the same time, in the course of investigating women administrators in the United States of America (USA), Shakeshaft (1989) contrasted this 'male-based knowledge' with research on women's leadership that focused on collaboration, power-sharing, caring and relationships. Hall (1996) on English women school leaders revealed an organizational culture of trust, openness and commitment. While Court (1994) in the New Zealand context, also built a picture of women in leadership positions who 'empowered' or shared power with others and created organizational cultures based on collaboration, communication and shared decision-making. Shakeshaft (1989) attributed women leaders' consultative, nurturing and non-hierarchical culture to Gilligan's (1982) 'ethic of caring' that contrasted sharply with ideas of 'male' competition, individualism and independence. As feminist perspectives on leadership are particularly illuminative of early childhood leadership, there is a danger in too closely associating characteristics of leadership with masculine or feminine values and qualities that leads both to stereotyping women and alienating nurturing men.

Scrivens (2002) from New Zealand, in a powerful and comprehensive overview of female constructions of leadership, suggested that there is still a lack of awareness of leadership concepts at the level of individual early childhood leaders who remain bound to male-oriented ideas of leadership and need to acquire wider frames of reference in order to think more clearly about leadership theory that confirms and validates their experience. Reay and Ball (2000) meanwhile have suggested that women behave in a supportive and caring manner at work largely because they are trapped in low-status and low-paid jobs that seldom demand competitive ways of working.

Kagan and Bowman (1997) from the USA have noted a general reluctance of early childhood leaders to identify leadership as part of their professional role and a slowness in understanding and interpreting findings and theories from other fields, for instance, business management, school leadership or women in education. Traditional notions of leadership vested in key characteristics or attributes, roles and responsibilities, power, hierarchy and influence of one person or position, rooted in a capacity to create vision and moral purpose, give direction and demonstrate effectiveness, presuppose a set of desired leadership traits, a stable set of skills and behaviours operating in a relatively unchanging environment. As noted by Kagan and Hallmark (2001: 8) such theory fails to take account of multiple, shared or joint leadership emerging in contemporary theory and has less to say to early childhood leaders of 'smaller, more people-oriented and informal programs'.

Changing world, changing theories

More recently, comparative perspectives on early childhood leadership in five countries (Australia, Finland, England, Russia and the USA) have extended understandings and opened up fresh theoretical discussions about the early childhood leadership phenomenon in relation to context and culture (Hujala and Puroila, 1998; Nivala and Hujala, 2002). Their International Leadership Project (ILP) identified a need to understand and describe early childhood leadership in a very broad context. From this perspective, Nivala (2002: 15) argued that the contextual model of leadership is a theoretical model which 'defines the structural framework of the factors and actors related to leadership and leading'. The context model is based upon Bronfenbrenner's (1979) ecological theory and draws attention to the operating environments of leadership that range from the circle closest to the leader (at the micro level) to the societal values and institutional structures that define leadership (at the macro level). Between these lie the meso level that constitutes the interaction or co-operation between micro levels and the exo level between micro and macro levels having an indirect effect on leadership. This model allows consideration of intercultural similarities and differences in the leadership phenomenon at a number of levels, as well as the incorporation of other theoretical orientations, for example, Giddens's (1984) structuration theory, Berger and Luckman's (1966) social construction of reality, the situated cognition of Rogoff (1984) and 'action' as described in activity theory (Engeström, 1999). From this perspective, leadership is 'conceptualised as a situational, socially constructed and interpretative phenomenon' (Hujala and Puroila, 1998: 8). It does not reside in the leader but has to be examined in relation to social interaction in the setting, the local community as well as a wider social and cultural context. Thus, leadership will need to be considered from the perspective of the followers as much as from the perspective of the leader (Gronn and Ribbins, 1996). What the ILP represents for early childhood leadership in all its multidimensionality is a real expansion of the theoretical and methodological questions being asked and research approaches being utilized.

Bennis (1999) has identified wider globalizing trends and influences on leadership. In describing a world in which political and technological complexity and change encourage collaboration and teamwork, he has also called for an end to traditional leadership or what he describes as 'exemplary leadership': 'a shrinking world in which technology and political complexities increase at an accelerating rate offers fewer and fewer arenas in which individual action, top-down leadership, suffices. The source for effective change is the workforce in creative alliance with top leadership' (Bennis, 1999: 71). His view is that post-bureaucratic organizations evolving into federations, networks, clusters, cross-functional teams and temporary systems need a new kind of alliance between leaders and the led, and a new and more indirect form of influence for leaders to be effective. In other words, leaders will have to learn an entirely new set of skills that are neither understood nor taught in business schools and, hence, rarely practised. In this 'new reality', intellectual capital rather than capital – 'brain power, know-how human imagination' – will be used as the criterion for success.

In line with current perspectives on organizations, Rost (1991; 1993) has described leadership as a dynamic relationship that is located within a group of people, leaders and collaborators working together to generate change. The leadership relationship in this context is one of influence in two directions:

leaders influencing collaborators and collaborators influencing leaders, with change that is effected reflecting the purposes of both parties. Gronn (2000) has argued that from this perspective leaders are actually more dependent upon followers than followers upon leaders. Thus the focus of leadership should be followership, followers' minds and social networks. Spillane et al. (2001) have created a framework for considering effective leadership by identifying not just the tasks completed and the actions taken, but also the influence of other people and the interactions within an organization. This 'distributed' perspective focuses on the processes of leadership as a complex relationship operating in specific social and situational contexts. It serves to underscore the importance of leadership in the early childhood field being recalibrated in line with current thought.

The world of social, economic and technological change that Bennis indicated, and characterized by Giddens (1990; 1991) as 'late modernity', is one that is destabilizing traditional family forms, school and work life, including the institutional arrangements made for early childhood, the social relationships within them and even the young children themselves. At the same time, we still have a traditionally highly structured work environment for early childhood leaders that takes too little account of the complex, contradictory and diverse demands inside and outside the contemporary work environment. As Ebbeck and Waniganayake (2003: 33) have concluded, there is a need to reassess leadership theories that address contemporary challenges in a changing and globalized world, and much to be gained from looking at advances in theory and research across disciplines: 'This provides new orientations or filtration systems against which to test our own views and beliefs about any aspect of knowledge and skills relevant to early childhood.'

Waniganayake (2000) has proposed the distributed early childhood leadership model with organizational learning at the centre and the possibility of more than one leader within the organizational setting or even multiple leaders or specialists within an early childhood centre who are experts in one area or expertise or domain of operation. As she noted, for leadership to work in the organizational context, all these leaders need to work together, in order to plan in a cohesive and strategic manner this participatory and decentralized approach. Given the rapidly changing societal context, it is argued that a distributed leadership model that relies on building relationships through existing knowledge and empowerment based on competence is a way forward. By these means, leadership emerges through creating a culture of learning and shared knowledge in collaborative ways.

Our leadership investigation

This was the international early childhood leadership context as our own early childhood leadership study in England was first being planned with a group of local leaders keen to explore leadership and willing to interrogate their own practice. A corresponding interest in studying early childhood leadership came from a team of four researchers, themselves representing a variety of interests and perspectives on early childhood leadership from school effectiveness to distributed leadership, from early childhood education to early learning and development in diverse and inclusive contexts, and working with multi-agency teams at the national and international level. What made the contemporary English context of such interest was the rapidly changing nature of the early childhood field, the sheer number of policy developments across the early childhood field over the previous few years and the particular emphasis being placed upon working together across agency boundaries to respond to the needs of children, families and the community. However, while the study itself was being undertaken at a time of great change, the challenge for the professionals involved remained the same – how better to work together in order to address more effectively the needs of young children and their families. For the researchers, the challenge was how best to capture the relationship between this context of great social, cultural and economic change, the leadership work itself and the dynamic interaction among participating staff in a set of diverse early childhood settings, its nature and significance.

▶ Asked where their ideas of leadership came from, our leaders and their staff held a range of views. Leaders were more likely to distinguish between learning informally from experience and formally from academic study. Their staff were less likely to have had formal training and more inclined to stress experience and personal qualities.

Practitioners' views I.1

Leaders' views concerning ideas about leadership:

- I didn't have a notion of leadership when it started. The first year was difficult. People had expectations of me as a leader. It was quite lonely. Where do you go? I was not sure who I should ask. I went on induction for leaders and did 'Headlamp' training for new heads. I contacted the University of Warwick for an MA in leadership then completed the MA with a module on leadership and management.
- Ideas of leadership came from observing other people, working with senior managers who provided role models (good and bad) and having direct links with assistant directors in previous jobs ... plus academic courses, my MBA for instance.
- Ideas of leadership came from a local two-year course 'Management in the Early Years' before I came into this job but it's only in the last few years that I have begun to consider leadership and management.
- I think my idea of leadership has developed from the nature of the job ...

(Continued)

(Continued)

- Well, I think that you just pick and choose the bits of management theory that suit your workplace, your environment and your team.
- You've got management skills, experience and qualifications ... it's a transferable experience you are utilizing in your decision-making otherwise what is the point of learning if you are not applying? I think the process is that you assess situations and you apply all the available resources ... and then you say ... to my best knowledge and my best judgement ...

Practitioners' views I.2

Views of staff concerning ideas of leadership:

- My idea of leadership came from theory and the practice of being in a leadership role. You have to be a different leader in different circumstances. Your workforce helps you develop as a leader.
- My idea of leadership has come from Chris (the head teacher) and Hilary (foundation stage leader) and experience. Different people have different skills. Hilary has a strong vision for leadership, a passion, an inspiration.
- Ideas of leadership are developed from the situations you find yourself in and experience, if you are confident in an area you are working in.
- Ideas of leadership come from experience of other leaders and how they manage people.

CHAPTER ONE

THE EARLY CHILDHOOD LEADERS' AGENDA

This chapter explains the main purpose of this book, its rationale and its structure. It identifies the starting points and key questions to be addressed: what do we know already; what leadership research applies; and what do we need to know? It also outlines what each chapter seeks to do.

1.1 Introduction

This book is about early childhood leadership in England at a time of great change, with young children and their families a high priority within national debate and plans in train for high-quality integrated children's services at national, local authority and community level. Our hope is that it will also make a contribution to the international debate about new constructs of early childhood leadership. By introducing new and emerging forms of interprofesssional leadership, new realities for the field will emerge and the knowledge base will expand. The Green Paper *Every Child Matters* (DfES, 2003a) and the subsequent *Children Act* (DfES, 2004a) had the overall aim to improve outcomes for all children through the reconfiguration of mainstream services around children and families. Key themes included strong foundations in the early years; a stronger focus on parenting and families; earlier interventions and effective protection for vulnerable and 'at risk' children; better accountability and integration of services locally, regionally and nationally; and reform of the workforce. The five outcomes for children that services should help them to achieve were:

• being healthy, that is enjoying good physical and mental health and living a healthy lifestyle;
• staying safe, that is being protected from harm and neglect;
• enjoying and achieving, that is getting the most out of life and developing skills for adulthood;
• making a positive contribution to the community and society and not engaging in antisocial or offending behaviour; and
• economic well-being, that is, being protected from economic disadvantage that might jeopardize life chances and achieving full potential.

The 10-year childcare strategy *Choice for Parents, the Best Start for Children* (HMT, 2004) and the *Childcare Act* (DfES, 2006a) to implement this policy built upon the Green Paper (DfES, 2003a) and *Children Act* (DfES, 2004a) with the aim to help deliver the outcomes by providing long-term goals and clear direction. Indeed, as the research that underpins this book was being carried out, local authorities were reforming their education and social services to create integrated children's services, with children's centres and extended schools being introduced by the leaders taking part in this study, a common assessment framework and an integrated workforce strategy, and a common core of training was being introduced together with a new integrated inspection framework for the early years developed by the Office for Standards in Education (OFSTED).

The Labour government had stated its commitment to eliminate child poverty by 2020 as a high priority. This led to a policy agenda from 1997 that has generated a national childcare strategy in 1998 (DfEE, 1998) that included expansion of nursery education and childcare from birth to 14 years and generated a programme of so-called Sure Start local programmes and early excellence centres, as well as a programme of neighbourhood nurseries. Also established was the 'foundation stage' as a distinct phase of early education for children aged from 3 years to the end of reception year in school (for 5-year-olds). As well as the *Curriculum Guidance for the Foundation Stage* (QCA, 2000), a *Birth to Three Matters* (DfES, 2003b) guidance framework had been introduced for all practitioners working with children under 3 years and now a single *Early Years Foundation Stage* framework (DfES, 2007) is unifying guidance from birth to 6 years, taking as a starting point the five outcomes set out above. The first ever *Children's Plan* (DCSF, 2007b) was published, setting out the future for children's services, with a vision of change to make England the best place in the world for children and young people to grow up in. The needs and wishes of families were to be placed first, with clear steps set out to make every child matter. This included an expansion of free early education places and an increase in the number of graduate early years professionals.

The agenda for change in early childhood services is complex and leadership across the sector, with children 3 to 5 years in private, voluntary and state provision, is critical to the quality of children's experience. Key findings from the Effective Provision of Preschool Education (EPPE) study (Sylva et al., 2004) indicated that settings integrating education with care provided the best quality and that there was a high correlation between well-qualified staff and better outcomes for children. All this argues for early childhood leaders who not only run effective, safe and caring environments, but who are also leaders of high-quality early education, care and development.

1.2 Context

Our focus is on early childhood leadership practice that is intended to make education, care and development more effective. To be useful, it will be both practical, in giving concrete details and examples of leadership practice, and principled, in the sense of providing a basis in both evidence and theory to underpin the practicalities. The endeavour arose from skilled early childhood leaders collaborating with researchers working in a university, with expertise in the area of gathering evidence and theory. The experiences, evidence and analysis provided by these leaders was an essential resource for this work. For this reason, we are assured that other leaders will take seriously and benefit from our leaders' experience. We have also benefited from the wisdom of Professor Viviane Robinson who reminded us of the need to redirect attention to effective educational leadership research so that we made stronger connections with learning, pedagogy and assessment and fewer links to 'generic' leadership skills. As she pointed out (Robinson, 2006: 63), generic leadership research provides important guidance about the influences and processes involved in leadership, and about the character and dispositions required to exercise the particular influence we call leadership:

> it provides little or none of the knowledge-base needed to answer questions about the direction or purpose of the influence attempt. In short, while generic leadership research can inform us about *how* to influence, and about the values that should inform the influence process (e.g. democratic, authoritative, emancipatory), it is silent about *what* the focus of the influence attempt should be.

She cited Firestone and Riehl (2005: 2) who recalled that:

> in the past educational leaders were judged routinely on their effectiveness in managing fiscal, organizational and political conditions … New leaders are increasingly being held accountable for the actual performance of those under their charge with a growing expectation that leaders can and should influence learning. Hence it is important to understand how leadership, learning and equity are linked.

This indicates the clear need to identify what effective early childhood practices and outcomes are – a theme to which we shall return.

1.3 What do we know already?

As Anne Nelson noted in the Foreword, the collaboration to be described here grew out of a leadership seminar jointly planned and presented by the University of Warwick and the local authority, that brought together researchers and 25 local early childhood leaders, identified by Anne, the local early childhood adviser, as exemplifying effective practitioners. These represented the full range of foundation stage provision thus involving private day nurseries, through voluntary daycare and foundation stage units in primary schools, to Sure Start programmes and an early excellence centre (now all designated as integrated children's centres).

Our starting point crystallized around three questions – what do we know already; what existing leadership research applies; and what do we need to know? The first two questions allowed the practitioners and researchers to pool their current knowledge before considering what the next stage of their joint investigation should be. The first stage of the process was to gather views on early childhood leadership. In order to achieve this end, the leaders were invited to consider five key questions:

- What does leadership mean in your setting?
- What factors contribute to the effectiveness of this role?
- What factors hinder the effective fulfilment of this role?
- What are your staff training needs?
- How can we build knowledge, skills and capacity in the field?

Participants worked in groups that allowed leaders at a similar phase of professional development and relevant experience to collaborate. Each group provided a written record of their discussion and then these accounts were analysed in order to identify key themes, issues and surprises.

Leadership in your setting

First, in terms of what leadership meant to the variety of leaders present in the diversity of settings represented, was having a clear vision and working towards this. Thinking strategically was emphasized and this was described as understanding the foci and direction that early childhood education was taking as well as the issues involved, in other words, awareness of the wider political, social and educational context. It also meant raising the profile of early years education and care and developing a shared philosophy. Fundamental to this was the recognition of its multidisciplinary nature. A central goal was valuing learning and having a commitment to ongoing professional development was important to this aspiration. In terms of generic leadership skills, having appropriate role models who had the ability to inspire, to motivate and communicate was emphasized.

Factors contributing to the effectiveness of this role

Second, in terms of factors contributing to the effectiveness of the leadership role, the ability to promote early years across a range of agencies and interest groups – the senior management team, staff, parents, governors and the wider professional community – was prerequisite. Stability in leadership with a firm commitment to working towards specific outcomes was regarded as the basis for this. Commitment to continuing professional development and support of staff was thought to contribute to effective leadership. Moreover, it was felt that effective leadership was underpinned by a range of skills that included confidence to empower, enable and delegate, motivation and enthusiasm, willingness to celebrate existing achievements, communication and listening, mediation and negotiation skills.

Factors hindering the effective fulfilment of this role

Third, in respect of factors hindering fulfilment of the leadership role, it was felt that there was a real lack of clarity at the national level about the foundation stage that has been in a state of change and development over several years. It was believed that a lack of status for the early years led to education for this age group being generally regarded as 'easy' and something that any professional could do. Lack of knowledge about early childhood was characteristic at all levels, from senior management teams, governors, local authority advisers, inspectors and trainee teachers. It was felt that for early childhood staff working in school settings, this could also lead to isolation and low levels of responsibility. Lack of status, it was thought, was reflected in a general lack of resourcing in terms of staffing, lack of time for planning, management training and professional development.

Staff training needs

Fourth, a need for accreditation of early childhood leadership and management at varying levels with appropriate funding was identified. Training, it was thought, should comprise knowledge of the principles, capabilities and skills of leadership. Theory and knowledge about early childhood education and care, current legislation and initiatives was regarded as important. The development of skills in devising and writing policy and design of the curriculum was regarded as important, as well as development of staff appraisal in whatever form (selection, recruitment, training, one-to-one observation, mentoring and 'moving staff on'). Effective communication skills for a variety of audiences, building and maintaining positive relationships and effective conflict management were also thought essential.

Building capacity in the field

Finally, how could new knowledge, skills and capacity be built in the field? National acknowledgement and recognition of the need for accreditation of training for early childhood leadership with identified funding streams for training and training the trainers was proposed. The need for trainers who knew the early childhood field in terms of knowledge and experience was emphasized. At the local level, cluster-group meetings with direct early childhood leadership training, support and advice was proposed, as was more time to reflect. Setting up networks and mentoring systems across the sector was also recommended. A need for an awareness of and links to existing National College of School Leadership (NCSL) programmes was indicated and, in particular, opportunities to have access to courses such as the new National Professional Qualification in Integrated Centre Leadership (NPQICL) programme (Whalley et al., 2004, together with the NCSL, DfES, 2007c) that was currently available only to children's centre leaders and deputies. It was clear that those present felt there were distinct training and development needs in the early childhood leadership field. The workshop also identified the need for a more systematic review of the formal knowledge base associated with early childhood leadership.

It seems clear from early childhood leaders' own accounts that they believed there to be generic leadership and management skills and practical applications that transferred across sectors. At the same time, valuing learning was at the heart of the process, with a related commitment to ongoing professional development. This highlights the need to move beyond theories, models and skills of leadership to test leadership impact on outcomes for children (Leithwood and Jantzi, 2005; Leithwood and Louis, 1998; Silins and Mulford, 2002). Indeed, an evidence-based review (Bell et al., 2003) has revealed the limited evidence of links between leadership and the processes of teaching and learning. The challenge for early childhood leaders, moreover, is to manage the challenge of increasing provision available while ensuring that high quality is maintained. The *Childcare Act* (DfES, 2006a) requires additional services, promising a children's centre in every community but with no additional resources. The challenge of recruiting, training and 'moving staff on' by the very leaders who will have responsibility for driving forward the new agenda is underlined. These leaders have the major responsibility for promoting outcomes related to health and safety, personal, social and emotional well-being as well as learning from 3 to 6 years and increasingly from birth to 6 years. All this is to be achieved in centres that demand well-trained staff with a variety of professional backgrounds in order to meet the diverse needs of both young children and parents. For the private and voluntary sector leaders there is the added tension of balancing affordability and sustainability.

This section of the chapter has focused on what leaders knew already and it has begun to consider what sort of leadership research applies, which is the topic for the next section.

1.4 What leadership research applies?

A lack of research

Despite the apparent lack of evidence for impact of leadership on learning outcomes, the influence of leadership has been described by Hallinger and Heck (1998) and Leithwood et al. (2004) as modest, though by Marzano et al. (2005) as quite substantial. Moreover, effective leadership has been accepted as a key constituent for achieving organizational improvement (Harris et al., 2002; Van Velzen et al., 1985). That said, a review of the early childhood leadership literature by the research team (Muijs et al., 2004) identified a scarcity of early childhood leadership research despite the high potential for activity in the field. There is a clear need to identify what effective leadership practice is in terms of processes and outcomes within the field of early childhood education and care, and within integrated children's centres. Theoretically based studies that allow different models and characteristics to be empirically tested are long overdue. Apart from the new NPQICL, open only to children's centre leaders and deputies, there is a serious lack of leadership development highlighted in the literature, which means many early childhood leaders can be significantly under-prepared for their complex leadership role. A few early childhood leaders with senior management responsibilities within the school as a whole may, if they wish, be able to pursue the National Professional Qualification for Head Teachers.

The nature of existing research

Overall, research on early childhood leadership is dominated by a relatively small number of researchers (for instance, Bloom, 1997; 2000; Rodd, 1996; 1997; 1999). Much of the literature is anecdotal and in some cases barely rises above the level of 'tips for leaders'. There may be reluctance to engage with concepts of leadership (Bloom and Sheerer, 1992; Osgood, 2003; Rodd, 1996). In most English-speaking countries, relatively few people have both early childhood and leadership skills (Bricker, 2000). Australian studies (in Victoria) have found that early childhood leaders have a narrow view of their role and feel discomforted by the management aspect of work (Rodd, 1996). Increased accountability and financial constraints in the sector as well as increased competition and frequent government policy changes demand a sophisticated leadership response (Hayden, 1997; Rodd, 1997). Literature in this area is not well informed by theory and research. Such theorizing as occurs is limited in scope and mostly does not connect with key concepts in educational, public sector or business leadership (Kagan and Hallmark, 2001). One reason may be the complexity of the field, characterized by a great diversity of institutions, state, private and voluntary. Rodd (1999) suggested that many women have difficulty in identifying with the concept of and need for leadership in the sector and that leadership styles used are very different from those used by male leaders. Other studies (Coleman, 2001; Evetts, 1994), however, offer no evidence for sex differences in leadership style.

Leadership is associated with quality provision

Leadership has been identified as a key element of quality provision (Hayden, 1997; Rodd, 1997; Stipek and Ogana, 2000). A number of studies have found that organizational climate is strongly influenced by the quality of leadership (Teddlie and Reynolds, 2000), with lower levels of staff turnover being associated with their involvement in decision-making (Whelan, 1993). In the early childhood field, job satisfaction levels have been found to be higher in settings with an open climate (Bloom, 1997). A high-quality work environment has been found to be related to lower levels of staff turnover, which in turn have been related to children's scores on child development and social and emotional scales in an Australian study (Hayden, 1997). In one US evaluation of Head Start programmes, committed, competent and respected leadership was found to exert a powerful influence on programme effectiveness. Leaders with less experience, less skill at training and supervising staff, in working with schools and the community, and less involved and committed, were associated with less successful programmes (Ramey et al., 2000). Indeed, leaders' experience has been related to centre quality in a number of studies (Kontos and Fine, 1989; Philips et al., 1987) as has the educational level of directors (Bloom and Sheerer, 1992; Sylva et al., 2004). A New Zealand study found that managers were often older and had worked for longer in the organization than other staff with a relatively low level of higher-education qualifications (Croll, 1993).

Roles and responsibilities of leaders

Much of the existing literature on early childhood leaders has focused on the multiplicity of roles they assume and their context-specific nature (Bloom, 2000). One English study of 79 early childhood managers identified the most common roles (Rodd, 1997). Of note was the focus on maintenance rather than development, that is, management rather than leadership function. A New Zealand early childhood project, defined leadership as having a vision, being able to articulate this vision in practice, strengthening links between the centre and the community, developing a community of learners, community advocacy and giving children leadership (Hatherley and Lee, 2003). Rodd (1999) noted that as well as influencing the behaviour of staff and planning and implementing change, a strong emphasis on working with and guiding parents was important in early childhood leadership. While Kagan and Hallmark (2001) suggested a number of early childhood leadership forms: community leadership; pedagogical leadership; administrative leadership; advocacy leadership; and conceptual leadership. Thus, many types of leadership and training may be required. Mitchell (1989) suggested that effective early childhood leaders needed to focus on the entire family, be strong communicators with parents and be able to liaise with a variety of organizations. Kunesh and Farley (1993) recognized the importance of the co-ordination role between family and community.

A lack of effectiveness studies

There appear to be few case studies of effective leaders or quantitative analyses of characteristics against effectiveness measures. Bloom (2000) suggested that early childhood leaders needed to be competent in the knowledge of group dynamics, organizational theory, child development and teaching strategies; technical, human and conceptual skills; and attitudes, including moral purpose. Rodd (1996) noted that professionals' views of early childhood leadership had become more mainstream in comparison with earlier studies. It should be noted, however, that a large number of these studies are not recent and, as such, might anyway have limited relevance in the present English context. A New Zealand study of early childhood managers identified a discrepancy between the managerial tasks carried out and the leadership tasks thought important (Bloom, 1997). Managers reported that staff were provided with a great deal of feedback on relationships and communication though they felt that this was not reciprocated. A more recent study by Carter (2000), however, suggested that teachers did not regard such support from their managers as important.

A lack of leadership development

The lack of early childhood leadership development programmes contrasts with counterparts in primary and secondary schools (Freeman and Brown, 2000). Interviews with professionals in Victoria indicated that most felt that leadership development and training would be useful (Rodd, 1996). A survey of 257 early childhood directors reported that they had received no prior development on leadership and management with 70 per cent feeling ill-prepared (Bloom and Sheerer, 1997). Other US studies have reported a lack of training (Caruso, 1991). Many English early childhood leaders have likewise received little management development and feel uncomfortable with professional development aspects of their role (Kagan and Bowman, 1997). A survey of 201 Australian early childhood directors found that less than half had received any management subjects in initial development and, although 49 per cent had done some in-service training related to leadership and management, 20 per cent felt that they were not prepared at all (Hayden, 1997). Early childhood directors claimed training was best delivered once they were already working in the job and were positive about its benefits (Rodd, 1997). Peer support was also seen as crucial in promoting growth and maintaining motivation (Poster and Neugebauer, 1998).

To date most reported early childhood development programmes have been small scale and localized (Bloom and Sheerer, 1992; Eisenberg and Rafanello, 1998; Mitchell and Serranen, 2000). Bloom (1997) identified a three-phase model of career stages, as beginning, competent and 'master' directors. This suggests that while there should be dedicated programmes incorporating basic elements of early childhood leadership and management at the beginning level, more differentiated programmes are needed at the competent level with coaching, mentoring and emphasis on transfer of knowledge and expertise at the 'master' level.

This section has examined existing early childhood leadership research and theory and the limited extent to which it provides high-quality information on how to raise the impact of leadership on child outcomes. This paved the way for addressing the third question – what do we need to know or find out?

1.5 What do we need to know?

Chapter 2, 3 and 4 form the heart of this book. Chapter 2 surveys the perspectives on early childhood leadership of nearly 200 practitioners. These were not only notions that leaders themselves held, but represented the views of staff throughout the organization, thus taking into account implicit models of leadership that existed at all levels within the setting and indeed the sector. It has been noted by Alban-Metcalfe and Alimo-Metcalfe (2000) that, where leaders' notions of leadership dominate, these notions may have no face validity with the population of practitioners in those settings. Chapter 3 then drills in more depth into the nature of day-to-day roles, responsibilities and characteristics of leaders and staff, their culture and collaborative team decision-making, the internal and external facilitators and barriers to their work. Chapter 4 then considers what precisely early childhood leaders do and what their daily tasks actually comprise. It follows leaders into their settings drawing on video records and diary reports. It introduces the major dimensions of leadership, management and administration in the context of roles, responsibilities, skills, qualities and dispositions, and uncovers the marked differences across the early childhood sector in the deployment of these key elements. Chapter 5 examines in more depth leaders' mixed and contradictory attitudes towards business and entrepreneurial skills.

Chapter 6 considers the journeys of individual leaders into leadership and explores the development of competence from beginning to 'master' leader. Chapter 7 introduces the leader as mentor and guide. Chapter 8 focuses on the particular challenge of leading multidisciplinary teams. Chapter 9 concentrates on leading in the context of change and the type of leadership that may be required. Chapter 10 picks up on and amplifies the many references to reflective learning by considering the use of action research by leaders. Finally, Chapter 11 reviews our starting points and reflects on the outcomes. Those interested primarily in practical applications may want to start with the questions and activities in the appendices that serve to stimulate discussion and analysis of leadership in different early childhood contexts. The Introduction, this chapter, Chapters 9, 10 and 11 help the reader to see the developments of early childhood leadership from a more theoretical and research-based perspective, although all chapters draw upon leaders' work in their own settings.

▶ Our leaders were asked what topics they would like to have included in an early childhood leadership seminar series. The most frequently requested topics were leadership, mentoring and curriculum development.

Practitioners' views 1.1

With respect to leadership, suggestions were as follows:

- Provide a year-long programme for early years leadership similar to primary leadership.
- Modules for leadership from the university to gain a qualification.
- Strategies for good leadership.
- Leadership techniques and management styles.
- Look at ways to reassess the impact of leadership styles on quality services for children.
- More in-depth exploration around the leadership and management role.
- Team-building, positive staff relationships, managing conflict.
- Policy and procedures to improve and implement changes.
- Consider who leads the leaders, how do we get leadership support at all levels?
- Recruitment and retention.
- Leadership in the global context.
- Network meetings for senior staff to talk 'off the record' about any of their concerns.
- Reading groups, booklists, references to documents and studies would be useful.

Practitioners' views 1.2

With respect to mentoring, suggestions were as follows:

- Mentoring skills and knowledge.
- Mentoring and supervision reviews.
- Mentor training.
- Further information on mentoring.
- Working together, accessing contact numbers for services that can support and what services are available.
- Mentors … more information please, we all need one!
- Where we can go for support and help.
- Counselling support.

Practitioners' views 1.3

With respect to curriculum development, suggestions were as follows:

- 'Birth to five' … what is it all about; how, when and why is it changing/how can we get the best out of this?
- The new foundation stage profile.
- Up-to-date legislation for the foundation stage.
- Changing standards, OFSTED regulations.
- New changes, current issues.
- Effective planning and experiences for young children.
- Improving standards in further education through working with colleges to increase quality of childcare students.
- Different approaches – Reggio Emilia, High Scope and Montessori.
- Starting a forum.
- Quick courses, bite-sized modules or courses for practitioners.
- Speakers from private and voluntary sectors.
- Less emphasis on schools.
- Playgroups, 'wrap-around' and 'after-school' clubs.

CHAPTER TWO

LEADERSHIP IN ENGLISH EARLY CHILDHOOD EDUCATION AND CARE

This chapter surveys the perspectives on early childhood leadership of a large number of practitioners working in a variety of contexts at a number of different levels. It covers background characteristics, leadership roles and responsibilities, and challenges in the current context. It identifies differences in views of leadership between practitioners with different qualifications, professional heritages and workplaces.

2.1 Introduction

Having established with our leaders what we needed to find out, the next stage was to set ourselves some clear objectives to shape our joint investigation of early childhood leadership. We realized that given the diversity in the field it would be important to involve private, voluntary and state sector providers and represent daycare, nursery and Sure Start children's centre-integrated provision. Furthermore, as we were to look in more depth at early childhood leadership it might not be possible to involve all 25 leaders who took part in the scoping exercise outlined in Chapter 1. This led to a further focusing on 12 settings, located geographically in a Midlands city and representing the full range of early childhood provision that included:

- three private nursery and daycare settings;
- two voluntary family centres;
- four nursery and reception classes in infant and primary schools, that is the foundation stage units (for 3- to 4-year-olds);
- three integrated children's centres that provided a range of services for children from birth to 4 years, their families and the community (one former early excellence centre and two Sure Start programmes).

This meant that we had achieved a maximum variation in types of early childhood establishments in terms of size, status and complexity. We had also ensured that participants had been identified by the local early childhood adviser on the basis of high-quality leadership practice and externally endorsed on the basis of OFSTED inspection reports.

2.2 Our objectives

We then set about generating a set of objectives that took account of what we knew already about leadership and what we needed to find out. In summary, our investigation aimed to:

- identify, describe and analyse what leadership meant to key participants in early childhood settings, that is, explore implicit models and 'folk theories' of leadership practice within the full range of early years settings and at all levels within the sector;
- consider the nature of the roles, responsibilities and characteristics of leadership in early childhood settings and explore how this affected their effectiveness;
- investigate the core components and characteristics of effective early childhood leadership, its knowledge, skills, attitudes and strategic intent, that is, its vision, goals and operational objectives;
- capture early childhood leadership practice and judge how it was understood and enacted;
- explore what types of leadership development programmes or preparations were required to maximize early childhood leaders' effectiveness.

2.3 What we asked our early childhood professionals about leadership

We decided that the best way to obtain a great deal of information in the shortest possible amount of time from the widest possible range of early years practitioners was to carry out a survey. We organized our topics in the questionnaire to cover background information, leadership roles and responsibilities, leadership in the current context, and training and development needs (see Appendix 2). Care was taken to address the initial objectives that we had chosen and we also took account of other recent and relevant surveys (for instance, those of

Bloom, 1997; Rodd, 1996; 1997; and Waniganayake et al., 2000) to check that essential elements had not been omitted. The questions we asked were mainly fixed-choice ones, using rating scales and ranking but also included were open questions to allow practitioners a less restricted response. The draft questionnaire was piloted with 10 leaders representing the full range of early childhood provision who were not taking part in our investigation. It was also scrutinized by Jill Rodd, a recognized international expert in the field, who kindly offered us her suggestions. A range of statistical analyses was carried out that enabled us to look in more detail at relationships between categories of response but these have been reported elsewhere.

2.4 What we found out

One hundred and ninety-four questionnaires were distributed across 12 institutions representing a range of early childhood settings. The survey targeted all staff in the 12 organizations and those fulfilling various leadership roles including 'middle' leaders, who were accountable to the main leaders identified by the study. One hundred and thirty-one questionnaires were returned (representing a 68 per cent response rate). Twenty-nine out of 36 staff carrying a leadership role responded (representing an 81 per cent response rate).

Characteristics of the respondents

Table 2.1 *Current positions of respondents*

Leadership role	Position	Number of respondents	Sub-total
Leader	Owner	2	
	Principal	1	
	Head of centre	2	
	Programme manager	1	
	Foundation stage leader	5	
	Nursery manager	4	
	Deputy NM	2	
	Team leader	12	
		29	*(22%)*
Non-leader	Early years worker/childcare worker	27	
	Administration	6	
	Teacher	14	
	Nursery nurse	14	
	Teaching assistant	9	
	Nursery assistant	6	
		76	*(58%)*
Specified 'other'	Other (including a range of other personnel from education, health and playwork as well as educational psychology and library service)	26	26 *(20%)*
Total		131	131 *(100%)*

As indicated in Table 2.1, 22 per cent of practitioners indicated that they currently had a leadership role. The distribution of leaders, non-leaders and other specified positions was thus fairly even.

Type of setting

Table 2.2 *Types of childcare settings*

Type of setting	Number of respondents
Integrated centre	52 *(40.0%)*
Private day nursery	17 *(13.1%)*
Voluntary day nursery	18 *(13.8%)*
State day nursery	2 *(1.5%)*
Primary foundation unit	24 *(18.5%)*
Infant foundation unit	2 *(1.5%)*
Other	15 *(11.5%)*
Total	130 *(100.0%)*

As shown in Table 2.2, positions held were distributed fairly evenly between types of setting. The 'other' category personnel were, in the main, co-located in an integrated centre and another setting such as a health centre, social work office or library.

Characteristics

There were only four male respondents: one in administration, one a teaching assistant and two with unspecified positions. Three of the men were between 50 and 59 years of age and the fourth between 30 and 39 years. Unsurprisingly, the profession remains dominated by women.

Table 2.3 *Age of respondents*

Age group	Respondents
Under 20	5 *(3.8%)*
20–29	36 *(27.5%)*
30–39	29 *(22.1%)*
40–49	41 *(31.3%)*
50–59	18 *(13.7%)*
60 or over	2 *(1.5%)*
Total	131 *(100.0%)*

The ages of responding practitioners were fairly evenly distributed between 20 and 49 years (Table 2.3). However, as Table 2.4 shows, there were differences between respondents in different positions and between leaders and non-leaders.

All those in leadership positions had had six or more years' experience in early childhood settings with the exception of two team leaders with three to five years' experience and two owners with two years' experience or less. By and large those in leadership positions, with the exception of owners, had spent more time in such settings generally than in their current position, whereas other responding practitioners had smaller differences between the two (Table 2.5). What this does indicate is that owner/leaders with overall responsibility for the quality of provision can in some cases have very little experience.

Table 2.4 *Median years in childcare and in current positions by positions of respondents*

Leadership role	Position	Median age
Leader	Owner	50
	Principal	40–49
	Head of centre	40
	Programme manager	40–49
	Foundation stage leader	40–49
	Nursery manager	40–49
	Deputy NM	40
	Team leader	30–39
		40–49
Non-leader	Early years worker/childcare worker	20–29
	Administration	30–39
	Teacher	40–49
	Nursery nurse	30–39
	Teaching assistant	40–49
	Nursery assistant	20–29
		30–39
Not specified	Other	40–49
		40–49

Table 2.5 *Median age groups by positions of respondents*

Leadership role	Position	Median years in early childhood	Median years in current position
Leader	Owner	2 or less	2 or less
	Principal	11–15	6–10
	Head of centre	11–15	5
	Programme manager	11–15	2 or less
	Foundation stage leader	11–15	6–10
	Nursery manager	21 or more	2
	Deputy NM	11–15	3–5
	Team leader	6–10	2 or less
		11–15	2 or less
Non-leader	Early years worker/ childcare worker	6–10	2 or less
	Administration	2	2 or less
	Teacher	6–10	2
	Nursery nurse	5	3–5
	Teaching assistant	3–5	3–5
	Nursery assistant	2 or less	2 or less
		3–5	2 or less
Not specified	Other	6–10	2
		6–10	2

Training

Table 2.6   *Highest levels of original qualification*

Level of qualification	Number of respondents
Postgraduate	11 *(8.4%)*
First degree	20 *(15.3%)*
NNEB	28 *(21.4%)*
Level 3 NVQ Early Years Child Care and Education	10 *(7.6%)*
Level 2 NVQ Early Years Child Care and Education	11 *(8.4%)*
Other	23 *(17.6%)*
Unspecified	28 *(21.4%)*
Total	131 *(100.0%)*

There were no particular associations between types of qualification and current position, though this may be because the sample surveyed was relatively small and so sample size may account for this finding (Table 2.6). As Table 2.7 shows there was evidence of differences between types of setting in which the respondents' current positions were located and level of original qualification. Disproportionately many respondents from primary school foundation units had a first degree or postgraduate qualification. Disproportionately many respondents from voluntary day nurseries had National Vocational Qualifications (NVQs) that are based on the existing competences of the practitioner in real-world settings rather than a course of training leading to a formal examination. These qualifications build upon practical capability supported by knowledge and understanding through training courses of individual candidates who are mentored and assessed and move at their own pace. They are particularly popular with childcare workers, many of whom came into such work through their own children and who have experience but no formal qualifications. Furthermore, this finding indicates that practitioners in voluntary daycare are likely to have fewer qualifications than those working in foundation stage units.

Table 2.7   *Highest levels of original qualification, by location of current position*

	Degree	NNEB	NVQ	Other	Unspecified	Total
Integrated centre	13	15	3	13	8	52
Private day nursery	1	3	4	3	6	17
Voluntary day nursery	3	1	8	3	3	18
State day nursery	0	0	1	0	1	2
Primary foundation unit	10	3	2	2	7	24
Infant foundation unit	0	1	0	1	0	2
Other	4	5	2	1	3	15
Total	31	28	20	23	28	130

Of the three men who reported their qualifications, one had a first degree and two had postgraduate qualifications. It is perhaps heartening that men who were attracted to work with our youngest children are those who are well qualified.

Those professionals with Nursery Nurse Education Board (NNEB) qualifications rather than a degree or other qualification were likely to have 16 or more years' experience in early childhood settings (Table 2.8). Since the NVQ replaced course-based NNEB qualifications in 1992, this finding is not surprising.

Table 2.8 *Highest levels of original qualification and length of experience*

| Original qualification | Total EY experience (years) | | | | | | Total |
	2 or less	3–5	6–10	11–15	16–20	21 or more	
Degree	8	2	13	4	0	4	31
NNEB	0	4	7	3	4	10	28
NVQ	6	6	7	0	2	0	21
Other	5	6	4	3	1	3	22
Unspecified	8	10	2	4	0	3	27
Total	27	28	33	14	7	20	129

Table 2.9 *Original training by target age group*

Target age group	Number of respondents
Birth–5 years	28 *(23.7%)*
Birth–8 years	50 *(42.4%)*
3–7/8 years	14 *(11.9%)*
3–11 years	3 *(2.5%)*
5–7/8 years	2 *(1.7%)*
5–11 years	6 *(5.1%)*
Secondary	2 *(1.7%)*
Other	13 *(11.0%)*
Total	118 *(100.0%)*

Of the 118 who responded, 66 per cent had training related to children from birth upwards, indicating that one-third of early childhood workers do not have training to work with children from birth upwards. Fourteen per cent had training from 3 years upwards and 7 per cent from 5 years upwards (Table 2.9).

As Table 2.10 shows, disproportionately many of the practitioners responding from primary school foundation units had not initially received training to work with very young children. This is an interesting finding, suggesting that many of those with graduate and postgraduate qualifications do not have experience of working with our youngest children.

Table 2.10 *Target age group of original training by type of setting*

| Type of early childhood setting | Target age group | | | | Total |
	From birth	From 3	From 5	Older	
Integrated centre	27	7	0	0	34
Private day nursery	12	0	1	0	13
Voluntary day nursery	16	1	0	0	17
State day nursery	1	0	1	0	2
Primary foundation unit	8	8	6	0	22
Infant foundation unit	1	0	0	0	1
Other	12	1	0	2	15
Total	77	17	8	2	104

Table 2.11 *Target age group of original training and subsequent training for early years work*

Age group for which initially trained	Trained for EY work after initial training?		Total
	Yes	No	
From birth	68	9	77
From 3	15	1	16
From 5	5	3	8
Older	0	2	2
Total	88	15	103

As shown in Table 2.11, half of those who reported no initial training for working with children under 5 years also reported no subsequent training. These included one owner, one foundation stage leader and three teachers.

Table 2.12 *Types of subsequent training for early years work, completed and in progress*

Type of training	Completed	In progress	Total
In-service EY training	74	7	81
Short course (LEA/ EYDCP)	75	4	79
Advanced certificate	1	1	2
Advanced diploma	3	1	4
MA (master's degree)	4	3	7
Further professional qualifications	13	8	21

All four of those who had completed master's degrees were in leadership positions, were between 30 and 49 years and had less than 16 years' experience in early childhood settings. Three of them were initially trained to work with children under 5.

Table 2.13 *Types of subsequent training for early years work, completed and in progress, for respondents without initial training for under-5s*

Type of training	Completed	In progress	Total
In-service EY training	16	2	18
Short course (LEA/ EYDCP)	14		14
Advanced certificate			
Advanced diploma			
MA (master's degree)	1	1	2
Further professional qualifications	3	3	6

The majority of subsequent training was in-service early years training or a short course (Table 2.12), especially among those without initial training for working with under-5s (Table 2.13). This suggests that those professionals in our survey seeking to extend training for work with our youngest children were likely to have had only relatively short courses.

Reported characteristics of our survey professionals should be regarded as merely indicative of those of the wider population of relevant early childhood personnel, and caution should be exercised in generalizing from these findings.

Roles, responsibilities and functions

Participating practitioners were offered seven aspects of the leadership role (and the opportunity to add another) and asked to rank the top five in order of importance (Table 2.14).

Ranking questions are difficult to analyse and to simplify analysis unranked items were taken to have a rank of 8.

There was a high level of agreement that the most important aspect of the role is to deliver a quality service. This finding is entirely consistent with the views of our original group of 25 leaders who took part in the seminar and the needs of the profession as stressed by Robinson (2006). This was ranked first by 53 per cent of respondents, so the median rank was also first. It also had the best mean rank (2.6). The aspect considered next most important was being accountable to and acting as an advocate for children, parents, staff, the profession and the general community, with a mean rank of 3.4. At the other extreme was adopting an entrepreneurial approach that is mindful of the competition with others in the sector, which nobody ranked first and which was included in the top five by only six people. Between these two extremes were: engaging in ongoing professional development and encouraging it in all staff; articulating a philosophy, vision and values; engaging in collaborative and partnership style of leadership; and being sensitive and responsive to the need for change and managing change effectively.

Table 2.14 *Ranks allocated to aspects of the early years leadership role*

| Aspect of role | Number of respondents allocating rank | | | | | Mean* | Median |
	1	2	3	4	5		
Articulate a philosophy/ values/vision	13	17	12	17	23	5.0	5
Deliver a quality service	70	15	15	8	7	2.6	1
Engage in ongoing professional development	2	17	35	27	29	4.3	4
Be accountable to and act as an advocate for all	24	45	17	14	9	3.4	2
Engage in collaborative leadership	8	6	17	16	31	5.5	5
Be sensitive/responsive to the need for change	2	18	21	34	19	4.8	4
Have an entrepreneurial approach to sector	–	1	2	2	1	7.8	8
Other	1	–	–	–	–	7.9	8

* Unranked = 8

Only the correlation between the quality service aspect and the professional development aspect was strong enough to be worthy of mention. It also serves as a reminder of the need for ongoing professional development in order to maintain high-quality provision. This finding is also in line with views expressed in the seminar. Older respondents tended to rank articulating values lower and ongoing professional development higher. Those in leadership positions ranked collaborative leadership more important than those not in such positions.

Indicators of leadership potential

Early childhood professionals were offered seven indicators of leadership potential at the start of early childhood professionals' careers (and the opportunity to add another) and asked to rank the top five in order of importance (Table 2.15). Ranking questions, as noted above, are difficult to analyse and to simplify analysis unranked items were taken to have a rank of 8.

A large consensus supported dedication as the most important indicator of leadership potential. This was ranked first by 51 per cent of respondents, so the median rank was also first. It also had the best mean rank (2.8). The aspect with the next best mean rank was willingness to work with others (3.6) but critical evaluation and trying new ideas (mean rank 3.9) was ranked first by more people. Indicators relating to teaching and professional experience tended to be ranked lower.

Table 2.15 *Ranks allocated to indicators of leadership potential*

Indicator	Number of respondents allocating rank					Mean*	Median
	1	2	3	4	5		
Dedication	67	13	11	14	7	2.8	1
Willingness to work with others	15	40	26	15	15	3.6	3
Attitude to lifelong learning	6	15	12	18	25	5.4	5
A variety of teaching experiences	1	8	18	15	19	6.0	8
Constantly questioning own practice	10	14	17	21	18	5.1	5
Guides and mentors during professional experience	1	8	20	13	20	6.0	8
Critically evaluates and tries new ideas/ways of working	18	27	19	28	15	3.9	4
Other	1	1	1	1		27.8	8

* Unranked = 8

Importance attached to dedication was associated with importance attached to delivering a quality service and engaging with ongoing professional development. Importance attached to self-questioning was associated with importance attached to accountability and advocacy. Mentoring and articulating values were associated. Critical evaluation and collaborative and partnership style of leading were associated.

Older respondents tended to rank dedication as less important. Given their probable longer service in the profession, it could be argued that they had already demonstrated their dedication! Those with more experience in early childhood settings tended to rank their willingness to work with others as more important. Those who were initially trained for working with younger children tended to rank critical evaluation as less important.

Personal characteristics of effective leaders

The question regarding personal characteristics of effective leaders was in Likert-scale form (Table 2.16).

Only being a calculated risk-taker, being business-oriented and being economically competitive had mean ratings at or below 'moderately important', with being business-oriented just above these. This again highlights survey practitioners' lack of value for business and entrepreneurial skills.

One statistical analysis is included here because of its particularly interesting findings. A principal components analysis was carried out in order to indicate how particular practitioner respondents differed in the levels of importance that they attached to particular leadership characteristics. (Component 1 is omitted because this showed only how much importance they attached to the leadership characteristics in general.) Components 2, 3 and 4 each contrast those respondents who attribute relatively high importance to one group of characteristics with those who attribute relatively high importance to another group (with a few so-called 'neutral' characteristics appearing to be of little interest). Table 2.17 lists the characteristics in each contrasting pole.

Table 2.16 *Ratings allocated to personal characteristics of effective leaders*

Characteristic	Number of respondents rating importance					Mean[1]	Median
	Very	Important	Moderately	Low	Very low		
Authoritative	15	57	38	12	4	2.5	2
Calculated risk-taker	6	26	46	29	16	3.2	3
Influential	41	58	20	6	1	2.0	2
Proactive	69	50	4		1	1.5	1
Empowering	54	45	19	5	2	1.8	2
Visionary	59	54	12	1	126	1.6	2
Professionally confident	82	42	4			1.4	1
Systematic planner	40	60	25		1	1.9	2
Goal-oriented	35	55	25	10		2.1	2
Assertive	50	52	22	2	2	1.9	2
Mentor and guide	79	40	7	1		1.4	1
Professionally confident	76	34	6			1.4	1
Kind/warm/friendly/ nurturing/sympathetic	89	30	7	2		1.4	1
Knowledgeable	75	45	7			1.5	1
Rational/logical/analytical	33	68	22	1		1.9	2
Coach	19	53	41	7	4	2.4	2
Economically competitive	5	36	47	30	7	3.0	3
Business oriented	10	44	33	34	6	2.9	3
Other	7			1	1	1.8	1

[1] Practitioners who did not rate a particular characteristic are omitted.

Table 2.17 *Schematic list of personal characteristic variables contrasted in principal components 2, 3 and 4*

	Principal component 2	Principal component 3	Principal component 4
Pole 1	Kind/warm/sympathetic	Visionary	Economically competitive
	Rational/logical/analytical	Professionally confident	Coaches
	Assertive	Knowledgeable	Mentors and guides
	Knowledgeable	Systematic planners	Proactive
	Goal-oriented	Proactive	Rational/logical/analytical
	Coaches	Kind/warm/sympathetic	Empowering
	Mentors and guides	Empowering	Business-oriented
		Rational/logical/analytical	Knowledgeable
			Kind/warm/sympathetic
Neutral	Authoritative	Assertive	Visionary
	Professionally confident	Mentors and guides	Calculated risk-takers
	Business-oriented	Goal-oriented	
	Economically competitive	Coaches	
Pole 2	Systematic planners	Influential	Systematic planners
	Calculated risk-takers	Authoritative	Goal-oriented
	Influential	Economically competitive	Influential
	Proactive	Business-oriented	Assertive
	Visionary	Calculated risk-takers	Professionally confident
	Empowering		Authoritative

It is notable that certain sets of characteristics always appear close to each other in each of the lists. The most surprising of these perhaps is the group consisting of being kind, warm, friendly, nurturing and sympathetic; being rational, logical and analytical; and being knowledgeable. Being 'warm, nurturing and sympathetic' may be a distinctive feature of early years providers and, as noted earlier, of female workers.

Those with postgraduate qualifications tended towards the first pole of principal component 2, favouring warmth, rationality, knowledgeability, assertiveness, goal orientation, coaching, mentoring and guiding (*leaders as guides*) and those with 'other' qualifications towards the second, favouring systematic planning, risk-taking, influence, proactivity, vision and empowerment (*leaders as strategists*). Those with NVQ qualifications tended towards the first pole of principal component 3, favouring vision, warmth, professional confidence, systematic planning, proactivity and empowerment (*leaders as motivators*) and postgraduates towards the second, favouring influence, authority, economic competitiveness, business awareness and risk-taking (*leaders as entrepreneurial and business-oriented*). Those with postgraduate qualifications may thus value the role of coaching, mentoring and guiding or 'moving staff on', while those with NVQ qualifications favour an empowering and motivating role. This contrasts with those with 'other' qualifications, probably from community development, health, library services or social work, emphasizing the leader's strategic role in a fast-changing context. Interestingly, while up until this point, survey participants had not emphasized business and entrepreneurial skills, those with postgraduate qualifications acknowledged the value of such competence.

What is particularly interesting here is evidence that people with differential initial qualifications and following different routes into the early childhood sector may have different views about early childhood leadership and different attitudes towards aspects of their role.

Aspects of leadership contributing to sustainability in current institutions

Participants were invited to rate the contribution of aspects of the early years leadership role to sustainability in provision in their own institutions with guidance being as to what the terms meant (Tables 2.18 and 2.19). The extent to which this led them to make associations with the previous question items using similar terms to those expanded here cannot be estimated. Suffice to say, the difference in format and terminology from the earlier question ranking aspects of the leadership role in terms of importance is probably likely to reduce associations with items in the previous question.

Table 2.18 *Expansion of aspects of leadership contained in the question*

Aspect of leadership role	Expansion
Community	Understanding and responding to local realities
Pedagogical	Bridging research and practice
Administrative	Focusing on administrative and financial management
Entrepreneurial	Vision, forward thinking, planning, taking risks
Conceptual	Vision to change in context of the broader social policy shifts
Career development	Enabling practitioners to see progressive and fulfilling career paths
Advocacy	Represents, brings to public attention and seeks to improve
Performance-led	Emphasizes efficiency, performance and technicist practice
Other	–

Table 2.19 *Contribution of aspects of leadership to sustainability in current institutions*

Aspect of leadership role	Level of contribution					Mean	Median
	1 Very high	2 High	3 Moderate	4 Low	5 Very low		
Community	58	42	24		1	1.7	2
Pedagogical	25	71	25	2	1	2.1	2
Administrative	13	55	45	7	3	2.4	2
Entrepreneurial	40	60	20	4		1.9	2
Conceptual	24	56	36	4		2.2	2
Career development	44	54	27	2		1.9	2
Advocacy	47	52	21	3	1	1.9	2
Performance-led	30	51	29	10	2	2.2	2
Other	2					1.0	1

(Note that those who omitted some items are omitted from Table 2.19 but included in subsequent analysis as rating 'moderate'. Those who omitted all items are omitted below.)

Community leadership was generally considered to make slightly more of a contribution than advocacy, career development and entrepreneurial leadership. Other aspects were a little further behind but not greatly.

It is interesting that entrepreneurial leadership is seen as making quite a contribution to local sustainability whereas the firm consensus was that having an entrepreneurial approach was the least important aspect of the leadership role. This is difficult to interpret and may reflect a recognition of local competition for places for 3- to 5-year-olds and further illuminate the importance attached by those with postgraduate qualifications to leaders as entrepreneurial and business oriented.

Overall, current position showed no strong evidence of association with any of these items, with one small exception. The evidence for respondents in leadership positions attributing greater contributions to entrepreneurial and conceptual (that is, vision to change in the context of wider policy shifts) is stronger than evidence for any other link and is well worth reporting (Table 2.20).

Table 2.20 *Mean ratings assigned to contribution to sustainability by aspects of leadership, by leaders and non-leaders*

| | Leadership position | |
	Non-leader	Leader
Community	1.79	1.75
Pedagogical	1.97	2.11
Administrative	2.51	2.32
Entrepreneurial	2.03	1.71
Conceptual	2.33	2.00
Career development	1.82	1.93
Advocacy	1.79	1.79
Performance-led	2.11	2.36

Impact of external requirements

Table 2.21 *Ratings for impact of external factors on the role of the early childhood leader*

	+1 Very helpful	0 No impact	-1 Unhelpful	Mean	Median
OFSTED	95	11	7	0.8	1
Competition	24	59	22	0.0	0
Performance-related appraisal	81	25	7	0.7	1
Changing policy	64	25	12	0.5	1
Staff scarcity	39	26	45	-0.1	0
Other factors	2	2	1	0.2	0

Staff scarcity is the only external factor that on average is rated negatively by early childhood practitioner respondents, since 39 respondents rated it as very helpful. However, it may be that the question (column 1) was taken to indicate 'large impact' rather than positive impact. A large number of people similarly rated OFSTED inspections as very helpful (Table 2.21).

Table 2.22   *Ratings for impact of changing on the role of the early childhood leader*

Leadership position	Impact of changing policy on EY leader role, by leaders and non-leaders		
	Very helpful	No impact	Unhelpful
Non-leader	34 (59.6%)	21 (36.8%)	2 (3.5%)
Leader	19 (70.4%)	2 (7.4%)	6 (22.2%)

There is strong evidence for a difference between leaders and non-leaders in their assessment of the impact of changing policy, with those in leadership positions being less likely to say this has no impact (Table 2.22). Given leaders' responsibility for instigating corresponding change in their organization, this finding is scarcely surprising

Who makes the decisions?

Given the total number of making decisions 'all the time' responses in Table 2.23 (144), it is likely that at least some of the practitioner respondents saw more than one group of people making decisions 'all the time'. It seems reasonable to assume at least some respondents have interpreted 'all the time' to mean 'a lot', 'some of the time' to mean 'a little' and 'none of the time' to mean 'not at all'.

Table 2.23   *Rating of preponderance of decision-making by various actors*

	1 All the time	2 Some of the time	3 None of the time	Mean	Median
Governors/trustees	23	62	18	2.0	2
Senior management	52	69	1	1.6	2
Middle management	17	93	3	1.9	2
Appropriate individuals	13	98	5	1.9	2
All staff	10	108	6	2.0	2
Parents and community	12	96	13	2.0	2
Child	12	87	22	2.1	2
Others	5	2	7	1.3	1

It is notable that for all practitioners the median rating for decision-making is 'some of the time'. The child was reported as having the least input to decisions, but only slightly less than parents and the community, all staff collectively and the governors or trustees. Thus, there is a sense in which it is perceived that everyone is involved to some extent in the decision-making.

Table 2.24 *Distribution of preponderance ratings for parents' decisions, by type of setting*

Type of early childhood setting	Decisions made by parents		
	All the time	Some of the time	None of the time
Integrated centre	10 *(20.4%)*	39 *(79.6%)*	0 *(0.0%)*
Private day nursery	0 *(0.0%)*	13 *(76.5%)*	4 *(23.5%)*
Voluntary day nursery	2 *(12.5%)*	14 *(87.5%)*	0 *(0.0%)*
State day nursery	0 *(0.0%)*	1 *(50.0%)*	1 *(50.0%)*
Primary foundation unit	0 *(0.0%)*	17 *(81.0%)*	4 *(19.0%)*
Infant foundation unit	0 *(0.0%)*	2 *(100.0%)*	0 *(0.0%)*
Other	0 *(0.0%)*	9 *(69.2%)*	4 *(30.8%)*

Table 2.25 *Distribution of preponderance ratings for decisions delegated to appropriate individuals, by type of setting*

Type of early childhood setting	Decisions made by parents		
	All the time	Some of the time	None of the time
Integrated centre	5 *(10.9%)*	40 *(87.0%)*	1 *(2.2%)*
Private day nursery	2 *(11.8%)*	15 *(88.2%)*	0 *(0.0%)*
Voluntary day nursery	3 *(20.0%)*	12 *(80.0%)*	0 *(0.0%)*
State day nursery	0 *(0.0%)*	1 *(50.0%)*	1 *(50.0%)*
Primary foundation unit	0 *(0.0%)*	20 *(100.0%)*	0 *(0.0%)*
Infant foundation unit	1 *(50.0%)*	1 *(50.0%)*	0 *(0.0%)*
Other	2 *(15.4%)*	8 *(61.5%)*	3 *(23.1%)*

Table 2.26 *Distribution of preponderance ratings for children's decisions, by type of setting*

Type of early childhood setting	Decisions made by parents		
	All the time	Some of the time	None of the time
Integrated centre	1 *(20.4%)*	37 *(79.6%)*	9 *(0.0%)*
Private day nursery	6 *(0.0%)*	7 *(76.5%)*	3 *(23.5%)*
Voluntary day nursery	5 *(12.5%)*	12 *(87.5%)*	0 *(0.0%)*
State day nursery	0 *(0.0%)*	1 *(50.0%)*	1 *(50.0%)*
Primary foundation unit	0 *(0.0%)*	20 *(81.0%)*	2 *(19.0%)*
Infant foundation unit	0 *(0.0%)*	2 *(100.0%)*	0 *(0.0%)*
Other	0 *(0.0%)*	7 *(69.2%)*	7 *(30.8%)*

Table 2.24 shows that professionals from integrated centres were disproportionately more likely to say that parents made decisions all of the time and less likely to say that they never made decisions. Given the emphasis in the original Sure Start integrated centre programmes on children's services being locally driven and responsive to the needs of families, this finding is not surprising. Table 2.25 shows that respondents from state day nurseries and 'other' settings were disproportionately more likely to say decisions were never

delegated to appropriate individuals. Since these respondents include different professional groups, with different value bases, ethical codes, regulatory bodies, traditional roles and boundaries, this finding is less surprising. It also highlights the hidden and less documented value differences between professions that must be acknowledged before they can be addressed and reconciled (Barr et al., 2005). Table 2.26 shows that respondents from private and voluntary day nurseries were disproportionately more likely to say decisions were made by children all of the time. In this context, the private and voluntary sectors clearly recognize that children as well as parents become clients of the services that they receive and, as such, are accorded independent views about improvement of these. Given the current interest in accessing and understanding children's perspectives on their own lives that have legal, political, economic and academic origins (for example, the United Nations General Assembly's, 1989, *Adoption of a Convention on the Rights of the Child*; the *European Convention on the Exercise of Children's Rights* – Council of Europe, 1996; and *The Charter of Fundamental Rights of the European Union* – European Convention, 2000) one might have anticipated a stronger emphasis from participants on children's role in decision-making.

2.5 What we made of the findings

In terms of our original objectives, first, early childhood leadership clearly meant different things to practitioners in different settings with a different emphasis being placed on leaders as guides, leaders as strategists and leaders as entrepreneurial and business oriented. This also suggests that the knowledge, skills and attitudes as well as strategic intent regarded as important may vary according to the qualifications of the early childhood practitioner concerned, as well as their professional heritage. The workforce was predominantly female and leaders were aged between 30 and 49 years. Second, in terms of overall roles, responsibilities and characteristics of early childhood settings, providing a quality service was regarded as being of the highest importance and entrepreneurial skills of lesser importance. Providing a quality service was associated with continuing professional development but, while the least qualified childcare workers appeared to have opportunities for 'on-the-job' training, most training received was in the form of short courses and in-service training. This is a reminder that quality, affordability and sustainability are linked to provision of better qualified staff. Given the emphasis being placed on high-quality provision, it is perhaps less surprising that professionals should rate accountability in the form of regulatory bodies such as OFSTED positively and staff scarcity should be regarded negatively.

This chapter has begun to uncover what early childhood leadership meant to a group of leaders and practitioners and examine the role, responsibilities and characteristics of leaders. It has also identified areas of difference in views between professionals with different qualifications and professional heritages and working in different settings, for example in the area of organizational decision-making. It has confirmed a unanimity in response regarding the fundamental importance of valuing learning and quality provision. It has also uncovered an ambivalent attitude towards the leader's entrepreneurial and business skills.

Attributing the mixed response regarding organizational decision-making to value differences between professionals would be simplistic, particularly so given the reported importance attached to dedication in the early childhood field. It is more likely that this mixed response reflects traditional notions of leadership associated with a productive work style, cultivation of a work culture and traits such as vision, ethics and courage still very prevalent within the workforce. There is also some slight evidence to support the view that commitment to parental participation and involvement, as well as to children's right to participation, varied across type of setting and might reflect the very different aims, purposes and origins of different early childhood services as well as the differing needs of client groups they served. On the one hand, integrated centres and their staff represent the English government's social inclusion agenda (Social Exclusion Unit, 1998; 2001a; 2001b) in terms of their 'joined up' services and agencies intended to revive communities and promote inclusion and equality. On the other, it could be argued that school personnel represent a more prevalent view among educational professionals that positions parents as 'clients' and 'consumers' but at the same time in need of professional attention and intervention (Moriarty, 2002; Vincent, 1996; Whitty, 1997). Marketization of education in England, it has been argued by Whitty (1997), has caused polarization despite a rhetoric of 'partnership'.

The combined views of our early childhood practitioners shed valuable light on the roles, responsibilities and components of leadership and they indicated certain areas that need further investigation. Chapter 3 thus provides a more in-depth consideration of leaders' and staff groups' perceptions and definitions of leadership; their views of roles, responsibilities and functions; their experiences of decision-making and culture; as well as perspectives on influences on leadership and their views on training.

► The differences in roles, responsibilities and components of leadership that emerged from the survey should also to be considered in the light of the very different purposes of early childhood leadership in different types of settings.

Practitioners' views 2.1

One of our foundation stage leaders described her role in terms of her original job description as a phase leader:

- Provide opportunities for staff to develop their interests and increase expertise.
- Work with class teachers and post-holders to implement agreed school aims in each curriculum area, to provide a broad and balanced curriculum for individual children.
- Work with curriculum leaders to ensure the suitability of curriculum guidelines and schemes of work for children in the foundation stage phase.
- Promote the professional development of staff in the phase.
- Attend to individual needs of staff and children in the phase, providing personal, pastoral and professional support.
- Play a leading role in various aspects of school life, including assemblies, community links and school management.
- Undertake particular administrative tasks which facilitate effective teaching and optimize the use of resources.

Practitioners' views 2.2

By contrast, one of our integrated centre leaders outlined the job of a children's centre manager:

- Deliver better outcomes for children under-5 and their families, through the development of integrated services in response to need.
- Support the partnership board in the monitoring and evaluation of implementation and development of the children's centre project, ensuring the full and effective participation of local families.
- Work in partnership within the local community and key agencies to provide a quality service to enhance opportunities for inclusion.
- Manage and lead the development of the children's centre project including the following core services – personal support for children and adults; childcare; promotion of health and well-being early learning opportunities; education, training, information and advice.

Practitioners' views 2.3

Different again was the description of a head of a former early excellence centre turned children's centre with its strong training purpose:

- Manage and develop the integrated provision of education, care and family and community support.
- Further develop and maintain the centre as a community resource, responsive to needs identified by local people in the community.
- Further develop and maintain partnerships with local primary schools and education providers to ensure continuity in the provision of education for local children and families.
- Establish and maintain the centre as a recognized model of excellent practice in the provision of integrated services for young children and their families.
- Work in partnership to implement quality training, recruitment and childcare throughout the area.

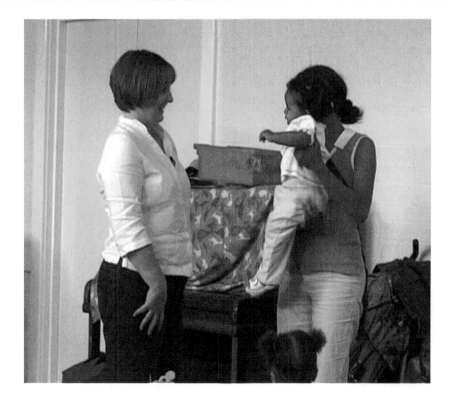

CHAPTER THREE

PRACTITIONERS' UNDERSTANDINGS OF EARLY CHILDHOOD LEADERSHIP

This chapter describes more in-depth conversations with leaders and staff in their setting. It identifies key themes of characteristics, definitions and perceptions of leadership; roles, responsibilities and functions of leaders; decision-making; internal and external influences on leadership; and training. Feelings of ambivalence towards business and entrepreneurial skills are uncovered and the nature of decision-making and organizational culture in a changing context considered.

3.1 Introduction

Conversations with leaders and group conversations with a range of other personnel in each setting provided the opportunity to probe in more depth areas of interest identified by our survey reported in the last chapter (see Appendices 3a and 3b for the specific questions asked). These are presented within key themes that clustered around leadership definitions and perceptions; roles, responsibilities and functions; decision-making; internal and external influences; and training.

3.2 Characteristics of the leaders and staff that we talked to

In terms of characteristics, leaders had been in their current posts for varying lengths of time (Table 3.1). There were nine white British females, one Indian-heritage female and one Bangladeshi-heritage male. Three led integrated centres, three led foundation stage units in primary schools (one was also a deputy head teacher), two led voluntary sector family daycare and two private daycare settings. One voluntary sector and one private sector leader/owner were in the process of changing to children's centre status. The staff represented a cross-section from their setting, including middle leaders where they existed, main-scale practitioners as well as governors.

Table 3.1 *Characteristics of respondents*

Leader interviews	Group interviews
Leaders interviewed had been in their current posts for varying lengths of time: • those working in foundation stage units in school settings showed the greatest stability, having been in post from 13 to 30 years; • integrated centre leaders, voluntary and private sector had been in post for a relatively short time, between two and five years; with the exception of one owner of private provision, who had worked in further education, all had worked previously in the sector.	Staff in the group interviews included: • parent governors; • nursery nurses; • reception class teachers; • family involvement officers; • children's service workers; • teaching assistants, and • community service volunteers.

3.3 Definitions and perceptions of leadership

Leaders and staff expressed compatible views. The values associated with this phase were described by staff as more 'caring and understanding'. Leaders stressed provision of quality care, raising achievement and staff performance. Staff also strongly emphasized children's achievement. Both groups identified clear vision and strategic awareness as important and role modelling as a means of setting standards. Coaching, mentoring, staff support and development were emphasized too. Juggling and balancing the complex needs of young children, parents and community was noted by leaders, while the leader's influence on staff and community was identified by staff. Keeping abreast with policy changes was recognized as a challenge by both leaders and staff (Table 3.2).

3.4 Roles, responsibilities and functions of leaders

With respect to roles, responsibilities and functions, leaders and staff stressed provision of high-quality education and care and children's achievements (Table 3.3). This was consistent with survey findings.

Table 3.2 *Definitions and perceptions of leadership*

Leader interviews	Group interviews
A number of common leadership themes emerged including: • values and needs of this phase, including raising children's achievement and staff performance being consistent not just with staff but in the provision of quality care; • having a clear vision and strategic awareness; • 'being a role model, setting the standard, letting people see and observe'; • leading others by coaching, mentoring, improvisation and support; • being at the forefront and keeping up to date with new initiatives, managing the rate of change in the sector; • juggling and balancing – 'a balance where everyone gets the best they can … balancing what is appropriate and safe in the context of the complex needs of young children, parents and community'.	Respondents identified specific skills and qualities: • values different from business and industry, 'more holistic', 'caring and understanding', 'identifying needs of others', raising children's achievement, 'what we're here for'; • having vision, giving direction, being a strategist, being a decision-maker, creative and a problem-solver; • providing a role model, guide and setting standards; • listening and giving advice, approachable, being a motivator, generating staff development; • leadership changed in response to policy changes; • influence on staff and community, 'more flexible in working' and 'multi-agency'.

Views concerning business and entrepreneurial skills were mixed as the survey had shown. The importance of maintaining budget and optimizing income, however, was stressed by both voluntary and private providers. One private provider linked business skills to sustainability but acknowledged the 'fine line between making it a business and making it a place for children'. Another acknowledged that it had been necessary to develop business skills but other professionals, such as accountants and solicitors could be relied upon. Leaders from the voluntary sector were reluctant to engage with this topic. One said, 'I would like to say no … but we need to have knowledge of business planning and funding in order to sustain ourselves'. The other said, 'I came here from the private sector because I did not like the idea of making a profit … exploiting those on low wages'. Two integrated centre leaders acknowledged the importance of entrepreneurial skills but indicated that they relied on others with more expertise. Another integrated centre leader noted that business experience was important but indicated that the public sector was different from the private sector – 'you don't have to make a profit and you have some responsibility which is moral and ethical as a public body'. Foundation stage leaders did not see this as their role: 'the head does most of this, budgeting'; 'I don't need entrepreneurial skills in my role'.

Table 3.3   *Roles, responsibilities and functions*

Leader interviews	Group interviews
Common themes emerged relating to the importance of high-quality education and care: • raising achievements, focusing on personal and social development, enjoyment and well-being; • understanding the local community (knowledge of children, families and other local provision); • the role of staff standards, aspirations and morale; • links to other organizations and networking. A mixed and ambivalent range of responses was received regarding business and entrepreneurial skills: • maintaining budget and optimizing income by maximum occupancy of the nursery (stressed by private and voluntary providers); • relying on the relevant expertise of others was stressed by foundation units and integrated centres; • business planning and funding was linked to sustainability; • business was a low priority; • profit-making was also exploitation of low wage earners. Responses to performance management were mixed, reflecting the differing practices and regulatory frameworks prevalent in integrated centres, a familiarity for those working in school contexts and an uncertainty for those in private and voluntary organizations.	Common themes emerged related to quality care: • raising children's achievements; • understanding the local community (or families using the service in the case of private providers); • positive leadership qualities, such as being approachable, visible, flexible and motivating and unhelpful aspects of leadership related to criticism, dictatorial approaches and lack of vision were identified; • links with other groups, such as nurseries, the church were identified. Business and entrepreneurial skills were thought to be either 'unimportant' or 'not as important' as other aspects of the leader's role: • becoming more important in the voluntary sector, and for private sector 'charging fees was very important or we would not have a nursery'; • 'can be delegated to others' was indicated by foundation unit staff; • 'of growing importance' in integrated centres; and • 'not a profit-making organization'. Staff had less certainty about performance management and whether it referred to achievement of staff or children.

Views concerning performance management were varied and reflected the very different professional groups, regulatory bodies and stakeholders served. In school contexts, a performance-management structure that included teaching assistants and mentors was described, in integrated centres target-led measures of success were indicated, while private and voluntary sector participants were less certain but inclined to think of staff performance as being judged in terms of children's achievements. Staff groups acknowledged the importance of staff quality being judged in terms of children's 'reaching their potential' but made little further comment.

Staff agreed that business and entrepreneurial skills were 'important but not as important as other areas'. There was a feeling that such skills were becoming more important but could be 'delegated' or 'handled by others'. Views were consistent with leaders' views though it should be noted that those in leadership positions were found to attach greater importance to entrepreneurial and business skills. The voluntary sector in particular emphasized that they were 'not a profit-making organization'. Talking to leaders and staff about entrepreneurial and business skills illuminated the mixed and ambiguous picture that emerged from the survey.

Nowhere more powerfully do early childhood practitioners' values and beliefs of people orientation, welfare and caring clash with the marketization and economization of English educational reform. Osgood (2003) has demonstrated how unwelcome new managerialism and entrepreneurialism is to an almost exclusively female group of practitioners who are committed to heightening their professionalism through preferred and more feminized ways of operating.

3.5 Decision-making

Decisions in general tended to be seen as 'top down'. Leaders felt that they 'had a big say at every level'. One said, 'I am a very powerful person'. It was confirmed that much of the decision-making at team level was collaborative. The opinions of staff about decision-making appeared to be more mixed though there was agreement that the leader made strategic decisions and teams made operational decisions (Table 3.4). Decision-making at the team level was thus emphasized and a sense of a collaborative culture conveyed. Overall, the organization was regarded as 'hierarchical at the strategic level and collaborative at the operational level'. Lack of visibility of parents and children is worth noting. While reference had been made to the distinctness of caring for young children and family, this was the first occasion that leaders themselves drew attention to the fact that by and large early childhood services were female-led.

Huffington (2004: 59) has suggested that 'the rate of change in organizations today requires more people to be involved in decision-making on the vision and strategy of the organization as it evolves day-to-day'. She saw this as increasing the power that people have in and over organizations and the 'sense of synchronicity between women's approach to leadership' that she described as 'based firmly on people, and the demands arising from the context'. This she saw made for a closer engagement by the organization, with the needs of people working within the organization as well as in the external environment of clients, partners and suppliers. The personal qualities and values identified as important in leadership by staff in our settings is consistent with views of women's leadership that emphasize the person(al) rather than role relationships or systems (Kagan and Hallmark, 2001).

As Waniganayake et al. (2000) found in the Australian context, comments made reflected the existence of traditional views of line-management style leadership within the group of professionals that took part in this study. At the same time, there is discussion of shared decision-making and teamwork that suggested decision-making was democratic.

Rodd (2006) emphasized the importance of decision-making in early childhood settings to the quality of the service provided since both the quality of work (the primary task) and the quality of life (group morale) are affected. Hence, decision-making style is related to characteristics of the leader, the group of professionals and the nature of the decision being made. Employees involved in the decision-making thus need to understand the whole organization. This in turn has implications for organizational culture. Staff recognized the need to be motivated, to work in collaborative teams that contribute to the working of the organization as a whole and, at the same time, show some concern for the communities, families and children they served.

Table 3.4   *Decision-making*

Leaders' interviews	Group interviews
There was general agreement that: • decision-making in general was seen as 'top down'; • day-to-day decisions were made by leaders themselves; • leaders had 'a big say at every level'; • much of the decision-making, however, it was felt, took place at the team level and was 'collaborative'. Factors influencing culture were: • size and scale of the organization; • absence of hierarchy; • focus on working with other professionals, parents and children; • female leadership; • rate of external change.	Views on decision-making seemed to be mixed from 'top down', through 'shared' to ' bottom up' but the role of the leader was clear: • 'involved at every level'; • 'ultimate decision-maker'; • role of the leader's line manager was also identified; • one group of voluntary providers mentioned children and parents might be consulted, while an integrated centre group noted 'parents have little voice'. Respondents' views on the culture had more in common: • the organization culture was 'collaborative'; • 'hierarchical at the strategic level and collaborative at the operational level'.

3.6 Internal and external influences on leadership

Leaders' views of the main internal influences on their role, both positive and negative, were staff, their development, commitment and motivation, their willingness (or reluctance) to change and staff scarcity (Table 3.5). This finding is in accord with the survey finding that staff scarcity had a negative impact.

Changing boundaries and expectations were also identified and, for the private and voluntary sector, resource constraints: 'it all boils down to money unfortunately and the quality of staff training'. Advisory teams were regarded as a positive influence and statutory requirements 'a spur to performance', although one private provider admitted a 'nervousness' about OFSTED visits. Group participants, for their part, identified characteristics of the leader as a major internal influence on their work as well as the training and development opportunities available. A range of outside hindrances was also identified including policies, procedures and inspections.

Table 3.5 *Influences on leadership*

Leaders' interviews	Group interviews
Internal influences on the leader's role related to: • staff (staff ratios), their commitment (their willingness/reluctance to change) and motivation and, in the case of integrated centres, the representation of different professions; • role of supervision, personal development plans and appraisal. External influences on the leader's role were: • external agencies/organizations as facilitators; • parents and the community as a source of support; • statutory requirements as a spur to performance; • strategic bodies as a controlling force; • inadequate/ring-fenced budgets as a constraint; • bureaucracy, paperwork and OFSTED were a challenge.	Internal influences on the leader's role were seen to be: • the characteristics of leader concerned, 'the leader's leader' and other staff; • having a mentor/being mentored; • regular training; • communication, administrative structures and buildings. External influences on the leader were: • external agencies/organization as facilitators; • colleagues, parents and the community as a source of support; • generous budgets that supported the vision and goals of the institution; • training courses. • policies, procedures and inspections as a constraint.

3.7 Training

In general, leaders regarded themselves responsible for both their own and their own staff's development: 'I think that you have constantly to question your own practice'; 'I can hardly be seen as continuing professional development (CPD) co-ordinator and not be seen as doing it'. Significantly, in terms of current leadership development experienced by participants, most had no experience. Staff, with few exceptions, had received no training and development in the area of leadership. Overall, a reciprocal picture emerged with leaders recognizing the important role of staff and their commitment, and staff, for their part, acknowledging the importance to them of their leader's characteristics (Table 3.6).

Table 3.6   *Training*

Leaders' interviews	Group interviews
Forms of leadership training and development included: • academic qualifications (master's degrees in education, business administration and the new NPQICL); • short courses, internal training, conferences and meetings; • contact with other professionals/talking to people; • reading; • experience was regarded as more useful than theory. Leaders regarded themselves as responsible for making decisions about their own training and updating.	Most respondents had no experience of leadership training though one mentioned a local authority day course: • formal courses were anticipated to be most helpful for leadership; • role models and 'nuggets ... what people say about leadership, books, studies and experience' were also mentioned.

3.8 Leadership in a changing world

In-depth discussions with leaders and staff illuminated attitudes towards entrepreneurial and business skills and clarified views concerning decision-making. While it was recognized that availability, affordability and sustainability were linked, there was deep unease about profit-making in a sector where many childcare workers were still very poorly paid.

In practice, decision-making in early childhood organizations was observed to be typically hierarchically organized, yet collaborative in culture. The vivid picture that leaders and staff offer is one of changing culture in organizations that is in itself a response to changing political, social, economic and technological contexts that in turn generate new challenges to leadership. Associated with these changes are corresponding shifts in structures within organizations and corresponding changed expectations as well as requirements of the workplace. As organizational boundaries, both internal and external become less rigid and less clearly defined, conventional organizational structures and roles will become redundant. In this context, these professionals recognized that leadership was needed to develop a shared vision and common purpose as well as a strategy for the future. In a very real sense, staff are articulating what they see as important for leadership in terms of direction, commitment and for the management of change. In a changed world in which traditional roles and boundaries are dissolving, it may be a real strength that early childhood leaders are predominantly women in a context where leadership, authority from work roles, organization and change are being redefined.

Chapter 4 follows leaders into their organizations in order to examine at first hand the impact of changed relationships between early childhood organizations and the changing external environment. This can be characterized as change in the traditional function of schooling for foundation units, with the introduction of the extended school day and 'wrap-around' care, and changes in governance, funding and outsourcing of services in the case of integrated children's centres. At the same time, the chapter will document corresponding changes to internal boundaries as these are renegotiated and settled roles, autonomy and control become more tenuous.

▶ The changing culture in early years organizations was seen as a response to new external challenges.

Practitioners' views 3.1

Leaders felt that organizations and individuals within them influenced the culture of their setting:

• A sense that a voluntary sector setting changing its status first to a neighbourhood nursery and then to a children's centre was not auto-matically made welcome by managers in the children's services – 'it felt as though people wanted to exclude us and the door was closed'.
• Clarity and autonomy within children's centres in delivery of services that the community expected was curtailed by strategic leaders in the children's services – 'these external forces are holding you back, the community expects you to deliver a service, people from diverse

(Continues)

(Continued)

disciplines have their own professional ways of working and professional ethics. You are manager in the middle'.

- Lack of understanding of integrated centre work in the children's services leaders – 'it would be nice if they had more understanding of what we are doing, I seem always to be telling people all over again about us!'
- Funding issues – 'ring-fenced budgets in children's centres'; 'money in terms of getting people in for quality training', 'the budget does not stretch far enough' in foundation stage units.
- Bureaucracy – 'government initiatives that you don't agree with' from foundation stage leaders; 'all that paperwork, nervousness of OFSTED visiting, keeping up to date'; and 'conflict between policies that change hours and the new nursery grant for a 38-week term when independent schools have a 33-week term', in the private sector.
- Marketing – 'competition with other providers, in terms of length of sessions, hourly rate and getting children into the nursery' in the private sector; and 'not being known locally, despite advertising' in the voluntary sector.

Practitioners' views 3.2

Views about the importance of business and entrepreneurial skills were mixed:

- 'I would like to say, no, but we are in voluntary organizations. We need to have knowledge of business planning and gaining funding in order to sustain ourselves.'
- 'In the voluntary sector, we are not a profit-making organization.'
- 'I think in today's climate you must have business skills otherwise the sustainability is compromised. There is a fine line between making it a business and making it a place for children in the private sector.'
- 'In the independent sector, we have to sell the place to prospective parents.'
- 'With charging fees, business and entrepreneurial skills are very important or we would not have a nursery' was echoed across the settings.
- 'It is of growing importance. We need to have business-management skills in children's centres. It's also becoming more important in applying for grants.'

CHAPTER FOUR

EARLY CHILDHOOD LEADERS' WORK

This chapter examines a typical day in the life of a variety of leaders working in a range of settings. It reveals differences in the amount of direct work with young children, with foundation stage leaders maintaining full-time teaching responsibilities. It shows that a considerable amount of time is spent in administrative tasks, particularly in the private and voluntary sector. Integrated centre leaders are observed to be working across organizational boundaries with other agencies and providers. The need to distribute leadership across the organization is considered. Finally, leaders report on the intensification of their work, their tiredness and the lack of time for reflection and self-evaluation.

4.1 Introduction

The reports that leaders offered in discussion of a typical day were entirely consistent with what we observed in practice when they were followed into their settings to explore a day in their lives. We asked them to keep a diary record of the day against a time line to complement the five hours of 'day-in-the-life' video-recording that took place. Later, leaders identified critical moments, events and activities where they were aware of using particular leadership knowledge and skills (see the diary schedule in Appendix 4). This offered insight into underlying thinking and decision-making and an opportunity for them to outline other events and activities not captured by camera at the beginnings and endings of the day. Later the video recording was reviewed and a selection made of 30-minute highlights that best represented their own leadership practice. For a final joint meeting, leaders identified one highlight to share with colleagues best demonstrating their leadership strengths, at the same time identifying areas for development, as well as potential opportunities and threats in their own context. Video highlights were also reviewed independently by three researchers and emerging themes compared and revised until consensus about interpretation was achieved. Event sampling within video highlights was then carried out. Leaders' diary records, video review and recorded comments provided triangulation for the themes that emerged as well as a background and context for professional development materials that were being prepared during the same period.

Leaders described a rich and varied range of activities that included meetings, paperwork, telephone calls, staff interactions, communication with parents and children, training and visiting other establishments, some events planned, others unplanned.

4.2 A typical day

Foundation stage leaders in primary schools reported that they still carried substantial 'hands on' teaching responsibilities that involved planning, liaising and co-ordinating with other nursery staff, teaching assistants and parents. Dedicated time for leadership responsibilities ranged from one half-day to one day per week. Interestingly, leaders with teaching backgrounds who no longer taught expressed regret at their reduced contact with children. This was demonstrated in their avowed determination to spend time with individuals and groups of children in teaching and learning contexts and to take part in games and constructional activities that were observed to take place.

Integrated centre leaders reported and demonstrated a 'mixture' of activities, with meetings playing a large part: 'one meeting a day or more, communication with staff, professionals from other agencies and parents from the centre, telephone calls and paperwork'. The differences between those integrated centre leaders who were working indirectly to serve the structures, processes and outcomes that surround working with parents, children and the community, and those integrated centre leaders who were more 'tightly coupled' to children's learning and development, through mentoring staff in assessment and record-keeping in one case or leading and coaching staff in curriculum design and development in another case, were striking.

Leaders of two private and one voluntary organization emphasized routine office administration within their spheres of activity and demonstrated this in practice, none of whom had secretarial or administrative support. Given that video-recording took place towards the end of the summer term it must be acknowledged that leaders were reaching a challenging period of the year when permanent staff were taking their annual leave and agency staff were required to cover for staff absence.

At the time of videoing, one voluntary-sector leader and one private provider were moving towards gaining children's centre leadership status, and a primary school foundation stage unit was introducing the extended school day. Hence, like other integrated centre leaders, they found themselves in a state of change in an internal and external environment that was increasingly complex, fluid and unpredictable with the 'loss of the stable state' (Schön, 1971). In this profoundly unsettled world, the boundary between the public and private sectors, as well as their relative values and practices, was less clearly defined and exemplified by the ambivalent attitudes of early childhood practitioners towards entrepreneurship and business in human services. Uncertainty about performance management and targets was opposed with practitioners' espousal of 'dedication' and 'quality provision'. In the midst of a transformation of children's services, including childcare and education, these professionals still cherished stability, social relationships and trust in leadership.

4.3 Roles, responsibilities and functions

The video highlights thus reflected both the varied range of activities that leaders reported and the palpable sense of change and development in the sector, identified at different points in prior discussion with them. Indeed, capturing early childhood leadership practice at a time of increased complexity and instability and illustrating how it was enacted and understood, was what marked out the distinctness of these leaders' work. By following the leader across a day in the organizational setting, it was anticipated that the realities of people's lived experience in early childhood institutions, early childhood leadership and relationships between professionals and leaders would emerge.

A number of ways of examining leaders' behaviour was considered and, indeed, tried out. One way of distinguishing the leaders in different early childhood sectors was the relative emphasis they placed on key leadership, management and administrative tasks in the context of their reported roles and responsibilities and their observed skills and dispositions. In order to verify this, an attempt was made to quantify these tasks through event sampling. This offered some framework or lens within which to locate leaders' diary records and the video highlights obtained. This showed a difference in the relative emphasis placed on day-to-day routine administrative and management tasks as opposed to more strategic leadership tasks. (Sample events are provided in Table 4.1.)

Another way of distinguishing leaders' work was by its direct (and client-centred) or indirect engagement with young children, their parents and community that Robinson (2006) emphasized. Compatible with this approach was investigating the relative focus of leadership work on functions that Hayden (1996) described as technical and mostly administrative or staffing, public relations and client oriented.

Foundation stage leaders

Foundation stage leaders retained major and direct responsibilities for planning, teaching, co-ordinating staff, and recording and reporting the progress of individual children. Administration, management and leadership duties were observed, if at all, in the relatively small amount of time formally allocated to these tasks or that was released through planned delegation to other staff and teaching assistants. What marked out the work of the foundation stage leaders most distinctly was its high intensity and pace throughout the day. Having a cohesive team that included other teaching staff, the school special educational needs co-ordinator, nursery nurses or teaching assistants, and external agencies such as the speech therapist, appeared to be a priority. This, it was observed, generated multiple leadership roles that required co-ordination of people (adults and children), time and resources and, hence, the curriculum. Relationships appeared to be both task- and person-oriented, with foundation stage leaders successfully completing work with and through others, while maintaining respect and trust. A good example of this was observed when an established foundation stage leader supported and 'led' her new and incoming head teacher through a parents' meeting at the same time as supporting other staff and parents. While the overall school management was reported as hierarchical in structure, effective communication and co-ordination strategies were observed to be achieved through ongoing face-to-face interactions with other staff that created a middle-management level, teamwork environment, allowing staff to feel that decision-making was shared as multiple leadership roles were discharged in the course of daily ongoing teaching processes. Much activity was 'invisible' in the sense that it began long before the school day started, with staff meetings and parents' consultations often being carried out after school and other administrative activities being taken home. These were either observed by the research team or in some cases accessed through leaders' diary records:

> 6.00 p.m. welcoming new parents ... 7.30 p.m. clearing up and thanking everyone. Home! 9.00 p.m. rang three newly-qualified teachers. 9.15 p.m. completing written weekly plan for Reception Year for photocopying tomorrow, checking all paperwork for zoo trip, checking emails. Bed before midnight will be early for me!

The foundation stage leaders observed were all very experienced and highly-skilled practitioners, confident in their leadership role to carry out the wide range of tasks demanded of them, to work collaboratively with co-workers to the maximum benefit of the organization, as well as supporting personal development of less-qualified staff through the qualifications framework.

Private and voluntary daycare providers

In contrast, those private and voluntary sector leaders who were not working towards children's centre status were observed to spend a large part of the day

Table 4.1 *Event sampling of 30-minute video highlights*

Shows frequency data (how many times an event occurred and the relative frequency of different events)

Roles and responsibilities (behaviours associated with events observed)	Administration (day-to-day systems and record-keeping)	Management (day-to-day financial management and monitoring of the needs of staff, children and families)	Leadership (future-oriented policy development related to staff, children, families and community in line with internal and external requirements)	Other
Integrated centre leader A	4 (Works with administrator in front office)	1 (Discusses new cook with another member of staff)	3 (Meeting with design team about new building)	1 (Talks aloud about work to researcher)
Integrated centre leader B	3 (Processes papers for new member of staff)	11 (Checks crying child in baby room)	5 (Meeting with building contractors)	2 (Talks to researcher about her work)
Integrated centre leader C	4 (Exchanges papers with administrator)	3 (Telephones to arrange welcome for new member of staff arriving in the holiday period)	3 (Visits parents' forum which is bringing together three disparate communities for first time)	2 (Explains to researcher background to matters being dealt with)
Foundation stage leader D	1 (Takes profiles to main office)	5 (Discussions about children's progress with staff)	3 ('Leads' her new head teacher in parents' meeting)	2 (Main duty teaching)
Foundation stage leader E	1 (Makes notes of staff discussion)	4 (Staff meeting with curriculum planning)	1 (Talks to teaching assistant about local training opportunities)	2 (Main duty teaching)
Foundation stage leader F	1 (Checks computer facilities)	1 (Liaises with speech therapist)	—	1 (Main duties deputy head and teaching)
Private sector leader G	1 (Form filling)	10 (Discusses pay and conditions with new member of staff)	3 (Networking regarding facilities for new children's centre)	1 (Talks to researcher about background to activities)
Private sector leader H	2 (Clarifies procedures for staff resignation)	9 (Staffing arrangements for summer period)	—	3 (Washes up and makes tea for staff)
Voluntary sector leader I	1 (Takes fax to office)	12 (Staffing arrangements for summer period)	—	—
Voluntary sector leader J	—	2 (Phones parent to apologize for missed session)	5 (Discussion of outcomes from staff away day)	2 (Discusses work with researcher)

engaged in general technical administrative and managerial tasks, related to matters such as staff cover over the holiday period, dealing with staff salaries, processing fees, co-ordinating the safe arrival and departure of children with their parents, talking to staff and the professional community. Neither of the leaders who focused on administrative tasks had employed an administrator, though one relied for support on two deputies who also carried out teaching responsibilities and the other relied on her childcare services team leader who was observed to spend most of her day providing the leader with administrative support. Their time was filled with indirect technical, staffing and public relations tasks.

The other private sector leader who was moving towards children's centre status also displayed leadership roles and responsibilities in facilitating staff development and training, directing curriculum policy formulation and development. Over the course of a day, although she worked indirectly with parents and children through her staff, she showed that she had a vision for the future and drew her staff into this organizational vision through, for example, the planning of visits to other provision and consulting with other providers. She was proactive in seeking opportunities, obviously enjoyed working with others both inside and outside the centre, was dedicated to her work and demonstrated her keenness to recruit the best people for the work in hand and had prior first-hand knowledge of running a business.

Integrated centre leaders

Integrated centre leaders and the voluntary sector leader working towards children's centre status were observed to spend time on a similar range of administrative and managerial tasks indirectly related to the client group. All had administrative assistance in this process though none had deputies. What appeared to distinguish children's centre leadership was its observed location within a complex organizational structure, systems and governance, attendant partnerships with other agencies requiring different policies and different regulations in order to plan and deliver services to meet joint outcomes, in line with changing legislation. In contrast to foundation stage leaders, integrated centre leaders were managing a changing and developing internal organization in the context of changing external priorities and requirements of different service frameworks as well as different performance and inspection imperatives. This required balancing the centre's vision and community needs with a changing government agenda, managing large capital and concurrent budget work observed through meetings and telephone calls with the local authority, builders, architects and other agencies such as social services, as well as personal reflections on future funding, staff development and concerns over longer-term sustainability.

Most noteworthy in integrated centre leaders' activities were the multiple domains of their activity-demanding multiple leadership functions related to working within a single organization. Responsibilities included large-scale personnel management, centre administration, community development, building external partnerships with stakeholders, as well as incorporating different teams of professionals, education and social work on the day of videoing.

Primary task

Analyses based upon key themes that have emerged from the Tavistock Consultancy Service, described by Huffington (2004a), that focus on the human dimension of enterprise and the multifaceted dynamics of the workplace have been promising and insightful in terms of understanding leaders' behaviour. Huffington (2004: 31) has drawn attention to the massive effect of internal and external change that has altered the psychological contract between organizations and their staff. In this context, leadership is needed to hold the organization together 'in a common purpose to articulate a shared vision, set direction, inspire and command commitment, loyalty, and ownership of change efforts'. These are the very skills and qualities identified by our leaders and staff in the previous chapter. In a very real sense, the video-recordings in the early childhood settings provided a unique opportunity to examine the relationship of the primary task that leaders and staff were employed to pursue, the meaning that this work had for them and what in practice they were observed to do. The original definition of the 'primary task' by Rice (1958) was of a task that a system has been created to perform, the priority it has over other tasks and the success with which this is performed. Miller and Rice (1967) later observed that the concept of the primary task provided a means to explore the ordering of multiple activities in the system where they existed and potentially a way to compare different organizations with the same or a different primary task. As emphasized by Obholzer with Miller (2004), however the concept of the primary task is defined, given its importance, it must be subject to ongoing debate in relation to organizational vision, direction, goals and functioning. Where the primary task is clear, as in the primary school foundation units, debate will be minimal but where an organization has multiple tasks as in the integrated centres, it becomes more complicated and there will need to be further debate.

Lawrence and Robinson (1975) developed the concept further to distinguish between:

- the 'normative' primary task, as the task that those working in the organization are expected to pursue;
- the 'existential' primary task, as the task that staff believe they are carrying out; and
- the 'phenomenal' task, as the task they are actually engaged in, whether or not they are aware of this.

Hoyle (2004) describes the optimal position as one where the normative primary task of an organization and the existential task are in alignment and staff identify with and believe in the task that they are employed to carry out. Where the normative and existential primary tasks are out of alignment, however, there could be resistant behaviour. This is demonstrated most clearly in the discomfort expressed by staff about business and entrepreneurial skills in the context of a profession they regard as caring and nurturing. A core leadership task could therefore be described as one of keeping the primary task in the forefront of staff's minds and continuously reviewing and modifying in the light of changing external circumstances. Where the task was clear, as with the 'enjoying and achieving' outcome for educators, there was little room for disagreement and great sense of purposeful activity observed. Similarly with integrated centre leaders with teaching qualifications this same strong sense of purposeful activity was being achieved through working directly with other staff. Where there were multiple tasks as in a children's centre – to improve outcomes for all children related to 'being healthy', 'staying safe' and 'enjoying and achieving' – there was greater complexity and scope for interpretation or misinterpretation. Obholzer with Miller (2004) stress the dangers of the primary task being corrupted by defensive processes arising from the work of the organization. Where there are multiple tasks, as in integrated centres, this raises a particular challenge not easily accessible through the course of a few hours' observation. On the one hand, the leader needs to maintain staff confidence and well-being so that the primary task remains manageable, despite changes in the outside world, and related anxieties can be addressed. On the other, the values, activities and outcomes need to be communicated to the external world of local stakeholders in the family, community and local authority.

Suffice to say at this point that the nature of the primary task was a vital ingredient in the leader–staff, staff–staff and staff–child relations and interactions. It was demonstrated in the patterns of interpersonal relationships between individual staff, the group or team and leader in the different settings. Foundation stage teams and their leaders, for example, showed high levels of commitment, dedication and emotional investment in working directly with children on the primary task to secure high-quality educational outcomes and raise their achievements. This appeared to provide a great sense of common purpose and attachment to cause. Other leaders worked indirectly but nevertheless intensively through their staff to lift the quality of performance of children and, hence, complete the primary task. This they attained through a range of strategies that had the intention of improving practice, such as coaching in fundamental activities associated with formative and summative assessment, record-keeping and encouraging curriculum development. Still others, who worked through other professionals and professional groups whose direct responsibility it was to deliver agreed outcomes for multiple primary tasks, at one step removed from children and parents, were inevitably more psychologically distanced and detached. Finally, some leaders were engaged in technical and administrative work that supported the completion of the primary task by dealing with everyday issues that, although less satisfying, were nevertheless vital to the smooth functioning of the organization.

4.4 Decision-making

Foundation stage leaders

Foundation stage leaders worked collaboratively at the team level with teaching colleagues, teaching assistants and other professionals in the setting. They were relaxed and friendly, 'hands on' yet task-focused, since they retained an overall responsibility for the quality of teaching and learning in the setting that was being fed into the wider decision-making within the overall school structures.

Private and voluntary providers

By contrast, the two private setting leaders and one of the voluntary sector leaders were observed to remain for much of the time in their offices making decisions related to money, staff and equipment integral to organizational functioning, as well as communicating and interfacing with the world outside, for example, discussing a recent chicken-pox epidemic with a local general practitioner. From time to time they consulted staff, participated in children's or parents' activities and involved themselves in the primary educare task of their staff.

Integrated centre leaders

The integrated centre leaders and voluntary sector leader moving towards children's centre status were observed co-ordinating multiple tasks, staff teams and projects though shared decisions related to operational matters and delegating decision-making to team leaders. But, as one participative integrated centre leader declared, the most exhausting aspect of open communication, shared decision-making and allowing 'everyone to have their say', was that it took considerable time, patience and energy. Democratic decision-making might be short-circuited through pressure of time, tiredness or the urgency of reaching a decision. Moreover, the integrated centre leaders themselves were typically located within a wider organization or authority that was observed to influence their decisions. As one leader mused, 'who leads the leaders?' However, as observed, it was the early childhood leader who was authorized by the organization to make decisions about staffing, finance and equipment, for instance, which was quite different in kind from sanctioning a team to execute a particular task. Power in the sense of being entrusted with the resources of the organization in order to implement decisions was also entailed and while this is different from 'authority' (or displaying an 'authoritative' style) staff clearly recognized that ultimately the leader would be judged in terms of the quality of the primary task of the organization.

A shift away from traditional styles of leadership

As indicated in previous chapters, a shift away from traditional, 'vertical' and hierarchical leadership to more flexible decision-making that takes place in conjunction with and in close contact with children, parents, community and other stakeholders is likely to be more suited to the needs of early childhood leaders and staff. This latter or 'distributed' model of leadership among individuals, groups and networks observed in integrated centres and foundation stage units calls for different skills in leadership and management. If staff are to become more involved in organizational decision-making and to understand the organization as a whole, this entails learning about and developing understanding about it over time. In turn, this is related to staff morale, and to how well led and motivated they are, as staff described in Chapter 3. It is also related to the way they are integrated and function as teams, as demonstrated by the foundation stage teams, for instance. It entails listening to parents, children and community as a whole outside the organization as well. The 'day in the life' observations of leaders uncovered many examples of cordial yet 'routinized' professional exchanges with parents that revealed little about the assumptions that each held of the other or the nature of parental participation.

Leadership in a time of change

There was a sense in observing these women leaders that they were leading organizational cultures in transition, as part of a movement away from traditional hierarchies and differentiation. In Chapter 3 this was described as vision-, strategy- and values-oriented; in other words, more person-centred, inspiring and influencing, as noted in the relationships between staff, other professionals, parents and children. This leads to authority that is negotiated and accepted but, above all, based upon shared values and trust (Mant, 1997). The survey and interviews made reference to mentoring, coaching and support from leaders. In turn, leaders were observed supporting new staff, celebrating the achievements of their teaching assistants and considering where the cook could gain appropriate NVQs. In most cases, there was high visibility.

Increasingly, the rate of change in organizations demands that more people are involved in decision-making related to vision and strategy. This may be very compatible with women's approach to leadership and hence leadership in the early years. It is leadership that responds to the needs of staff working within the organization as well as the external needs of other agencies, parents and the community. As emphasized in discussions with staff in the last chapter, it is about personal qualities and values that coalesce around common goals. In summary, traditional ideas of role, authority and power have had no place here. Purposes and primary tasks change and traditional boundaries no longer exist. What these women leaders exemplified was the shift from a traditional authority to one based on influence, relationships, collaborating with staff and interacting with families.

4.5 Influences on leadership

Major building projects

The challenge of change and growth to existing organizational cultures was an ever-present feature of the video highlights, with major new building work being planned and carried out and extended day provision being planned. Leaders of integrated centres were observed in meetings with builders, visiting building sites, discussing plans with colleagues and architects, in disputes about pathways and visiting adjacent settings to get ideas about fitments and furnishings. They spoke of and were observed finding themselves taking on major operational tasks, necessary to the changing nature and scale of their organizations, with a demand for financial management and administration with technical expertise or responsibility required for which they had no training or experience and, consequently, must learn 'on the job'. Crucial to this process was the capacity of leaders and staff to accommodate to change, to have a clear vision, to recognize existing knowledge of those around them and to empower others on the basis of areas of expertise and inclusivity in terms of diverse interests, cultures and capabilities. Of note too was their capacity to entertain and own uncertainty and self-doubt, and express this when observing their own videotaped behaviour, for instance, when participating in a meeting of building contractors in the case of one integrated centre leader or attending a parent forum comprised of three disparate communities in the case of another integrated centre leader.

Challenge of change

Early childhood leadership was observed to be centrally concerned with the management of internal and external change. Early childhood organizations were located within a radically different and shifting environment. Few early childhood professionals have been unaffected by the current political, social and economic change, bringing in its train cultural change to patterns in the workplace and in family life. This has necessitated adaptation to new ways of working by individual staff, staff teams, leaders and their organizations.

In this context, internal and external boundaries, structures and roles have become more fluid and old hierarchies less well defined, as experienced and expressed by our early childhood professionals. Throughout, there was an observed emphasis on vision and strategy for the future as a core function of early childhood leadership. At the same time, there was a reported emphasis on core values and the needs of children, parents and community, by active and dedicated early childhood staff. It is clear from the video highlights that early childhood leadership is about the management of internal and external change and that it requires structures and processes to exploit the opportunities in the external environment while maintaining sufficient equilibrium within the organization to protect core values and tested practices of practitioners. What emerges is the sign of personal cost to leaders who will not compromise in terms of values and provision of the highest possible quality in the primary task of the organization, in the context of day-to-day practical responsibilities and challenges of a new building emerging outside, for example, or maintaining a voluntary or private organization as it changes core roles and functions in order to qualify for children's centre status. Recognition by leaders of the speed and intensity of work, their visible tiredness and declarations that no leave can be taken until that building is completed masks a confidence based on previous experience that the enterprise in hand has to be manageable and challenges to this along the way will be absorbed. Hargreaves (1994) has recorded the intensification of educators' work related to the multiple innovations and imposed policy changes. What were less prominent in surveys, interviews and video observations were parents and community. Meetings and exchanges with parents took place during video-recordings but while they had a presence it was less easy to judge the substance of the relationships, their perceived value and inclusion.

4.6 Training

The need for new skills, knowledge and understanding across the sector

The need for new skills and understanding and, hence, training reform across the sector was another feature of the video highlights. Celebration and displays for parents of new 'on-the-job' NVQs and a recently acquired foundation degree provided a means of creating a positive organizational climate in foundation stage units. Welcoming trainees on work placements, greeting both newly qualified professionals as well as new members of staff was part of creating an inclusive environment in integrated centres. Such activities marked the new pathways into early childhood work being found and exploited for teaching assistants, nursery nurses, parents, cooks and dinner ladies.

Many of the issues that underpin the current changes in training, qualifications and workforce reorganization have been highlighted by previous chapters – the continuing perceived low status of the work, the variation in qualifications across the sector reflected in our survey findings as well as the need to work to the *Every Child Matters* agenda with its integrated workforce that was outlined in the opening chapter of the book. At one extreme are qualified teachers and leaders with master's degrees and, at the other, are staff with NVQs, developed initially at levels 2 and 3 to replace the course-based NNEB. Not represented in the survey, but nevertheless important in the sector, have been the new entrants with early childhood studies degrees and the Sure Start sector endorsed foundation degrees as well as the development of networks of childminders with a requirement to work towards level 3 qualifications. Rationalization and workforce reform may emerge from the Children, Young People and Families Workforce Development Council (CWDC) that seeks to bring together the playwork, health and school-based workforce, with strong representation from the early childhood sector. At the time of writing, an 'early childhood professional' at graduate level, has been created and individual settings will be encouraged to move staff through this training to the qualification with the support of a vast new Department for Education and Skills (DfES) transformation fund.

The lack of leadership training

The important role of leadership within this new workforce is yet to be determined. As observed from the video highlights, leadership of multi-agency teams with the primary task of raising children's achievements in the context of improved physical, mental health and safety is a challenge. The new NPQICL piloted by the NCSL with the Pen Green Children's Centre (Whalley et al., 2004) has been rolled out for delivery by universities and colleges providing leadership training to leaders and deputies in integrated centres drawn from community development, education, health and social work backgrounds. It has national standards and parity with the National Professional Qualification for Headteachers. This leaves unexamined the needs for development in leadership for the diverse range of settings included in our study.

Already, short courses for 'pre-NPQICL' are being developed and the interest in these attests to a felt need for development of leadership training more widely across the sector. As this section has indicated already, only leadership training that takes account of the varied journeys into leadership that these professionals have experienced can begin to address their very diverse developmental needs. It is a matter, however, for Chapter 6 where the important role of leadership within the early childhood workforce is reconsidered and the particular challenges of the workforce re-examined.

4.7 Collective views on the video highlights

The impact of internal and external change on leaders

When the leaders met to share their successes and challenges and compared their video highlights and experiences, there was much laughter and many exclamations at the pace of their work, their own (tired) appearance and the difficulty in taking a break as daycare and 'wrap-around' care continued to be provided through traditional school holiday periods. In terms of successes, they applauded themselves on responding to a new national childcare strategy in the local context and 'holding focus' in what they regarded as unique circumstances. They noted that new career pathways were opening up and yet, at the time of their meeting, early childhood leadership training was still confined to those leading in children's centres. They still saw themselves as 'leading by example' and responding intuitively 'on the spot', identifying the challenges and dilemmas of the human and 'feeling' side of their work. In many ways, looking at their own practice, as outsiders, uncovered not only what they understood and attended to, but also the underlying emotions, stresses and tensions that influenced the processes of decision and action, negotiation and change, conflict and creativity. This experience reminded the leaders of the undercurrents of their own emotions and states of mind and the relationship of this to their own social behaviour and hence group dynamics. It was also a broader reminder that the changes in the external environment and corresponding internal organizational changes did not leave leaders or staff unaffected. They shaped what early childhood practitioners felt and the way they behaved in obvious and less obvious ways. What female leaders bring to this is a willingness to make this discomfort and uncertainty a source for information and learning rather than a weakness to be hidden. In turn, fluidity and change in traditional boundaries and structures in organizations is leading to new conceptions of leadership and followership, hence, changes in thinking about task and role, power and authority. Here our leaders showed themselves able to draw confidently upon their personal and emotional resources as well as professional role requirements in order to be responsive to outside change as well as deeply attuned to their practitioners' understandings of and commitments to the primary task, and the impact on this of changes being made.

Leaders' expertise outstripped their children's service managers'

Leaders characterized the changes in the early childhood sector in terms of changed local authority structure and increased bureaucracy that was not moving as fast as staff in settings in terms of creating new dynamic patterns in relationships between individuals, teams and the organization. Moreover, there was a sense that senior local authority personnel might not always understand what needed to be done. The extension of days and hours of working was regarded as a challenge in respect of maintaining quality in provision, in team-building and training. Unstated was a recognition that constant change took its toll on the quality of the primary task in a climate of vigorous accountability and target-setting. The increased multi-agency dimension to work created a number of challenges associated with information-sharing and the difficulties in leading a team that might not necessarily be co-located, in the context of more fundamental differences in work culture such as pay, conditions and professional ethos. Here, leaders drew attention to the hidden and poorly documented value differences between professionals and between stakeholders that have to be made explicit and acknowledged before they can be addressed. The status of work in the sector in general was still regarded as low, although changing. However, it is clear that raised status, pay and esteem will be required in order to recruit and retain practitioners of the standard that young children and their families deserve. The current changes in structure and organization of promotion in school contexts, it was felt, might not necessarily advantage early years leaders.

Unease at provision of 'for profit' childcare services

The business and entrepreneurial side to the work was regarded as a particular challenge, given that 'it was hard to make a profit in deprived areas'. Moreover, the tougher edge of 'customerization' and increasing emphasis on 'consumer' and 'client' did not sit comfortably with their commitment to collaboration, partnership and development of people in organizations and their notions of external relationships. This aspect of leaders' work is considered in more detail in Chapter 5.

Culture of over-consciousness

Job and task overload was a recurrent feature, and the need to make time for reflection and self-evaluation was acknowledged. The culture of 'over-consciousness' first identified by Evans et al. (1994) in respect of early years teachers' response to the introduction of the National Curriculum and assessment is still a problem and, indeed, many of the teachers of that generation are the leaders of today. A number of questions are raised. Who leads the leaders and where does (or should) such support come from? How do leaders assess their success in the knowledge that different leadership capabilities will be required for different circumstances? With the exception of one voluntary sector leader, it was noted that while leaders might have line-managed supervision, they did not have a mentor. Also raised was the question of professional and interprofessional learning and development entailed in preparing individuals for collaborative practice, cultivating collaboration in groups and teams. This is considered in more detail in Chapter 7 while Chapter 6 takes a closer look at journeys into leadership.

▶ Leaders' own diary accounts were illuminating in revealing the pace of work in foundation stage settings, where leaders typically still retained a full-time teaching commitment; the greater emphasis on role differentiation and administrative duties of the private and voluntary sector; and the flexible arrangements for working within and outside the organization to secure the involvement of other agencies in the children's centre teams.

Practitioners' views 4.1

The foundation stage leader kept a running record of her day:

- 7.40 a.m. Saw caretaker – no chairs for meeting at 2.30 p.m.
- 7.45 a.m. SH a teaching assistant let us know that she had passed NVQ3.
- 7.50 a.m. Setting up of nursery.
- 8.00 a.m. Saw HP (reception-class teacher) regarding books/Jolly Phonics display for 2.30 meeting.
- 8.40 a.m. Saw head and checked that he knew about SH (the NVQ).
- 8.45 a.m. Checked teaching plan with DB (teaching assistant).
- 9.00 a.m. Opened door for nursery children.
- 9.15 a.m. Register and introduction of number game and concept of adding.
- 9.35 a.m. Outdoors, focus on skipping and den-making.
- 10.00 a.m. Fruit and milk. Discussed groups' activities.
- 10.25 to 11.00 a.m. Activities.
- 11.10 a.m. Office. Letters to new parents. Letter to fruit supplier.
- 11.30 a.m. Children go home.

(Continues)

(Continued)
- 11.35 a.m. School office to send fax.
- 11.35 to 11.45 a.m. Met with DB.
- 11.45 to 12.00 meet with AN (SENCO) regarding IEPs.
- 12.45 p.m. Children in.
- 1.00 p.m. Register. Counting/explanation of number game, as in a.m.
- 1.20 p.m. Outside (see a.m.).
- 1.30 p.m. Saw new head teacher regarding running new parents' meeting.
- 1.45 p.m. Fruit and milk. Get changed ready for meeting.
- 2.15 p.m. Children divided into groups for activity. HC (a teaching assistant) came into the nursery. Already appraised her of activity.
- 2.20 p.m. Into hall to greet/talk to parents.
- 2.30 p.m. Meeting started including introduction to new head and reception staff.

Practitioner's views 4.2

The leader of a private nursery also kept her running record of a day in her life:

- 10.00 a.m. NN handed in her notice to leave. Not unexpected but had to advise that terms and conditions stated that staff must give one full calendar month's notice which meant that proposed leaving date was not acceptable.
- Explained to parent how child's clothing was accidentally flushed away. Humour and tact required and parent good-natured about it.
- 4.00 p.m. Member of staff unhappy about holiday leave entitlement for fixed period.
- 5.00 p.m. Had discussion with parent whose child was bitten by another child.
- 5.30 p.m. Discussion with parent concerning booking through summer vacation.
(Most of the day spent on the computer sorting out staffing during the summer holiday period.)

Practitioner's views 4.3

The leader of the children's centre that had been an early excellence centre described her day:

- 8.15 a.m. Arrived at centre. Needed to check cover for one staff absence and look at training room diary to check usage. More rooms needed! My room given to provider development manager for supervision at 10.00 a.m. Nursery staff member on non-contact time to be moved to another part of the centre for 10.00 a.m., too.
- 9.00 to 10.00 a.m. Time to look at 'to do' list and action some calls and letters. Begin to process new appointment made yesterday. Set out training room and ask for drinks. (K had organized!)
- 10.00 a.m. Site meeting between ourselves as clients, property services from LEA (Project Managers and G the building contractor).
- 11.30 a.m. Walk on site. First time to see first-hand what the second build will be like. Very exciting. Decision to be made regarding height of plug sockets whilst on site.
- 12.00 noon. Dishwasher to fill from morning meeting.
- 1.00 p.m. Quick check that centre operating OK and architect asked for decision regarding wall on site. Went into nursery and began an interaction with child. Informed of concern about a member of staff.
- 2.00 p.m. Another meeting with auditor of company accounts. Very aware of group dynamics. This time, more younger than older and male than female participants. My role became one of trying succinctly to sum up what we were trying to say (by we, I mean, the governors). Meeting productive.
- 3.30 p.m. Meeting with Sarah and senior management team.
- 4.45 p.m. Meet with candidate for partnership post, outreach family worker. Candidate interviewed by social services already. Very taken with candidate. Talk to social services. Tomorrow to action process.

Practitioner's views 4.4

Another private provider described her day. Mainly office:

- 8.45 p.m. Spoke to parent about vouchers.
- Checked rota to see if any spare members of staff for cover of meetings, if needed.
- Saw parent about purchase of double buggy. Agreed.
- Work on computer updating timetables (ongoing throughout the morning).
- Collected fee payments.
- Survey by telephone with Learning Skills Council (pre-arranged as they needed to speak to owner).
- Spoke to architect on phone for hours! Needed information from him and kept saying to him – 'while you are on the phone'.
- Architect needed information from me regarding fixtures and fittings in new nursery by the middle of next week, therefore arranged to visit a nursery (NNI) nearby who have recently opened.
- Went into kitchen to discuss stock control with A.
- Sorted B's certificates, ensuring staff training qualifications are up to date.
- Discussed nursery summer outing with A and S.
- Rang parent regarding July fees. Discrepancy. Was disputing the amount with A earlier in the morning. Discussed on phone and agreed amount. Discussed holiday times on the phone.
- Asked S if she was able to sort out staff so that she could visit nursery with me.
- 12.15 to 12.45 p.m. Lunch.
- 12.45 p.m. M, previous employee, visited. Showed her new areas of nursery and talked to other members of staff.
- As unable to discuss 'Birth to Three Matters' with J, gave her a grid to start writing examples.
- Gave L, our new MA who will start in September, information on nursery.
- Staffing with S, the manager. Part-time and full-time staff needed in September.
- 2.30 p.m. Visited nursery with S.
- 3.35 p.m. Telephoned four prospective candidates to arrange visit to nursery.
- Discussed new menus and shopping with A for next two weeks.
- Discussed September hours with N and O.
- Discussed possibility of new stair-gate with J. Did not agree as too many obstacles in small area. Door should be kept closed. No hot water. S sorted out but told staff must put in problems book.

Practitioner's views 4.5

The leader of a children's centre, formerly a Sure Start project described her day.

- 8.30 to 10.30 a.m. *Administration and contracts*. Working through post, making contact with other professionals on my list and dealing with telephone calls from others. This particular morning, most of the incoming calls related to staffing issues and reflected the fact that many staff were about to go on holiday and needed to share information and ensure that handover of responsibilities was smooth. (This included me, too.) Currently we have a number of staff with personal issues and I needed to spend time catching up on their progress and trying to support them in sometimes stressful circumstances. I also have an open-door policy so can be visible in the centre for parents. Incoming mail was particularly large because I had been out of the programme for two days and there was therefore three days' worth.
- 10.30 to 11.30 *Visiting the Parents' Forum event*. Travel to SA for a parents' forum, organized by the family involvement worker and information team. Circulate with parents and interact with staff. Also observe quality of activities that we offer. Met with parents and their children who are actively involved in the Sure Start partnership board. Also parents I had met at a previous Sure Start event, a non-English-speaking group, who are now using our services. Tried to circulate and interact with all staff at the event to thank them for their efforts and observe them in their work.
- 12.00 to 2.00 p.m. *Meeting regarding Social Services' involvement in hate crime recording*. Met with Primary Care Trust officer responsible for health inequalities and City officer responsible for community safety. Discussed and planned future involvement in the development of hate crime reporting centres. Sure Start personnel to be trained to take reports and support people disclosing incidents as children's centres to become hate crime reporting centres.

CHAPTER FIVE

'I DON'T LIKE THE IDEA OF MAKING A PROFIT ... EXPLOITING THOSE ON LOW WAGES ...'

This chapter revisits leaders' and practitioners' views on entrepreneurial and business-oriented approaches to early education and childcare. It aims to review what leadership meant to our participants in respect of business and entrepreneurship; evaluate their perceived roles, responsibilities and characteristics in relation to business and entrepreneurship; and link their views to broader national and international policy trends and divisions between care and education.

5.1 Introduction

One significant area of leadership where ambivalent and contradictory attitudes by project leaders and staff could be discerned, related to their views concerning business and entrepreneurial skills. Indeed, this mixed and contradictory attitude threaded through the various stages of the project. Kagan and Bowman (1997) noted previously the general reluctance of early childhood leaders to identify leadership as part of their professional role and slowness in recognizing and making sense of theories and results from other fields, in this case, business management. Taking account of this, one might anticipate mixed feelings and attitudes towards notions of entrepreneurship, competition and power. At a broader level, these concerns reflect deep-seated and generally recognized unease about the division between care and education policy that continues in this country as in some other Organization for Economic Co-operation and Development (OECD) countries (Bennett, 2003). It can be characterized as a significant lack of investment in and supply of services for under-3s and the recent growth of the private sector. This chapter sets out, first, to review the attitudes of our project participants. They emerged in the initial survey, were illuminated by the interviews, and made manifest in the 'day-in-the-life' observations. These viewpoints are then placed within the wider context and consequences of imbalance of government investment in care services for under-3s and over-3s.

The survey

In terms of roles, responsibilities and functions, adopting an entrepreneurial approach that was mindful of competition with others in the sector was ranked first and included in the top five by only six people in our survey. Meanwhile, mean ratings for being business oriented and economically competitive as personal characteristics of effective leaders were at or below the 'moderately important' level, with being business oriented just above these. Being economically competitive was thus deemed at least moderately important by almost 50 per cent and, although just over one-third (35 per cent) viewed being business oriented as important to an effective leader, almost as many (32 per cent) believed that this characteristic had low or very low importance. At the same time, it was acknowledged that entrepreneurial leadership made quite a contribution to local sustainability, indicating an awareness of a demand-led market for care and education places. The interview data provided an opportunity to pursue these contradictory viewpoints in greater depth.

The interviews

Views of leaders, when asked directly in interview about the importance of business and entrepreneurial skills, however, were similarly mixed and contradictory. Two children's centre leaders and a school leader agreed that these skills were important, and qualified their response by admitting that business skills had had to be learned as they had no experience in this field and, moreover, financial decisions were shared by other members of the senior management team. Two other leaders from school settings agreed that such skills were important and again stressed that the head or senior management team took responsibility, for example: 'We will try anything to get money for projects but this is not really my role. I don't think I have these skills but I would try them.'

One private setting leader also agreed that such skills were 'probably important' and that 'such skills have had to be developed'. She claimed that she possessed those skills but 'relied upon solicitors and accountants to do these other things'. Yet another leader pointed out that her private, not-for-profit setting had a 'comfortable amount of money for resources' but observed that 'parents here spend a lot of money hence there is constantly pressure to achieve high-quality results'. In other words, she recognized the market-led context of her work and parents' expectation of a return in terms of outcomes for children on their investment in terms of fees. Another children's centre leader acknowledged that he had run his own business in the past but stressed:

> we are not a profit-making organization and have some responsibility which is moral and ethical as a public body, though some of the private sector may not have that.

This reinforced the view of the leaders that a market-driven return-on-investment approach, in other words profitability, sat uneasily with early childhood institutions that have ethical responsibilities in relation to choices made and practices engaged in.

Another private owner indicated that business skills were 'necessary for sustainability' but added 'there is a fine line between making it (the day nursery) business-like and a place for children'. Another voluntary sector leader with experience of the private sector replied:

> I did not like the profit end of the private sector. That is why I like being in the voluntary sector.

Staff, for their part, agreed that business and entrepreneurial skills were 'important but not as important as other areas' and, as with the leaders, believed such skills could be delegated to others. Throughout, a distinction seemed to be being made between the technical skills and practices required to run an effective business and a reluctant complicity in a system that provides childcare in a context of economic competition and change rather than (and opposed to) seemingly democratic and ethical practices. A strong picture emerged of a care ethic sitting uneasily alongside for-profit motives.

'Day-in-the-life' video recording

What arose from leader observations was domination by economic and business activities in private for-profit, voluntary not-for-profit *and* the welfare-oriented children's centres. Private and voluntary sector leaders at work, in practice, spent a large part of the day tackling general administrative tasks that related to the day-to-day financial aspects of their business arrangements, such as staff salaries, processing fees and dealing with small matters involving petty cash. On a larger scale, children's centre leaders were observed to be managing large capital expenditure and concurrent budget work, and personal reflections revealed concerns about future funding as well as future sustainability. Observations of state sector school-based leaders confirmed that their activities focused on the core business of educating 4- and 5-year-olds through public sector funding that was either administered elsewhere (as they affirmed) and/or took place outside teaching hours.

One might easily conclude that the observations merely mirrored the fragmentary nature of an English early childhood system that had developed with an imbalance between lack of public investment and supply of care services targeted for birth to 3-year-olds and an increased investment directed to education of over-3s, accompanied by a rapid expansion of the private over public sector. Overall, survey, interviews and observations point to a fracture in the psychological contract between early childhood institutions, their leaders and staff. Returning to the concept of primary task introduced in the previous chapter, there is a gap between the 'existential' primary task (the task that leaders are committed to and believe they are carrying out), the 'phenomenal' task (what they are actually engaged in) and the 'normative' primary task that those working in the organization are expected to pursue (Lawrence and Robinson, 1975). It is an indication that early childhood leaders' work cannot be fully understood and appreciated without reference to the broader early childcare and education policy context.

5.2 Early childhood education and care policy

As a result of changes to patterns in the labour market and child-rearing from the late 1980s to early 1990s, the policy of many governments has been to invest in early childhood services. The value of high-quality early childhood experiences to children's long-term social-emotional and cognitive development and school achievement has been increasingly recognized as a result of such research as the High/Scope Perry Preschool Study (Schweinhart, 2005), EPPE study (Sylva et al., 2004) and recent *Lancet* series (for example, Engle et al., 2007) on the economic cost to society of under-5s not developing to full potential. The need, on the one hand, to maintain economic prosperity by helping families combine work with childcare and, on the other, to address child and family poverty has kept provision of early care and education on the national and international agenda. Over a similar period, a series of early childhood education and care policy reviews of 20 countries in the OECD began in 1998 (Bennett and Taylor, 2006). These revealed a worrying trend in many OECD countries in the level of regulation of services for children under 3, where much of the sector is private, professional training and qualifications are poor and, therefore, variations in practice ensue.

At least two distinct approaches can be identified. A unified approach to lifelong learning and development from birth to school age is made available to all children whose parents wish to participate, is exemplified by the social pedagogy tradition of Nordic and Central European countries and is delivered by highly-qualified staff. By contrast, in a number of other countries including England, there are significant age-related differences, with training requirements for work with children birth to 3 significantly less than for children 3 years and older. Requirement for work with over-3s is typically a level-5 qualification on the International Standard Classification in Education (ISCED), United Nations

Economic, Scientific and Cultural Organization (UNESCO) 1997, with a focus on early childhood education/pedagogy (Oberhuemer et al., 2010, in their study of EU professionals).

Moreover, as Penn (2007) has noted, while a part-time nursery education entitlement is available to 3- and 4-year-olds in England, a substantial part of this nursery education is still provided by the private and voluntary, as opposed to the state sector. Bennett and Taylor (2006) have argued for broad guidelines and frameworks that promote more even quality across preschool age groups and provision. It is acknowledged that this would require most countries to double annual investment per child to ensure appropriate child–staff ratios and highly qualified staff. This is regarded as particularly important in the reduction of child poverty and diversity, as inclusion in high-quality universal provision is regarded as the most effective and most equitable approach. It would also require an improvement in recruitment, professional education and training, working conditions and pay of early childhood workers. By these means it might, however, be possible to achieve the ethical and democratic values to which our early childhood leaders aspire.

5.3 Early childhood professional and workplace issues

As noted already, levels of qualifications and pay vary considerably across the sector and in relation to ages of the children concerned. Moreover, the sector is served by a variety of providers from the private, voluntary and independent sector to state provision. On the whole, those working within the state-maintained sector have higher qualifications and command higher salaries. With *Every Child Matters: Change for Children* (DfES, 2004b) an integrated approach and universal services model was introduced. Related to this and relevant to this chapter, *Choice for Parents, the Best Start for Children: A Ten-Year Strategy for Childcare* (HMT, 2004) acknowledged the need for a 'step-change' in the quality of the workforce, training, qualifications and skills, heralding a commitment to a strategy to address the unevenness in provision, in particular, to ensure graduate-level leadership for daycare settings. Moreover, *Every Child Matters: Next Steps* (DfES, 2004c) proposed a consultation on the workforce strategy, including pay and conditions. The government's response to consultation, *Children's Workforce Strategy: A Strategy to Build a World-Class Workforce for Children and Young People* (DfES, 2006c), set out plans to increase qualifications levels and introduced a new Transformation Fund (replaced by a Graduate Leader Fund in 2008). *Children's Workforce: Building an Integrated Qualifications Framework* (DfES, 2006d) emphasized the need for further reform and an integrated qualifications framework that was supposed to be operational from 2010. Since 2006, a new early years professional (EYP) has been introduced to lead practice in the early years foundation stage. The aim of the government was to have EYPs in each of the 3,500 children's centres planned to be in place by 2010, in every daycare setting by 2015 and with two EYPs in daycare settings for the 30 per cent most disadvantaged areas. The Children, Young People and

Families Workforce Development Council (CWDC) was given the task of developing the professional standards for the EYPs (DCSF, 2008a), with graduate status supposedly equivalent to qualified teacher status (QTS).

In practice, the maintained sector has not recognized equivalence of EYP with QTS, and issues of pay and conditions remain unresolved. Meanwhile, an update to the *Children's Workforce Strategy* appeared, (DCSF, 2007a) and *The Children's Plan* (DCSF, 2007b) committed the government to further expansion of free early education places and an increase in the number of graduate EYPs. *Building Brighter Futures: Next Steps for the Children's Workforce* (DCSF, 2008a) brought a renewed commitment expansion of early education provision and consolidation of the workforce, as noted above.

Sylva et al. (2004) had shown that the qualification level of a centre head was associated with its overall quality ratings. Since that time, English policy has required a significant increase in the number of graduates in the private, voluntary and independent early childhood sector and a nationally recognized integrated centre leadership qualification has been introduced. Issues related to pay and conditions continue to be ignored and leave unexamined the broader characteristics of the early childhood workforce employed in the private, voluntary and independent sector.

5.4 Making a profit: the role of the private sector

Sumsion (2006) investigated the possible implications of the rapid growth of the corporate sector in childcare services in Australia. She was interested to investigate whether corporatization affected the nature of provision, the ways in which it might do so and whether these changes might conflict with other social goals. She regarded this as a reflection of the pervasive neo-liberalism facing all western societies, making complex decisions concerning childcare policy against a backdrop of commitment to consumer choice, competitiveness, profit maximization and a reduction in the state's role. 'Neo-liberalism' is thus used here to indicate the way in which consumer choice (in this case childcare) characterizes public sector reform and individual competitive entrepreneurship is encouraged. Unable to identify evidence of the impact of corporatization, she put together a series of questions related to market operation and effects as a means of interrogating privatization in the early childcare sector, such as:

> Who benefits? Who is disadvantaged? How does power operate and how are its effects made visible? How is power mediated by ideologies and for what purposes, and what are the implications for social justice? (Kincheloe and McLaren, 2005, cited in Sumsion, 2006:105)

In terms of market operation and effects, the Laing and Buisson (2010) review of private day nurseries provides interesting insight into the corporatization of the children's nursery market. They noted that an estimated total of 290 nursery groups (with three or more nurseries) accounted for one-fifth (20.5 per cent) of total nursery places in 2009, with the top 20 groups accounting for the bulk of corporate market share, (at around 9.6 per cent of total nursery places. As they conclude from this:

> In what remains a very fragmented sector, the largest groups have only minor shares of the total market with the leader *Knowledge Universe* holding a 1.7% share. (Laing and Buisson, 2010: 2)

Some contraction in the net nursery stock (by 3.4 per cent) during 2009 owing to the recession was noted, although market conditions for many had started to improve. On average, UK nurseries were operating with a reduced vacancy rate of 17.5 per cent at March, 2010, compared with 20.5 at the start of 2009. The average fees charged per child by private sector nurseries were £150 per week, or £30 per day.

Meanwhile, the biggest cost for a nursery provider is staff, although this can vary from provider to provider from as little as 50 per cent to 70 or 80 per cent, which can be the difference between making a profit and struggling to break even. Indeed, a recent survey (DCSF, 2008b) indicated that 30 per cent of full daycare providers made a profit or surplus, 33 per cent reported that they were covering costs and 18 per cent reported they were operating at a loss. Apparently, a further 19 per cent claimed not to know.

With the government requirement to employ more graduates will come expectations of higher salaries. Since ratios of staff to children are fixed by law, older children may be assumed to be 'more profitable' (with a one to eight ratio) than babies (aged 2 and under with a minimum ratio one to three and 2- to-3-year-olds, a ratio of one to four). According to Laing and Buisson, in 2009 the average wage for a qualified nursery employee was £7.74 an hour and for unqualified staff an average hourly rate of £6.15. Even so, this is considerably less than a graduate employee whose higher salary might be balanced by taking on more trainees. Premises represent the second largest cost, with utilities and food representing other regular incurred costs.

With respect to quality, a recent report from Her Majesty's Chief Inspector (OFSTED, 2009) reports that 95 per cent of early childhood provision is at least satisfactory with 65 per cent good or outstanding and 5 per cent inadequate. Well-established provision offers higher quality, although areas of socio-economic disadvantage are below that elsewhere and therefore more likely to be in the public sector.

Such an analysis, does raise the question of whether, and to what extent, private providers are inclined to provide more than minimum quality care, to promote pay, conditions and professionalism of their childcare workers and to commit to a broader ethical agenda.

5.5 Preschool care and education plc?

As noted by PriceWaterhouseCoopers (2006), since the early 1990s, the childcare market has seen strong growth in volume of places and in fees. Supply, however, remains highly fragmented, with the largest provider commanding 1.8 per cent of the market share, and the top 40 private providers 10 per cent of total places. There is some evidence of 'consolidation' or takeover but not much likelihood of this increasing very much at a time of market uncertainty that could reduce parent choice and market flexibility still further, and impact on outcomes for children in terms of standards of care. Meanwhile, local authorities (LAs) were seen to be focusing more on meeting goals related to the children's centres and extended schools agenda, and free entitlement to nursery education for 3- and 4-year-olds. It was noted by PricewaterhouseCoopers that working families unable to afford the full cost for a childcare place and not in a position to take advantage of children's centre capacity might not find their needs served. Unequal access to provision, which may in any case be of lower quality, by parents and children from disadvantaged background is likely to ensue.

Ball (2007) has concluded that education policy is increasingly regarded in terms of its economic value and contribution to international market competitiveness and, as noted by our project leaders, the bottom line for business is profit. Privatization of daycare means that new people, locally, nationally and internationally, are making it their business to influence early childhood policy. Sumsion (2006) has reminded us of the need to keep in mind, ethical obligations and moral values when considering the role of private sector and privatization.

A major area of concern focuses on government's reluctance to rationalize the early childhood workforce in terms of qualifications, pay and conditions. It reflects an unwillingness to destabilize the private, voluntary and independent sector contribution and a preference to leave early childhood professionals' salaries, and hence status and esteem, subject to market forces. But as Owen and Haynes (2010) concluded, only with raised status, pay and esteem will it be possible to attract and retain early childhood professionals who will provide the highest standards for young children and their families.

The OECD early childhood education and care review led Bennett (2003) to consider the consequences of the imbalance of public investment and supply of services for under-3s and over-3s. A key point he made was that early childhood provision cannot be left entirely to the market. Significant public funding is necessary to support a sustainable and equitable early childhood system. A simple market model with a well-defined product, competition and choice for a well-informed consumer will not work in the case of early childhood provision. Here, as noted above, disadvantaged consumers from 'at risk' backgrounds cannot exercise choice, and not all provision is of good quality. The consequence is inequality of opportunity for parents to receive appropriate public support in their child rearing, inequality of access to occupation, salary levels, career prospects, life earnings and pensions for working mothers and, hence, sex inequality.

▶ Our early childhood leaders expressed a range of views concerning the importance of business and entrepreneurial skills.

Practitioners' views 5.1

- I would like to say, 'no', but we are in voluntary organizations. We need to have knowledge of business planning and gaining funding in order to sustain ourselves.
- In the voluntary sector, we are not a profit-making organization.
- I think in today's climate you must have business skills, otherwise the sustainability is compromised. There is a fine line between making it a business and making it a place for children in the private sector.
- In the independent sector, we have to sell the place to prospective parents.
- With charging fees, business and entrepreneurial skills are very important or we would not have a nursery.
- It is of growing importance. We need to have business-management skills in children's centres. It's also becoming more important in applying for grants.
- Marketing – competition with other providers, in terms of length of sessions, hourly rate and getting children into the nursery – is important in the private sector.
- Not being known locally is a concern, despite advertising in the voluntary sector.

CHAPTER SIX

JOURNEYS INTO LEADERSHIP

This chapter traces the practical paths or journeys into leadership and explores the support needed at different points in a leadership career trajectory, as beginning, competent and master leaders. It reveals that leaders are rarely supported through their career cycle.

6.1 Introduction

As our survey revealed, the English early childhood workforce is still overwhelmingly female, with qualifications and hence levels of pay that vary very widely despite the introduction of the *National Framework of Qualifications* (QCA, 2001). Remodelling of the childcare workforce has its origins in the *Every Child Matters* Green Paper (DfES, 2003a) with a new *Children's Workforce Strategy* consultation paper (DfES, 2006a), the setting up of the Children's Workforce Development Council and the creation of an 'early childhood professional' at graduate level through various pathways, supported by a Transformation Fund. A list of skills, knowledge and practical experience that early years workers will have to meet to achieve the new professional status has been published. The hope is that this will allow early years practitioners to be able to progress to a situation where the new professional will have pay, status and conditions that match the profession of teaching and in time lead to the new NPQICL.

6.2 A journey?

It is no surprise that Bloom (1997) described the narratives of 20 early childhood directors' careers and professional development as 'navigating the rapids'. She cited Bateson (1989: 10) who observed that 'the act of composing our lives is oftentimes improvisation, discovering the shape of our creation along the way, rather than pursuing a vision already defined'. Bloom likened becoming an early childhood 'director' or leader to improvisation, noting that such people lacked insight into their career motivations and did not have a well-conceived plan for achieving the professional experiences that would help them fulfil career goals. She identified metaphorical themes that captured the personal career experiences of leaders she interviewed. One of these was a journey: 'going on a road trip – lots of surprises, a few road-blocks and detours, but never a dull moment'; 'a never-ending road that is rough and smooth, curvy and straight, wide and narrow, and taking me to the place I want to go, with many rewarding stops along the way'; 'being on a road trip – I sometimes encounter heavy traffic, detours, wrong turns, and near-miss crashes, but I'm headed in the right direction'.

Leadership as narrative

Gardner (1995: 14) in his anatomy of leadership also captured leaders' stories or narratives as dynamic and unfolding over time, in which: 'they – leaders and followers – are the principal characters or heroes. Together, they embark on a journey in pursuit of certain goals, and along the way and into the future, they can expect to encounter certain obstacles or resistances that must be overcome'. Hunter and Egan (1995) affirmed the power of creating and sharing stories, narratives and reflections. They considered that in composing such stories and narratives, questions are addressed, such as: how have they shaped who I am and what I might become; what kind of world do I wish to live in; how ought we to live; what is the right action to take; how do I care for others, for myself; what values and commitments are most important to me and why; what can I learn from such stories and visions? Richardson (2002) described narratives about contexts in which the writing is produced as 'auto-ethnography' or 'writing-stories', indicating that some stories are painful and others are joyful. Above all, they sensitize us to the potential of such writing in illuminating ourselves, our workplaces and work spaces.

Gronn and Ribbins (1996: 464) described three ways in which biographies of leaders' careers in context facilitated theorizing about leadership. First, they may be inspected for evidence of the development and learning of leadership attributes; second, they provide an analysis of the ends to which leaders have directed their attributes throughout their careers, within shifting demands and available options; and third, a comparative analysis of leaders' career paths as revealed in biographies can address broader questions about leadership attributes in different organizational, cultural and societal contexts.

Leadership as career phases

Gronn (1993; 1994) argued that leadership might be thought of as four broad career phases or stages: formation, accession, incumbency and divestiture. Formation relates to the socialization into institutional norms and values (for instance, morality, belief or authority) by the key agencies of family, school and reference group by generating conceptions of self, work style and outlook. Accession follows preparation and concerns the positioning of potential leaders for advancement while demonstrating credible and creditable performance. Incumbency involves the induction into the new leadership role and organizational norms. Divestiture of leadership, planned or unplanned, voluntary or involuntary may be either smooth or traumatic. Moving through these four stages is linear, sequential and chronological, and indeed can be viewed from within the particular historical or social and cultural contexts within which the events took place.

6.3 Career paths of early childhood leaders

Early learning experiences of leaders

The absence of a focused path towards leadership in the case of early childhood careers is unsurprising given that the field overall lacks a clear framework, established progression routes and, as the next chapter shows, lacks the kind of mentor relationships that serve to guide and coach at critical career points.

Six of the 11 leaders who we interviewed had been teachers, some for a very long time (in one case for 31 years), three had been nursery nurses, one a social worker and another, a community development worker. Some had worked in a variety of posts such as play scheme worker, youth worker, teaching in secondary and further education, running a business, engaging in freelance work and setting up a voluntary organization. All but one had been in leadership posts for three to six years, the majority for two to three years.

At the beginning of their leadership careers, three appeared to have had support from a previous incumbent, in one case being granted a day a week to study, in another case given the loan of 'loads of books' and in a third case inheriting a system of documentation. Two talked about support from other employers and one from a husband with business and information technology (IT) skills: 'we ran a business but we didn't have a clear idea about being in a childcare setting'. One of those who did not receive support complained of 'frustration at not being given proper, thorough and clear direction before starting the project'. Another reported that:

> At that stage a supportive head would have helped – I had a head who said that
> it was my job to get on with it. I learned my leadership skills through what I saw
> around me and role models as to how not to do it. I developed my own style,
> dependent upon my own beliefs and characteristics.

Yet another reported her predecessor was the main barrier:

> She had built partnerships with various organizations across the city but when she left, the responsibility for this did not pass to me. The fault lay with the person, not the role. I spent 18 months trying to get on the partnership boards … I tried picking up the pieces because things were left undone.

The last leader reported that: 'As a new head I didn't know who to phone. I used a new link inspector but he was far from empathetic which was not good – therefore I stopped telling him anything.'

Asked if they had a role model at the time, all but two replied 'no'. One elaborated – 'in the first year, I just fumbled through with available staff'. Another affirmed that although the head was not a role model she was a mentor – 'who gave support and confidence and gave me staff who were competent and experienced'.

Further professional development of leaders

In terms of further professional education and development experienced, all four integrated centre leaders had completed master's programmes, one a Master's in Business Administration (MBA) and the other three programmes that included modules on leadership and management. Asked which experiences had been most useful, five thought that 'all experiences were useful' and one remarked 'I have applied some of them'. Another one mentioned the benefit of short courses. Two thought contact with other professionals provided the most useful support, although in one case this was in the context of course attendance, while the other valued 'talking to people about generic issues'. One rated personal experience more than theory: 'theory has its place but you learn as you go along with background knowledge of management, business planning, budgeting and so on'.

What is most striking about these accounts is the leaders' own sense that becoming competent at something new, in this case leadership, came primarily from experience of doing it, in this case leading. It is equally clear that experience is not enough on its own. Having someone else to help reflect upon and make sense of this experience helped to construct knowledge, but new experience, in turn, allowed this knowledge to be applied to new situations. Everyday experience and real-world situations were central, but so was help from someone else in order to review these everyday activities and processes. There was a general acknowledgement that short and long training and award-bearing courses had had their place but experienced 'others' and one's own daily experience were what really supported the learning journey and helped to develop practice. What emerged quite spontaneously from this group of leaders was a cycle of concrete experience, reflective observation, making sense of experience (or abstract conceptualization) if not performing differently (or active experimentation), a process akin to Kolb's (1984) learning cycle. Moreover, it was felt that there was a place for leaders' action, reflection, theory, and trying things out.

Advice for new leaders

Asked what advice they would give to other early years beginning leaders, our leaders suggested:

- 'Stick at it, know yourself, really understand the impact that you have on all other people, like staff, governors, community and children. Don't be scared but understand the implications of relationships.'
- 'Treat and work with others as you would want to be treated.'
- 'Inspire people and find inspiration in others.'
- 'Take opportunity to visit each other ... have a knowledge of the range of provision that is out there.'
- 'Listen to people, be flexible, adapt to change and enable other people to do the same.'
- 'Try to maintain the enthusiasm for what you are doing in the face of bureaucracy.'
- 'Believe in yourself and be confident because everyone is an expert.'
- 'Do it only if you are willing and really enjoy it!'

A strong theme that emerged was building capacity in other people. However, as one leader emphasized, 'leadership is a lonely place' to which a leader in our team responded on reading this, 'it certainly is!'

As emphasized in previous chapters, Huffington (2004b) suggested that women leaders are creating a real shift in organizational life. They describe an inhospitable organizational culture that does not inspire people to follow and, at the same time, they are struggling to create a different values-driven culture that concentrates on treating people as individuals. Moreover, there is an indication that younger people may want different things from work and life – with good working relationships and friendly working conditions (Doyle, 2000).

Leadership as a career cycle

In terms of the leader's career cycle or professional journey there was a sense of change and development from one of barely surviving to one of confidence-building, enthusiasm, reflection and inspiration. No two leaders, however, responded in the same way as career development depends upon the particular experiences, circumstances located within a particular life history and socio-biography. Bloom (1997: 35) identified three stages of leadership: the beginning director, the competent director and the master director.

The beginning directors experienced concerns about their adequacy, their ability to handle the demands of the job and their desire to be liked and appreciated. They also harboured concerns about the quality and impact of their programme or primary task. Many, but not all leaders (or directors) that she spoke to had a survival focus – being preoccupied with meeting the multiple demands of the job and their status personally in the organization and externally in the field.

The competent director emerged through a period of competency-building after between one and four years in the job, when it shifted from 'struggling to juggling'. At this stage, the director was no longer concerned about merely coping but concerned about meeting expectations, internal and external, with a shift to concerns about managing them better.

The master director had reached a higher level of reflection and competence: 'the metacognitive ability to stand back and reflect on *how* they are doing *while* they are doing it' (Bloom, 1997: 36). Master directors also stressed the importance of the 'role model' and 'mentor'. Interestingly, while our leaders stressed the importance of role models and mentors to them at the beginning of the leadership cycle, coaching, mentoring and support was one of a number of current roles and responsibilities that they now fulfilled, particularly so in the case of foundation stage leaders who stressed the importance of their professional practice on the lives of children, their families and community. They were thus both process- and outcome-oriented, aware of the challenges in their leadership role yet demanding of themselves and others of the highest standards of achievement for their children. Other staff in their settings meanwhile responded in much the same way as their leaders when projecting back to their early experiences of leadership, emphasizing 'training courses and academic study' and 'experience and role models'. These responses also echoed the responses made by our wider group of leaders, much earlier in our initial meeting. (Appendix 5 provides a series of self-questions that relate the journeys into leadership through to competent and mastery leadership.)

While leaders in foundation stage units prioritized their time to focus directly upon children's enjoyment and achievement, leaders in other settings shifted their attention to planning, vision-building and working indirectly through other staff to deliver multiple tasks on multiple fronts. Review of the video highlights enabled them to acknowledge the difficulty in standing back, reflecting on and analysing the effectiveness of their leadership style and applying the outcomes of these reflections to future actions. Despite this, as leaders revisited the video-recordings showing their own performance in the context of local and regional conferences, their capacity to think self-critically continued to deepen and their capacity to interrogate their own practice increased.

6.4 Support through the career cycle

The reported changes that exemplify the thoughts and experiences of the leaders' journeys or career cycles could serve as a stimulus to identifying broader trends in early childhood leadership professional development needs. Of note was the beginning leaders' reported lack of support and survival or subsistence level of functioning. The perceived attractiveness of receiving mentor support from a more experienced colleague was evident. Despite an emphasis being placed on future-oriented leadership skills, the need for developing everyday technical expertise in administration and management for the beginning leader may receive too little attention. This is where a more experienced peer might adopt a coaching approach to help new leaders develop their capability and begin to realize their potential. Skill in juggling and balancing in the competent leader phase can be enhanced by the appropriate distribution of tasks to other trusted staff in order to create leadership at all levels. This serves to flatten hierarchies, create horizontal networks, interaction and interdependence across tasks within an organization and promote strategic partnerships with families, communities and other providers.

Providing leaders with knowledge that will help them more fully to comprehend the career development path they follow and the experiences they encounter can be achieved through coaching and mentoring. It will stimulate reflection, review and refinement of this personal experience and guide new leaders on their way. This of course is one obligation for the master leader, who can make a real contribution to the professional learning and development of others in the profession. This was seen in the case of some of our leaders, who, having received no mentoring themselves, were now engaged in tutoring, coaching and mentoring their colleagues on the NPQICL, on local authority short courses and at conferences that have emerged from the project.

'Navigating the rapids' calls for technical expertise, the calculation of risks and the countering of obstacles in the early stages of leading. Greater knowledge of the career cycle 'journey' with mentoring and coaching along the way to identify a roadmap, to steer round 'detours' and to survive 'near-miss crashes' will better equip leaders to manage their own progress and development.

▶ Leaders described their own journeys into leadership, the paths they had taken, roles that they had fulfilled.

Practitioner's views 6.1

At the time of my involvement in the project, I was Foundation Stage Phase leader, teaching in the nursery. My previous teaching experience at this school (over 14 years) included a brief time in Key Stage 1 (for 5- to 7-year-olds) as Phase leader but was predominantly in the Reception year of the Foundation Stage. Prior to this, I was teacher-in-charge of a 60-place nursery unit in a multicultural area of the West Midlands. During my time at the present school I was fortunate to undertake two secondments within the local authority, developing and using the skills and experience I had gained as an early years practitioner. The first secondment was for two years on a 0.2 (FTE) basis working as a partnership teacher supporting practitioners in the non-maintained sector deliver an effective curriculum of high-quality experiences to 3- and 4-year-olds. The second secondment was as a children's centre teacher 0.2 (FTE), providing practical teaching support for early years practitioners. At present, I am continuing to share and to develop my early years experience in a full-time role as a senior partnership adviser in the City early years and childcare team, leading a new team of experienced practitioners to support and advise on effective practice in the early years.

Practitioner's views 6.2

I was one of the first integrated centre leaders to receive the NPQICL and left my job as Sure Start programme manager in order to be part of the NPQICL roll-out. For three years I led, managed and developed a Sure Start local programme that has now developed into two children's centres, supported by a multidisciplinary team of 37. This role also involved supporting a multi-agency partnership board, including local parents. The local programme ensured the delivery of high-quality early education, health and lifelong learning opportunities in two neighbourhood nurseries and a range of community settings. Before I was the programme manager of a Sure Start local programme I was early years partnership worker, learning support assistant and field development worker with the Preschool Alliance. I was also deputy director for an early excellence centre for four years and then an early educational development officer.

Practitioner's views 6.3

I am head of centre at an early excellence centre that has become a children's centre. I had been in post for seven years when I became head of the nursery. Since then I have seen the site change from being two buildings, one a portacabin hut for family services and one a Second World War 'horsa hut' housing a nursery school into a purpose-built early years centre. We still have two buildings today but now fit for the twenty-first century! Today three services operate from the centre: a nursery education service, a family service and a provider development service. These services offer a range of advice and support to families with young children and also for the range of workers in the education and childcare sector. Before this position, I was a nursery teacher and I have also taught reception-aged children. I trained as a mature student after running a playgroup in a village hall when my children were small.

Practitioner's views 6.4

I am a qualified teacher with over 25 years' experience in the education service, including primary, secondary and further education organizations. Four years ago our company acquired its first nursery. The company is jointly owned by my husband and myself, and it has two main operations: the daycare division which I run and my husband's IT management consultancy. We acquired our daycare setting in a relatively run-down state and have since invested substantial time and funds to bring it to its current position. It now operates to full capacity (12 babies, 8 toddlers, 8 preschoolers) and we have achieved a good OFSTED rating together with 'Quality Counts' accreditation.

About two years ago, we successfully applied for funding to open a children's centre in a suitable property that has now been substantially renovated and is due to open soon as a 50-place day nursery (18 babies, 16 toddlers, 16 preschoolers), subject to OFSTED registration. The centre also has a community room and we employ two development workers to build links with the local community and appropriate agencies (for example, Job Centre Plus, Primary Care Trust, Social Services). This project, including the planning, design and construction phases, has taken a substantial amount of my time over the last year.

My time will now be spent overseeing the activities of both settings and working with my managers to ensure that we maintain appropriate resources, equipment, recruitment/employee relations, policies and procedures, marketing and communication processes.

Practitioner's views 6.5

I am children's services co-ordinator in a voluntary sector organization and a registered charity. This provides a range of services including support and accommodation for families in crisis, training opportunities for parents, counselling services and a registered nursery. We have been approved as a children's centre and work extended the nursery facility to increase the number of places. I have worked here for six years during which time a number of changes have taken place. From a small crèche facility we moved to full early years care and education. We then became a neighbourhood nursery. I have worked with and continue to work with many very motivated and interesting people who have a range of skills and expertise and this in itself has aided my growth as a leader. In my post here I have had two line managers both of whom have been key in my development. Before coming to the present organization, I worked in the private sector as a nursery manager. The nursery in which I spent most years as manager was a newly opened one at that time. I then went on to become a trainer and assessor and worked again for a private provider. In this post I worked across the Midlands with NVQ students. It took me some time to find the right place. I worked in no less than three nurseries before I finally found an organization that wanted the best for service users and employees. I finally found it and here I have stayed since!

CHAPTER SEVEN

MENTORING AS A LEADERSHIP STRATEGY

This chapter looks at mentoring as a strategy for staff development. It considers learning from experience and the nature of mentoring in the leadership context. It suggests that individual and group mentoring have a significant role to play in professional learning and development.

7.1 Introduction

If, as has been hinted in previous chapters, decisions by staff are to be taken away from the centre or hub of the organization or setting and shared across their job functions as well as contacts that they make with the external environment, then the organization itself must first be a learning community. It requires deep understanding by staff of the primary tasks being carried out, the contributory tasks being executed at various levels as well as the establishment of a new set of complementary roles that involve a greater personal authority and individual administrative and management competence and independent decision-making by all staff. At the same time, new work structures inevitably mean renegotiation of roles and accountabilities, creating greater uncertainty and ambiguity in an already fast-changing outside world. The challenges and potential benefits from new organizational structures and leadership will need to be supported by mentors and coaches working within the organization at different levels. The previous chapter has shown that our leaders themselves were rarely supported in this way through their career cycle. Staff interviews similarly revealed that they had little such experience and while 'books had their place' and 'courses confirmed what you were already doing', 'experience was more useful': 'a lot of it is what you are picking up day to day from hands-on experience'. Indeed, development days run by the leader, they felt, were the 'best way to deal with things, working with problems and ... steps to leadership'. Both leaders and staff confirmed that everyday experience was central to their learning and any organizational development strategy mounted would need to provide opportunities to help them review and learn from these experiences.

7.2 Learning from experience

Leaders *and* staff in our project felt the lack of and need for a mentoring approach to enhance capacity and develop potential by learning through experience. The use of more experienced professionals within the setting to act as mentors involves not only the setting up of a mentoring scheme but the creation of coaching for teams in order to establish a learning organization. It has different purposes at the different points in any individual career cycle. In principle, it could be argued that everyone should have the benefit of a mentor. In practice only one of our leaders was receiving regular mentor support. Mentoring has a clear role to play in the support of new staff. It can help more experienced and usually female staff to reassess their career aspirations. Hence, it can provide support for transition into the setting or organization, for the setting of long-term career goals as well as offer support to more experienced staff working in particular contexts or conditions of external change. More generally, if mentoring becomes an integral part of the early childhood setting there is a genuine chance that the organization will become a learning community and the culture will become one where learning, self-development and development of others through reflective conversations is the norm. In turn, this should create greater job satisfaction and less staff turnover. Moreover, given the current rate of change, where relations between the organization and the external world are increasingly fluid and unpredictable, stable staff interactions and interdependence may be challenged and individuals' (leaders' and staff's) relationship to the organization and to their own work needs to be re-examined.

Ten years ago, Rodd (1996: 123) proposed that leadership can and should be taught to aspiring and actual leaders. If, as suggested in the last chapter, leadership can be approached from a developmental perspective, 'it is important for individuals to be committed to lifelong learning, to be able to regularly reflect upon and learn from experience, to extend ... professional knowledge and to participate in professional development activities'. This requires self-awareness of one's own strengths, skills, values, interests and limitations, and a willingness to seek actively feedback from other staff, parents, colleagues and peers. Also important is the transfer or application of existing skills to new contexts, as noted by one of our integrated centre leaders who possessed an MBA, and who had wide experience of working as a social worker, community worker, setting up voluntary organizations, working on a freelance basis and serving as a planning and development officer. Furthermore, many previously-acquired 'people' skills (roles and responsibilities associated with leadership), professional management and administrative skills as well as warm, caring and nurturing attributes, will already be in place and can be transferred to new contexts and situations. This suggests that there may already be many experienced people within (or outside) the setting or organization who can act as listeners, who can challenge and extend learning from existing experience and offer advice.

7.3 The nature of mentoring

Interestingly the one leader in our project who was receiving mentoring was doing so from both the line manager within the organization (the director of her voluntary organization and a trained counsellor) and externally and in an informal capacity from a former adviser. But before proceeding further a more fundamental question needs to be addressed – what exactly is 'mentoring'? As is widely known already, the word 'mentor' has its origins in Homer's *Odyssey* and relates to the entrusting for care and education of Odysseus' son to Telemachus, when he set off for Troy. In terms of common usage, a mentor usually helps a less experienced person or colleague to learn from experience in order to improve performance through an accepting and non-judgemental relationship.

This suggests that the role of the line manager with responsibility for the conditions of service, performance of the member of staff and pay awards may sit uneasily with the role of mentor. It also suggests that skill in mentoring or helping in analysing and learning from experience in a non-judgemental yet sufficiently challenging manner calls for particular skills and attributes. It is also about values and ethics. Barr et al. (2005) have formulated principles for all interprofessional learning, arguing that it should be: collaborative, that is, it should be a microcosm of collaborative practice; egalitarian, in that it minimizes the status differences between participants; experiential, in the sense that it draws on professional experience and is thus a powerful tool in modifying attitudes; reflective, from Schön's (1983; 1987; 1991) perspective of 'reflection-on-action' or learning from experience; and applied, in that it implies the learning must be understood, revisited and reflected upon. Barr et al. also argued strongly that interprofessional learning should go beyond self-directed adult learning to group-directed interaction and understanding that revisiting and reflecting on learning is essential for learning to become embedded. They developed Kirkpatrick's (1967) four-point typology of educational outcomes (learner reaction, acquisition of learning, behavioural change and changes in organizational practice) to six categories:

Level 1 – reaction (learners' views on the learning experience);
Level 2a – modification of attitudes (change in reciprocal attitudes);
Level 2b – acquisition of knowledge/skills (including interprofessional

collaboration);

Level 3 – behaviour change (transfer to and change in professional practice);

Level 4a – change in organizational practice (wider change in the organization);

Level 4b – benefits to clients (improvements in health, well-being and education of children, families and communities in the case of early childhood contexts).

Outcomes of individual change in the studies Barr et al. reviewed tended to be based on self-report. However, there was also evidence of reported changes in organizational practice and in outcomes for clients.

7.4 Establishing appropriate ground rules

Individual mentoring requires the establishment of appropriate and agreed ground rules in the context of a trusting relationship, identifying priorities and setting specific goals, reviewing progress and making adjustments if necessary and, finally, continuing with another similar cycle or moving on. As noted above, the degree of learning can be judged in terms of changes in behaviour, attitudes and understandings. Thomson (2006: 62) has described the cycle as:

- *Establishing rapport*: exchanging expectations and agreeing how to work together.
- *Setting direction*: determining and prioritizing the mentee's initial needs and goals.
- *Making progress*: addressing the mentee's issues, reviewing progress, and identifying new ways of working.
- *Moving on*: reviewing what has been learnt that can be used in the future, and allowing the relationship to end or evolve.

This suggests that the mentor and mentee must each be clear about their mutual obligations to achieve agreed goals as well as open and transparent in establishing success criteria.

As noted by Ebbeck and Waniganayake (2000) in the Australian context, a key outcome of traditional one-to-one mentoring can be that it facilitates the maintenance and continuation of a particular style of leadership if it instils dependency. They suggest that a collective model of mentoring, where a whole group is mentored, offers an alternative approach. They argue that a collective model of mentoring is more powerful in establishing group relationships, commitments to learn and creates new understandings and knowledge. This perspective is in line with Barr et al. (2005) who emphasized group-directed learning and collective responsibility for collaborative action and competence. Team and organization change will be revisited in a subsequent chapter. Suffice to say at this point that as a strategic approach it helps to build a learning community or common culture within an organization. Moreover, the same challenges posed by authority structures and positional leadership in the selection of appropriate group and individual mentors remain to be resolved.

7.5 What does learning from day-to-day experience really mean?

Mentoring and the early years professional

It may be useful to look in more depth at what mentoring might look like in practice from the perspective of the early years professional (EYP). If it is accepted that mentoring is focused on learning, then the purpose of mentoring is to help staff by enabling learning to happen. If this relates to learning a specific skill in the short term, the term 'coaching' is often used, while 'mentoring' tends to be reserved for assisting in longer-term, career-oriented learning. Clearly the EYP's duties encompass a variety of specialist roles and responsibilities, from room leaders, through family support workers in children's centres to advisers and owner-managers in a variety of contexts and settings. No matter where they are located in their current work context, a particular strength they have is recent and relevant learning experience. Mentoring is a relatively simple process that simply requires the people involved (mentor and mentee) to know what is expected of them. In fact, 'developing people' to become more effective, whether it is the EYP herself or those staff for whom she has responsibility, through such processes as coaching, mentoring and feedback, helps them learn from their everyday activities. Deep and meaningful learning can come from ordinary everyday experience. However, it is necessary to go further, by reflecting on and making sense of experience in order to create new knowledge. In due course, this new knowledge is strengthened when it is transferred to new situations and the knowledge is thereby transformed. This has been described by Kolb (1984) as the learning cycle. It entails learning from experience; reflecting on this experience; making sense or meaning of it; that leads to performing in a different way.

If real learning needs real experience combined with reflection to make sense of that experience, this suggests that a professional development strategy requires two things. First, real, everyday experiences and, second, assistance in developing processes to review those experiences. Such an approach is not only more effective but less expensive than formal courses and accreditation. Indeed, accredited courses also make good use of such strategies; the NPQICL, for instance, encourages journalling as a means of recording and reflecting on experience, not just describing what happened but considering what patterns of motives and feelings, thoughts and behaviours emerge and what new decisions may be needed, what decisive action is to be taken or commitment made. To be a strategy for developing people in the EY workplace, however, a third ingredient is needed – the commitment of the person who leads, whether that be the EYP herself or some other person in a senior management position. This is because the leader who encourages such actions must be willing to develop herself as well as those she works with. Moreover, mentoring, that is, encouraging reflection and giving feedback, requires time, a precious commodity in a busy early childhood setting.

Practical knowledge

Our leaders' reported learning bears a strong resemblance to Schön's (1983) notion of reflective practice that has at its core, a personal and practical knowledge. This could also be described as craft knowledge, local knowledge or 'situated' knowledge. Perhaps its defining feature is that it is *tacit* knowledge, that is, not necessarily consciously 'known' or easily articulated by the person concerned but embedded in stories, case studies and images. This is very different from the scientific knowledge or theory found in formal courses and discussed in the previous chapter. Practical knowledge guides practice and helps staff to decide what to do in particular situations. It leads to practical principles that establish rules of conduct, and support professional judgement and strategic decision-making. Above all, it is a reminder that professionals produce and possess their own knowledge and that this is developed from participating in and reflecting on action or experience. Finally, practical knowledge leads to the notion of the professional as *producer* of knowledge that is created and used in the field. This can be contrasted with the professional as consumer or *user* of other people's formal knowledge to be found predominantly in traditional courses of professional development.

What mentoring offers

It has already been noted that the learning cycle can be used as a strategy for developing people. The role of the mentor is just that – mentoring can be established as a key development process in an early childhood setting. Typically it refers to an informal relationship when someone with experience helps another person with less experience to enhance her learning or development. Moreover, EYPs in training are placed in the interesting position of being both mentored and at the same time required to demonstrate their own mentoring skills while on placement. This is particularly challenging because first and foremost mentoring by definition is a relationship, and a relationship outside of a line management role. Then there is the further tricky issue of whether the role of the mentor includes giving advice and guidance. Given that the goal is the mentee's learning and development, the learning cycle in this context must be a cycle of empowerment. The more the mentor takes control, the higher the risk of a cycle of dependency developing. Mentoring is useful in helping someone to learn by reflecting on their experience; in developing confidence and skills; in planning career development; and it can be used to deal with issues of performance or problems/tensions in professional relationships.

The benefits of being a mentor are both personal, in terms of satisfaction and gaining a fresh perspective on the setting and professional, in terms of helping to build a more effective working environment. The expectations for the mentor will be that time is made regularly, that a positive relationship is established with the mentee, and good listening skills established.

Setting up internal mentoring has to take place within a context of agreed ground rules discussed in the previous section, an expectation of participation, an understanding of basic roles, responsibilities and purposes and, ideally, some choice of mentor. Moreover, there should be opportunity to review the process, share the experience and, where necessary, refocus the process. One variation of this is to establish peer mentoring. Here staff within a setting can be encouraged by the EYP to pair up, share, reflect on and review experience in the workplace and support one another in carrying out agreed actions. Another variation is action learning, where a group of colleagues or a team work together to solve a work-related problem or issue. It will have the goal of carrying out work-related tasks with a similar cycle of preparation (agreeing aims and planning), action and review. Whichever strategy is adopted, a means of encouraging a group of people to continue their professional development journeys is provided.

Two basic skills are required for mentoring: listening and questioning. First, listening is the way the relationship between mentor and mentee is built up and respect displayed. Second, listening is essential to understanding the position of the mentee. Third, listening will be demonstrated by the provision of a summary of what has been said at the end, partly to check understanding and partly as a prompt to check that nothing has been left out. Fourth, in order to question effectively it is necessary to have listened carefully as questioning and listening go together. Open questions are usually to be preferred as they prompt fuller responses and stimulate deeper exploration. Furthermore, questions prompted by listening are more likely to build on what has been said and move the conversation forward.

A mentee-centred approach will require a number of stages: discussing and agreeing goals; drawing out mentee's experience, encouraging reflection and self-evaluation; stimulating learning from increased self-awareness and discovery. The GROW technique (Gallwey, 1974) is a powerful technique that makes use of skilful questions and a clear structure:

G – goal (questions focus on what the mentee wants to achieve).
R – reality (questions about the 'reality' in which the mentee is operating).
O – options (questions the practical options that the mentee might choose to achieve goals that she has set).
W – will (questions focus on the 'will' to actually take specific action to implement one or more of the options previously chosen).

Using the GROW model: case study 1

The GROW model is best seen as a means of structuring a conversation. It can also be used effectively to help a group of people to explore an issue, particularly in an area where they have some joint investment.

A self-help group of EYPs noticed that participants on the full EYP pathway often seemed to have only a modest amount of experience of working with young children. They resolved that they would take responsibility for finding ways to increase the experience of these participants (*goal*) through asking themselves: what are we trying to achieve; what would success in achieving this look like; how would it feel, and so on? For *reality* they considered: why should this lack of experience become an issue to the qualified EYPs themselves; what, if anything, had been done already; and, if so, what was the effect? They agreed that the lack of experience could become their responsibility, if such trainees came to work in their setting. They then moved on to consider *options*. Various suggestions were made such as offering visits to settings or shadowing experienced EYPs. After generating a set of options it was agreed to rate them on their practicality, in order to determine which option/s to pursue (*will*). They considered their deadline for making a decision, the amount of support needed, and the first step(s) to be taken. In the end, they agreed to set up a local network for trainee EYPs, after brainstorming what they knew already about existing networks through local authorities, training providers and the Best Practice Network. They also considered the range of conferences, events and training activities available through the networks. Finally, it was acknowledged that while it was important to support the trainees, it would be more valuable to encourage them to set up the network themselves – maybe even using an initial GROW cycle.

Using the GROW model: case study 2

As experience develops, the GROW structure and its questions can be used flexibly in a number of different ways. One EYP created a silent model with a group of her colleagues in a setting. In this version, each person identified a real issue that they would like to spend 20 minutes exploring. Five questions were generated round each of the four steps in the GROW model. Participants simply recorded their own answers to each question, without saying anything.

It is not likely that every step will require the same amount of attention. Sometimes it may seem to take ages to identify the goal, on other occasions this is not the case. It can happen that examining the reality causes a shift in the goal to be achieved. Overall, the structuring of the exercise around the answering of 20 questions is a powerful tool that guides the way to problem-solving. At the same time, the silent method loses a distinctive feature of mentoring – listening to what the person concerned is saying and asking the right questions at the right time, in order to move thinking forward.

The GROW model can also be used to structure team meetings – addressing such questions as: what do we want to achieve; what is the current situation; what could we do or what options are available; and what will we do? Whichever model is used, the value lies in listening and questioning and avoiding a 'telling' approach.

A mentoring style of leadership

The challenge is to cultivate a mentoring style of leadership with the team in order to build a community of learners who systematically learn from experience. It demands a time to reflect on the nature of the relationships that the EYP currently has with each person with whom she or he works and has conversations. A useful exercise is exploring the ways that relationships can be built through conversations with colleagues in the setting and considering how this contributes to a learning organization.

► One EYP described the process in the following way:

> After I gained EYPS I felt that I was different in a number of ways. The changes did not come straight away and I think that they are still taking place. I think that I am at the start of a professional journey. Initially, I tried to make sure that every-thing was perfect (planning, assessments, administration, and so on) and that it was my sole responsibility to keep everything together. I set myself an impossi-ble job. Instead of trying to do everything myself, I allow my staff to share that responsibility. I have learned to use a variety of leadership styles (collaborative, authoritive or coaching) depending on the situation. The coaching that I myself received as a result of the EYPS has helped me to recognize that the leadership task had to be made much more manageable. I now approach the job with more confidence and enthusiasm. I think that I have gained insight. I also feel that I am more thoughtful and reflective. Practically, it means that I now enjoy the day-to-day challenges and welcome opportunities to share problem-solving with other staff in the setting.

7.6 A framework for staff development

The previous section has suggested four areas of focus for staff development (individual or group) first identified by Caruso and Fawcett (1986) in the US context: an orientation for new staff; on-the-job training and development; career development, available to all staff; and fine-tuning for skilled practitioners. There is a role for mentoring at each of these levels and, at times, for bringing together people with different kinds of development needs for group mentoring sessions. When practitioners are encouraged to clarify who contributes what to the primary task of the setting or organization and reach agreement on expectations for children, families and community and one another, they are likely to function more creatively and productively. Using different groups for such meetings within and across roles introduces novelty, variety of perspectives and also boosts morale. Planned, ongoing, face-to-face staff development as well as small- and large-group meetings on a regular basis can be enriching. Specific individual-focused mentoring at different phases of professional development will challenge without generating feelings of being overwhelmed. As Caruso and Fawcett (1986: 194) noted, when balanced with experiences that bring all staff together, 'mentoring can build relationships among individuals, increase communication, work on common problems and issues, and maintain high spirit and morale'. (See Appendix 6 for guidelines for setting up a mentoring scheme.)

7.7 Mentoring for the leader

Given the identified change and mobility within the field from the most highly qualified leader to the least qualified new entrant to the profession as well as the rapid growth of early years consultants, it is important that the benefits of mentor support for the early childhood leader are explored in more detail. Challenges that arise from change at personal or organizational levels or in the external environment need to be identified and dealt with, as well as areas of work generating personal satisfaction. In the current context, rates of change in the English early childhood sector and associated time demands create particular barriers and, as noted by our private and voluntary providers, lack of finance prevents the procurement of additional administrative staff to perform the necessary supportive roles creates another. Mentoring can help the leader to maintain an active response to work pressures, a stimulus to continuing with new learning, a perspective on balancing the family and out-of-work interests with career progression and, as noted above, the creation of a work setting that offers support and opportunity for responsibility and autonomy. For all of these reasons planning, designing and implementing an effective mentoring system for leaders and their learning communities is essential.

The previous chapter has identified different challenges at different points in the early childhood leader's career cycle. Major areas of stress for early childhood leaders include an inability to separate their personal and professional lives and the personnel-oriented tasks of finding suitably qualified staff, dealing with high turnover and doing whatever possible to retain good staff. Bloom (2000: 16) carried out interviews with nine early childhood directors that identified hardest and easiest job functions. These directors found interactions with other adults as 'easy and enjoyable' but acknowledged that working with adults, particularly staff management, was the most difficult aspect of their current duties. This again points to the need for a professional support system with deep knowledge of the situation-specific demands of the post that is able to provide opportunities for problem analysis and problem solution as well as acknowledge that the problems experienced are common to the sector and not unique to the particular leader concerned. This also suggests that long-term support systems and relationships among early childhood leaders are essential. Culkin (1997) drawing upon the 'burnout' literature (for example, see Cherniss, 1995), suggested that 'lifelines of support' for the transition into the position and ongoing support for establishing networks with other directors thereafter combat burnout. As noted already by one of our leaders, this is a lonely position that places leaders in isolation and often in an authority position in respect of friends. Culkin (1997: 192) specified the 'lifelines' of support that help to avoid burnout:

- having support for the transition;
- cultivating a suitable temperament (qualities of warmth, nurturance and open-ness essential for the primary task will need to be complemented by a number of other skills and styles that require a more proactive, assertive and instru-mental professional); and
- training and education, including formal preparation in knowledge skills and attributes relevant to the job that increase confidence and enable the leader to rise above the daily challenges of the post.

A range of promising practices and future possibilities emerge from these lifelines that include leader-led support groups to meet with colleagues, share ideas and solve problems together, associated workshops for specific topics, for example, staff retention, training to become leader mentors and leader training for applications that facilitate multiple teaching/learning strategies, distance learning and video-conferencing that relates to quality provision with associated websites, ongoing communication and networking for personal, professional and staff training.

Leaders play a central role in the creation of quality provision for young children and their families in the climate and culture of their organization and, hence, professional growth for staff. In order to discharge this function, leaders will need to have ongoing support for leader development.

7.8 Future possibilities

The position of the early childhood leader has reached a critical point in its development. Leadership in early childhood will need to draw upon, if not generate, more complex models of organization as the whole field expands and transforms and new career frameworks emerge. Staff development may continue to be constrained by financial considerations. While we may hope for a future with increased training opportunities for succeeding generations, ongoing professional networks, mentors and electronic links as well as specific training will continue to offer an inexpensive and valuable resource.

Strategies for developing leaders over time and in the context of change in this chapter have focused on learning in context. As observed by Fullan (2001: 126):

Learning in the setting where you work, or learning in context, is the learning with the greatest payoff because it is more specific (customized to the situation) and because it is social (involves the group). Learning in context is developing leadership and improving the organization as you go. Such learning changes the individual and the context simultaneously.

Opportunities to learn through study groups, action research and the sharing of experiences in support groups, create real supports for leaders. A number of other promising 'learning in context' practices from the Canadian context included:

- intervisitation (regular schedules of visits across a district to view implementation of initiatives);
- monthly leader support groups to discuss strategies and progresss towards goals;
- leader peer coaching (or 'buddying'), full-time mentor leaders coaching individual leaders on a regular basis;
- 'supervisory walkthrough', or on-site visits to address individual needs and provide guidance;
- district institutes that focus on topics such as standards and assessment;
- leaders' study groups, investigating presented areas or a problem of practice; and
- individualized coaching (or mentoring), that includes all newly appointed leaders, and is led by principal mentors.

While the practices above were identified as appropriate to the field of school leadership, their goal to develop leaders at all levels lends a particular relevance to early childhood leaders who are equally responsible for establishing a culture of learning, a corresponding primary task of caring for and educating young children and families, and providing a social life and interpersonal relations for all those working within the institution. When responding to change, collective capacity will be needed in order to deal with a culture of change and an increasingly complex society.

The change that is taking place in the English context with its focus on improving outcomes for all children emphasizes working together across agency boundaries to respond effectively to the needs of children and families. While Waniganayake and Hujala (2001) outlined major issues confronting early childhood professionals in diverse societies such as Australia and Finland, the current English policy changes that bring together education, health, social care and welfare of children, are introducing fresh challenges in the form of inter-agency and multidisciplinary working for the early childhood leaders that early childhood leadership research and publications have yet to address. Accordingly, Chapter 8 focuses on the particular challenges of leading multi-agency teams, where children's centre leadership is distinguished by its location within a complex organizational structure and governance, building on partnerships with other professions that have different policies and different regulations in order to plan and deliver services to meet joint outcomes, in line with changing legislation. Chapter 9 then examines the particular need for interprofessional education at a time of great change. Chapter 10 develops in more depth some of the ideas introduced in this chapter related to reflective practice and action learning. It looks at the way change in practice can be carried out and how critical reflection can help leaders to understand the process.

▶ One of our leaders tried to articulate the role a mentor had played in her professional development and how this was different from the support that might be provided by a peer or line manager.

Practitioner's views 7.1

Here (in a children's centre) there is no blueprint for the job ... There are leaders with similar sorts of experiences and you do have the opportunity to share that ... That's really important. But sometimes you need time and one of the difficulties that we have is that that doesn't always happen ... But you need to be able to share your fears and that's where the mentor comes in. That mentoring role is so good because sometimes there have been times when we have been facing – all of us – actually, something too complex. Sometimes you just burden someone else with your issues that they don't really need. So, at one level, peer support is good but often you need somebody who is completely outside and you are not burdening them.

The year I've had mentoring has been really important to me. My very first mentoring session I actually ... had no idea what I'm here for. I don't know what it's about ... actually the way mine has evolved is really useful. I think it's that ... it may not fit always but the reality is ... your experience of that issue is what frames your thoughts about it ... how you feel about it is how it is for you and it doesn't really matter if it's not actually the truth we have to unpick.

I was on a course and an issue that I was dealing with at that time came up. Another person asked me one question and that completely put everything into perspective and influenced my whole thought from there on about how I operate, how I understand other professionals. I did take it on and I discussed it a lot in my mentoring sessions. But it was discussions within a peer group that had actually raised it. So it's peer and professional support – but line management is totally different. A line manager, I think, is in too powerful a position to manipulate things in your own interest ... which is where mentoring helps. The mentoring helps put it in all the right value perspective in your head. You know, to tease out the bits that are important and bits that aren't.

It's now recommended for lots of people but it's pastoral and a lot of leaders have mentors that they pay for out of their budget. So it's money well spent really. Because you may lose a member of staff because you haven't handled things very well or you burn out because you're taking on too much yourself and it's very costly … so mentoring is a built-in safety mechanism.

CHAPTER EIGHT

THE CHALLENGE OF LEADING MULTI-AGENCY TEAMS

This chapter takes a detailed look at models of multi-agency working, facilitating factors and barriers, and the challenges in practice as experienced by a large group of professionals. Case studies of particular professional groups (speech and language therapists, a special educational needs team and a social worker) are presented in order to tease out both the strengths and challenges of such work.

8.1 Introduction

As noted earlier in the book, since 1997 the English government has invested heavily in early childhood services with the introduction of Early Excellence Centres, Sure Start and Neighbourhood Nursery programmes. This has led to a dramatic increase in the number of integrated centres offering education and care, family support, adult training, health and welfare services. With the introduction of children's centres as central to the delivery of services to families, this work has increased rapidly (see the government's strategy for *Special Educational Needs: Removing Barriers to Achievement*, (DfES, 2002); Green Paper, (DfES, 2003a); the 10-year childcare strategy, *Choice for Parents, the Best Start for Children*, (HMT, 2004); *National Service Framework for Children*, (DoH, 2004), setting standards for health and social services and the interface of those services with education; and the *Children Act*, (DfES, 2004a). Children's centres, originally conceived as serving the poorest wards, have been projected as a universal service to support all children and families through early years education, high-quality and flexible childcare, involving parents in their children's learning, adult learning, family support and outreach services, child and family health services, support for parents and children with special needs, and forging links with Job Centre Plus as well as other local training providers, further and higher education institutions.

Not only do leaders of children's centres come from different disciplines and have different training but, in their role as providers of 'service hubs' within the community, they are recruiting and employing staff themselves from a range of disciplines related to health, social care and welfare, and education. This means that children's centres have a significant role to play in developing the childcare workforce and offering new staff training opportunities at a time when the leaders themselves may have had limited leadership training opportunities. Given the stress in government policy on working across professional and organizational boundaries, it is important to consider that despite the potential to help solve complex societal problems, multi-agency working may require more resources of time, effort, creative thinking and money than single agencies and, as such, additional resources may be justified. Since there may be a range of models, methods and motives for engaging in interprofessional or multi-agency practice, as well as interdisciplinary research and development, it is important to be clear about what is involved.

8.2 Challenges to collaboration

A range of factors may challenge collaboration between different agencies and professional groups such as:

- poor communication between professionals and the range of professional languages and discourses that they use (Pietroni, 1992);
- the sheer complexity of the social problems that practitioners may encounter (real and perceived);
- the changing nature of family structure and hence the loss of support networks of the extended family;
- the increased population migration and mobility within and between countries that also serves to weaken kinship ties;
- the nature and variety of existing professional 'partnerships' that include different sectors of early childhood services (statutory, voluntary and private);
- the number and types of professional or agency groups involved, primarily from education, social care and welfare, and health-related fields, but including financial support and income maintenance;
- professionals working from a range of practice settings and not necessarily, or even probably, co-located;
- the value differences within and between professions that arise from

professional traditions and customs acquired before, during and after training;
- a professional knowledge base or discipline that may have origins in the natural sciences, for health-related fields or social sciences for education and social work;
- differences in relative status, income and career progression that may create professional rivalry;
- the different but related policies and priorities for practice and staff professional development and improvement across the field;
- the nature of the professional 'teamwork' involved, its structure and function, the mix of professionals and their formal relationships (Øvretveit et al., 1997);
- workforce reform with national standards for under-8s daycare and childminding (DfES, 2003c), the 10-year childcare strategy (HMT, 2004) and the rationalization of qualifications, the single Early Years Foundation Stage from birth to 5 years, and the continuous quality service improvement and inspection framework (DfES, 2006c).

Given the many factors that influence relations within and between agencies and professional groups, it is essential to identify the challenges and benefits that working in multidisciplinary teams can raise in considering the designing and leading of harmonious integrated services for children and families. It serves to highlight the complexity of working towards a shared philosophy, vision and principles with parents, children, community and all partners as well as developing shared identity, purposes and common working practices with all. It is a challenge for integrated centre leaders and it is a challenge for local authorities with the primary duty and responsibility for delivery of integrated services.

8.3 Questions to ask

Given the importance to early childhood leadership of multi-agency work, the key challenge is developing accessible, integrated services through partnership that are experienced as coherent and continuous by children, families and communities. Two key questions are raised for consideration:

- How much do we really know about effective multi-agency working?
- What are the key factors for their success and what kinds of challenges are raised?

8.4 What do we know about effective multi-agency working?

Sloper (2004) in a review of the literature on multi-agency working concluded that there was little evidence on the effectiveness of multi-agency working itself or of different models of such working in gaining improved outcomes for children and families. That said, consistent findings on facilitators for and barriers to joint working have been uncovered. At the organizational level, facilitative factors have been identified in the areas of planning, implementation and ongoing management. Planning, for instance, is found to be supported by clear aims and objectives, defined roles and responsibilities, staff commitment, strong leadership and a multi-agency steering management group, an agreed timetable for implementation of changes, linkages into other planning and decision-making processes and good systems of communication, information-sharing and adequate IT systems. Meanwhile, ongoing management and implementation demands shared and adequate resources, recruitment of the right staff, with the right experience, knowledge and approach, joint training and team-building, appropriate staff support and supervision, monitoring, evaluation of the service and reviewing policies and procedures in the light of changed circumstances. Existing professional and agency cultures as well as previous experience of multi-agency working have also been found to help. A corresponding *lack* of such facilitating factors was inevitably found to create barriers. Other factors such as constant reorganization, frequent staff turnover, lack of qualified staff, financial uncertainty, different professional ideologies and agency cultures were also found to hinder joint working. It was noted in the review that there was a clear need for methodologically sound local evaluations of multi-agency services, as well as multi-site studies that investigated the effects of different facilitating factors and models of working on outcomes for parents and children and included exploration of costs on effectiveness (Atkinson et al., 2002; Cameron et al., 2000; Liabo et al., 2001). As Milbourne (2005: 677) has noted, the idea of inter-agency work is not new but 'current policy approaches neglect to consider the diverse models of collaboration that practitioners may need to develop in practice'.

8.5 Models of multi-agency working

Atkinson et al. (2005: 8) identified five models of multi-agency activity based on their purpose:

Decision-making group – providing a forum for professionals from different agencies to meet, discuss ideas and make decisions.

Consultation and training – for professionals from one agency to enhance the expertise of those of another by providing consultation and/or training for them.

Centre-based delivery – gathering a range of expertise together in one place in order to deliver a more co-ordinated and cohesive response to need.

Co-ordinated delivery – to draw together a number of agencies involved in the delivery of services so that a more coordinated and cohesive response to need could be adopted.

Operational-team delivery – for professionals from different agencies to work together on a day-to-day basis and to form a cohesive multi-agency team that delivered services directly to clients.

Interestingly, decision-making groups and co-ordinated delivery were the most frequent types of multi-agency activity encountered within their sample, while operational-team delivery was the least frequently encountered. It was found by Atkinson et al. that many initiatives, in practice, were a conglomerate of these models and it would appear that this would also be the case for integrated centre provision. It should also be noted that the majority of models were focused on organization of professionals and that did not ensure families received a co-ordinated service. Moreover, as Watson et al. (2000; 2002) stressed, there was little evidence to show the extent to which models are implemented or what effects they have in practice. Where members of different agencies worked together, a more holistic approach could be achieved when a 'primary provider' or key worker took responsibility for delivering a direct and unified programme and the family were seen as equal partners. This finding is consistent with Robinson's (2006) call to focus on strategies that work directly on strengthening the conditions that enable effective practice and weaken the effects that hinder it.

8.6 Organization of professional groups

Sanders (2004) went further to question the very term 'multi-agency', noting distinctions among *groups* of professionals, occupations, sectors, agencies and disciplines as well as a differing focus of *operations* of work, teamwork, collaboration, co-operation and integration. Furthermore, he noted the disadvantages and barriers of working together such as costs in terms of time taken away from contact with clients to liaise, consult, co-ordinate as well as administrative and communication costs. In respect of primary health care teams, Øvretveit (1990) noted barriers to efficiency associated not only with lack of time but with understanding the purpose of interprofessional practice, understanding the roles of others, professional rivalry, exclusion of significant others (non-professionals), ownership of resources, discrimination and racism, and ways of ensuring that assessment is effective.

Øvretveit et al. (1997) identified significant dimensions of teamworking: degree of integration, membership of a permanent work group; processing pathways of clients; and management (how the team is led and how practitioners are managed). Indeed, a very important aspect of team functioning is the creation of management structures and the corresponding exercise of professional autonomy. There is also a need to establish responsibility for managing the total resources of the team that relates to job descriptions, reviewing of work and performance appraisal/supervision. In the case of the latter, where supervision may be undertaken by a senior staff member, this may be clinical advice where the supervisee remains accountable for the quality of work undertaken, clinical supervision where the senior staff member is accountable for the quality of supervisee's work, management monitoring to ensure adherence to agency procedures and full management, where the manager assumes responsibility for both clinical and organizational components of the role. Øvretveit et al. then proceeded to describe five types of management and supervision structure for teams: *profession-managed, single manager, joint manager*, a mixture of the previous two; *team manager-contracted*, who contracts in services of other professionals; and *hybrid*, based on the other four models.

As noted by Glass (2006), given the lack of experience of multi-agency early years services, the challenges to creating multi-agency management structures should not be underestimated. In terms of effectiveness, a recent report by the National Evaluation of Sure Start (NESS), Melhuish et al. (2005) set out to consider links between aspects of Sure Start local integrated centre programme implementation and levels of effectiveness judged in terms of child and parental outcomes for 150 programmes included in their impact study. The 18 dimensions related to:

- *what was implemented* (service quality, service delivery, identification of users, 'reach', reach strategies, service innovation and service flexibility);
- *the processes underpinning proficient implementation of services* (partnership composition, partnership functioning, leadership, multi-agency working, access to services, evaluation use and staff turnover); and
- *holistic aspects of implementation* (vision, communications, empowerment and ethos).

Their results indicated that links between the processes of programme implementation and impact on children and families living in programme areas could be detected, with better-rated programme implementation (what they did and how they were doing it) linked to beneficial outcomes, especially for parents. The fact that the effects of programme implementation were found to be slight might have been associated with the time it takes for programmes to reach full capacity in programme delivery. Furthermore, although effective leadership and multi-agency teams were categories included in the evaluation and data were collected from a national survey, interviews, delivery plans, organizational charts and annual reports, no further light was shed on these dimensions. In this context, the difficulty of demonstrating the indirect effect of leadership should not be underestimated, as noted by Robinson (2006).

8.7 Views on multi-agency working from four integrated centres

In order to capture changing perspectives on multi-agency working in local Sure Start integrated centre programmes, we worked in more depth with two of our integrated centre leaders as well as two of their colleagues who together led four local integrated centre programmes in the same location as our overall leadership project.

We used multiple ways to gather information over a three-year period in the lives of the four local Sure Start integrated centre programmes between 2003 and 2006 as they shifted towards children's centre status. The centres had been established over periods of time from one to five years, yet all served very distinct social, cultural and ethnic inner-city communities. An initial survey of 79 staff and partnership board members and 34 follow-up interviews with representatives of particular agencies, their lead professionals and parents explored facilitating factors and barriers to multi-agency working. We then followed up this work with case studies of three single- and joint-agency working: with the speech and language therapy team representing health, an early years worker, educational psychologist and outreach worker representing special education, and a social worker representing social care and welfare, using interviews, document analysis and, in one case, observation of professional training being delivered.

Those who took part included team members from the integrated centre programmes, representatives from the accountable body – in this case the primary care trust (PCT) – and the lead agency or local council, members of the programme partnership boards, including parents, as well as representatives of specific agencies and their professional leaders.

The survey questions were focused on multi-agency activity, key challenges and the key challenges for their success, drawing upon a study of multi-agency working of Atkinson et al. (2000; 2002a) and Tomlinson (2003) from the National Foundation for Educational Research (NFER). These were piloted with professionals from a range of backgrounds; for example health, education and psychology. The in-depth interviews then probed areas highlighted from the survey, in particular, topics that had generated mixed and ambivalent responses. For the case studies, interviews explored views of the professionals concerned, their professional leaders and integrated centre leaders themselves on the distinctiveness of their role, facilitating factors and barriers, targets and effectiveness. Documents gathered included person specifications and service-level agreements where available and information related to professional activities, such as leaflets for parents and other professionals, data related to targets and outcomes as well as records of work carried out. The quality of evidence available varied from service to service, reflecting in part differing contracts and therefore relationships to the management structure of the integrated centre programme of the agency concerned as well as the leading agency.

8.8 What we found out

It was noted above that a real challenge was posed for local authorities with the primary duty and responsibility for delivering integrated services to children and families. Our survey confirmed this.

As Figure 8.1 shows, views about the influence of local authority structures and boundaries on multi-agency working were mixed with half of our respondents feeling they facilitated, slightly less thinking they hindered multi-agency working and with a sizeable minority (11 per cent) reporting that they had no particular influence. The factors thought to facilitate multi-agency working within the integrated centre programmes were related to being able to use systems and people already in place in order to advise or to promote this type of work.

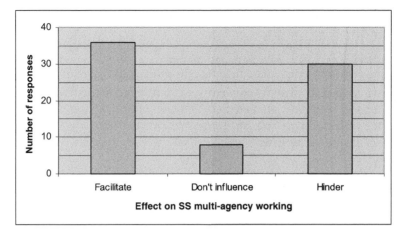

Figure 8.1 *Local authority structures and boundaries*

Working relationships within the teams and with the parent agencies of team members, as well as with other voluntary and statutory agencies, were seen as both facilitating and as a force for development of multi-agency working, thus enabling integrated centre programmes to deliver services that were needed.

> Working closely with other organizations enables our integrated centre to 'fill the gaps'.

Practical factors thought to hinder multi-agency working related to geographical boundaries, where these were different for the various agencies involved with the integrated centre programme. Different terms and conditions of work, holiday allowance, pay scales and policies and procedures, as well as staff employment matters were also highlighted.

Staffing arrangements and time investment of integrated centre programmes

The majority of respondents (three-quarters) thought that resources in the form of staffing arrangements and time investment were facilitative of multi-agency working, with the rest claiming either that they were a hindrance or that they did not to know one way or the other.

Qualitative responses suggested that time given to setting up new services was seen as essential to establish joint working.

> Being able to work closely with the multi-agency team influences our work together.

Individuals' and local programme teams' expectations and priorities

The vast majority of respondents thought that resources in the form of staffing arrangements and time investment in local integrated centre programmes facilitated multi-agency working, while a few thought them a hindrance or claimed not to know.

It was felt that staff had a high expectation of working as a multi-agency team. The development towards a fully-integrated team, however, appeared to be slower than desired. This was felt to be due to several factors. Staff not being clear about their roles within the team was considered a concern. Concern was also expressed regarding management of staff who, in many cases, remained line-managed and supervised by the parent organization and the tensions or problems this could cause were emphasized.

> The development of multi-agency working has been slow. 'Baggage' brought by the local programme members and in some cases, the professional management being maintained within the statutory agencies needed to be overcome.

Aims and objectives of local integrated centre programmes

Aims and objectives of the local programmes were regarded by the vast majority as facilitative of multi-agency working, with just a few stating that they did not know. It was emphasized that the aim of the integrated centres was to empower and provide a service for the communities they served, reflecting their needs.

> The aim of the programme is to deliver services in a different way, responding to community needs to work with families at most risk, to ensure their children have the best possible access and start in life.

It was generally agreed that the integrated centre aimed to work in a multi-agency manner. The centre also acted as a conduit, bringing together, and helping other agencies in adapting to a multi-agency style of working.

> A number of agencies in the area would not get together formally if it were not for the local integrated programme.

> Planning ensures complementary working to clear aims and objectives.

Confidentiality and information-sharing strategies between the various agencies

Views about confidentiality and information-sharing strategies between the various agencies involved were mixed (Figure 8.2).

Rather more respondents thought that these strategies facilitated rather than hindered such work, with a minority feeling that they had no influence.

Several had a positive experience of this process. It was acknowledged, however, that this was a problem for all four integrated centres and that systems and protocols needed to be developed to reduce the amount of time wasted by staff and, indirectly, families on this matter.

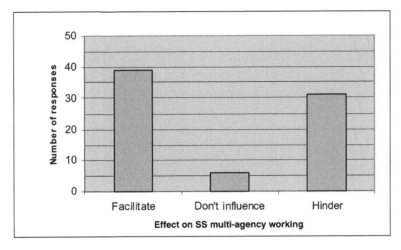

Figure 8.2 *Confidentiality and information-sharing strategies between agencies*

> Strategies need to be in place to facilitate multi-agency working. Organizationally, different agencies have different strategies that are not mutually understood.

These difficulties appeared to occur both across organizations that worked with the local integrated centre programmes and across the multi-agency team itself, due to the nature of local team members' employment conditions.

The accountable body for its part was highlighted by several respondents as a hindrance.

> The lack of information-sharing has ground to a halt several very positive programmes we have tried to put into place. Mostly on behalf of the accountable body!

The need for sharing information was seen by many as essential in order for the services to provide successful services.

The need for development of a common language across professional groups working in the local integrated centre programmes

As emphasized earlier in this chapter, respondents felt a need for development of a common language across professional groups working in local integrated centre programmes. The overwhelming majority of respondents felt that there was a need for a common language across professional groups, while 7 per cent did not and 6 per cent did not know one way or the other.

> Common language reduces isolation and increases partnership working which is essential in order to be effective.

There was also a strong sense that the language used should be accessible for parents. Overall, issues were highlighted about the difficulty in developing a universal language across professionals, representing different disciplines. It was also suggested that 'effective communication channels [could] overcome issues of different "languages"'.

Budgets and finance arrangements

As to whether budgets and financial arrangements created a conflict within and between agencies, a general lack of programme funding, a raised concern about sustainability and a recognition of the need to create more effective use of resources, views were very mixed. Given that the local integrated centre programmes have now become designated as children's centres with control and funding handed over to local authorities and 'ring-fencing' of Sure Start money abolished since 2008, without regard for their commitment or capacity to provide adequately resourced centres, these findings are challenging (Figures 8.3 to 8.6).

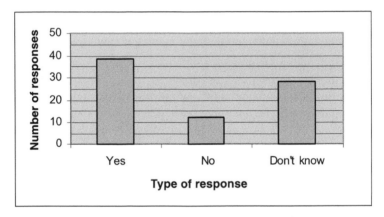

Figure 8.3 *Concern about conflicts within or between agencies that provided staff*

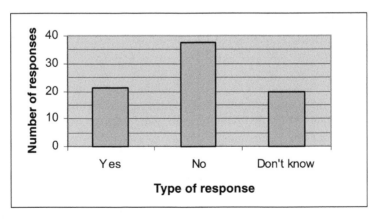

Figure 8.4 *Concern about general lack of programme funding*

Tensions, specifically between the lead agency and accountable body, were highlighted by qualitative responses. There was believed to be a need to establish good agreements between the two in order to reduce possible conflicts of interest.

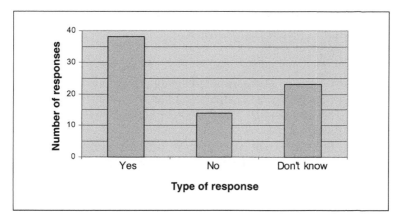

Figure 8.5 *Concern about sustainability of the services and, thus, uncertainty of funding*

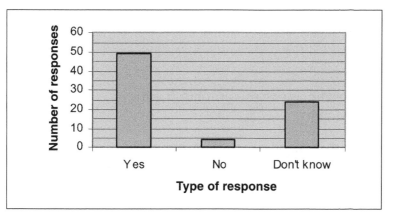

Figure 8.6 *A need to create more effective use of resources (human and material) by reducing repetition and overlap*

> There is always concern about conflicts when partnership working is in place, however, a good agreement reduces the prospect. Duplicate services to parents means a waste of resources.

> We need a more radical approach to reduce competition and ensure collaboration across agencies.

It was noted by more than one local programme that services were started up when the programmes did not have their own buildings from which to operate.

This was felt to be unacceptable.

> To start programmes with no buildings or venues is ludicrous.

Roles and responsibilities adopted by individuals working within local integrated centre programmes

The majority of respondents felt that issues around roles and responsibilities adopted by individuals working within the integrated centre concerned the need to understand better the roles of others, and half reported conflicts over areas of responsibility. The vast majority recognized the need to go beyond existing roles to work in new ways.

It was felt by some that in the past understanding others' roles and responsibilities, as well as the need to work in new ways had proved difficult.

> These have all been challenges to most of the individuals and agencies involved.

This was felt to be an area in which most felt the need for continued improvement.

> It is vital that all team members understand the role of others in order to effectively offer service.

Several respondents with different roles within the integrated centres understood the initiative to be about 'blurring the edges of your role to take new responsibilities and to work in a new way'.

Aims of specific agencies competing with local integrated centre programme aims

Respondents were mixed in view and less certain of whether or not aims of specific agencies competed with local programme aims as a result of different government targets, differences in target groups and different emphases on preventative versus crisis intervention (see Figures 8.7 to 8.9).

It would appear from the responses that the aims of some agencies were regarded to be identical with those of the local programme. With others they were seen as different.

> Targets are different from [agencies] which need not be a cause of 'competition' but complementary.

Still others recognized that complementary working, although ideal, was hindered by existing working cultures.

> A strategic approach would have been helpful. But a culture of competition for initiatives/funding hinders this.

> The flexibility provided within the integrated centre to achieve targets with new ways of working, many of which, being successful have not been recognized by mainstream services.

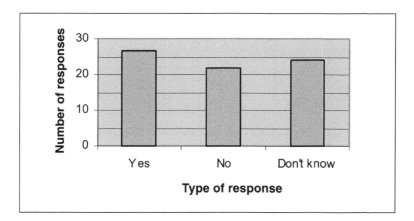

Figure 8.7 *Differences in the target groups*

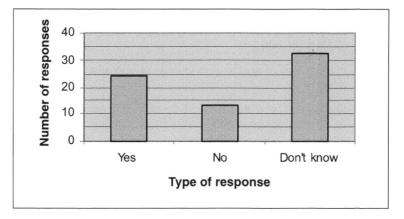

Figure 8.8 *Different government targets*

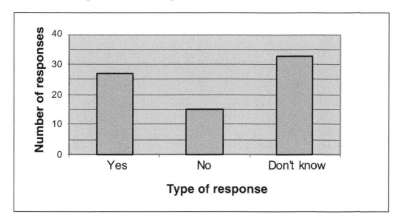

Figure 8.9 *A focus on preventative work versus crisis intervention*

Several respondents expressed the view that the ethos of all agencies was changing and becoming much more prevention focused.

> There is a general move towards preventative work that places integrated centre work at the heart of the government's agenda – which all agencies are beginning to recognize.

Non-financial resources creating challenges

The majority of respondents felt that non-financial resources created a challenge to multi-agency working. Areas highlighted were allocation of time, provision of staff and physical space in which to work together effectively.

Responses also revealed that availability of non-financial resources were thought to create a challenge, resulting in a less effective delivery of services than might otherwise be the case. Buildings and venues from which to work were slow to become available and recruitment of staff to carry out such work was also slow.

Physical space in which to work was perhaps the largest problem across all local integrated centre programmes. Programmes became operational without their own or adequate facilities. Even when facilities were open there might not be enough space for all staff.

> New offices, but no storage and teams too large for premises.

> We barely have enough room to work now. Building work due now is intended to reduce our space further. There is insufficient room to meet with parents/groups at the present site. It is against safe working practices to leave anyone working in the office on their own.

These observations provide further interesting insights into staff's own perspectives on the change and development taking place in the field, that complement those expressed in Chapters 2, 3 and 4.

Communication within and between agencies working with the local integrated centre programmes

The majority of respondents felt that poor communication within and between agencies created problems between those working at different levels within agencies, with half reporting that this could create different availability of professionals from different agencies and undermine successful multi-agency work through poor communication between different local government departments.

A clear understanding of each other's roles and the cultures of the agencies from which they originated was felt to be important to alleviate some of the problems, or potential problems that might occur within the teams. In some cases this was felt to be due to a lack of communication between the agencies involved.

> Because protocols have still not been agreed.

It was also highlighted by several respondents that, despite these problems at the strategic level, the local programme teams were delivering services in a multi-agency manner.

Although we are made up of different agencies we all work very well as a team.

The effect of professional and agency culture on integrated centre practice

Respondents' views on the effect of professional and agency culture on professional practice were mixed. A quarter felt that multi-agency working did disrupt existing agency cultures, values and ways of working; half claimed it did not and the rest did not know one way or the other. Nearly two-thirds, however, felt that specific policy and practice differences hindered shared practice. The majority felt that different data management systems affected information-sharing and did impact upon shared practice (see Figures 8.10 to 8.12). (Appendix 8 examines in more depth the multiple sources of values and potential value conflict underpinning multi-agency working.)

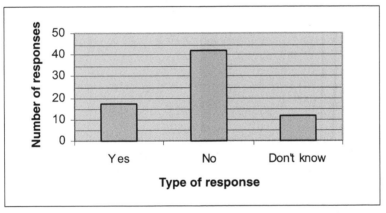

Figure 8.10 *Multi-agency working disrupts existing agency cultures (values and ways of working)*

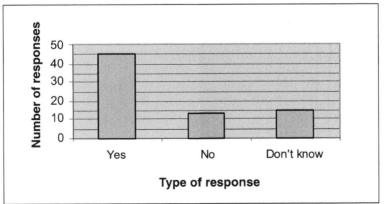

Figure 8.11 *Specific policy and practice differences hinder shared practice*

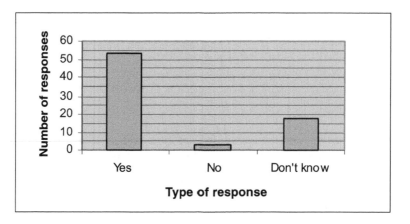

Figure 8.12 *Different data management systems which affect information-sharing impact upon shared practice*

Sharing information between professionals working for the local programmes as well as within agencies involved with them was regarded as problematic, with comments suggesting that staff were 'still awaiting some baseline information'. It was noted, however, that attempts were being made to eliminate such problems.

The strategy of the management in the local integrated centre programmes

In terms of management strategy, the vast majority felt that multi-agency working was strongly supported and promoted at management level in order to remain credible at delivery level but were less sure whether management strategy drive was organized carefully to carry along the various participants from each agency. A majority did feel that the integrated centre management strategy encouraged like-minded individuals who sought new ways of working in order to meet shared goals and work across existing management structures.

Overall, qualitative responses indicated that the management strategy of local programmes supported multi-agency working and these new ways of working were imperative to success. There were felt to be problems at the level of leading agencies, whereby the work at local programme level was being hindered.

> I don't believe that there is enough discussion and agreement at senior management level. However, there is a willingness to make it work lower down – at programme manager level.

Training opportunities for team members

The vast majority believed that additional multi-agency training to meet the extended role of agencies would be helpful and shared an active desire to engage with other agencies at the delivery level. Views were more mixed as to whether there should also be 'single agency' development.

Additional responses indicated that it was generally felt training in a multi-agency manner was necessary in order for team members to develop understanding of each other's roles:

> Knowledge is vital to the success of the local programme; this can only be gained by sharing of information through training.

The vast majority of respondents believed commitment and willingness of team members to be involved in multi-agency work was sustained by an active desire to engage with other agencies at the management level, at the delivery level and by a 'bottom-up' as well as a 'top-down' management approach. This finding is consistent with the findings reported in Chapter 3.

Specific responses indicated strongly that there was willingness to be involved in multi-agency work at both the strategic and operational level and that both helped to sustain this work.

> 'Bottom-up' allows practitioners to feed back voices of the local community and to identify gaps in provision. 'Top-down' allows for clear protocols and clear line management in areas of emerging practice to be clarified.

Leadership or drive of individual integrated centre programme managers

The majority felt that leadership or drive of individual integrated centre leaders demonstrated clear strategic direction, showed tenacity to overcome obstacles to progress, and could bring together the team in order to bring about change and overcome obstacles.

Overall, respondents were very positive about the leadership of the local integrated centre programmes. Some of the problems that had been dealt with were highlighted as examples of the strength of the programme leaders.

> Delivered services even without having buildings. Operated without adequate, or no base – homeless.

These findings are illuminating in their insight into both facilitating factors and barriers at the local level and assessment of the role of integrated centre leadership. Views on leadership were very positive in terms of providing strategic direction, having tenacity and bringing the team together to overcome obstacles. Commitment of staff teams to sustaining multi-agency teamwork was also stressed. Aims of the integrated centre were seen to facilitate multi-agency working. Barriers were also identified in the form of local authority structures and boundaries, uncertainty concerning budgets, and non-financial resources of staffing, time and space, hence, sustainability. It was acknowledged that knowledge and understanding of roles and responsibilities within and between agencies was important and that the aims and culture of individual agencies could conflict with or disrupt multi-agency working. The need for additional training was identified. (Appendix 9 provides an exemplar framework for planning, implementing and reviewing a team exercise.)

Interprofessional training needs

The implications are that further interprofessional development is needed in order to develop collaborative teamwork that addresses tensions in working relations within and between agencies in a context of instability and change. But this is training that needs to go beyond information exchange towards a fundamental reconception of a workforce that is flexible in approach and in career progression, that takes place over time through learning both in the workplace as described in earlier chapters and also through more sustained professional development that addresses values, culture, roles and expertise. Championing integrated working throughout the integrated centre and within the local community is one thing but, significantly, this is a new challenge for local authority personnel themselves who may be 'line managing' integrated centres with less experience and expertise than the leaders themselves. One response to this situation, as noted by Glass (2006), where commitment to excellent provision is uncertain, is an increase in control and prescription at a time when resources are almost certain to be reduced.

8.9 A closer look at the challenges of multi-agency working

Despite real enthusiasm of the local integrated centre programme members concerned, the survey respondents suggested that effective multi-agency working had not always been easy to achieve. Multi-agency work by its very nature could disrupt existing professional and agency culture, and conflicts over areas of responsibility could arise. Establishment of common aims within and across agencies was regarded as essential but, in practice, was less straightforward to establish, with new roles and responsibilities needing to be made explicit at all levels and effective communication developed to increase understanding of these. Practices established to protect confidentiality were still creating tensions and information-sharing strategies could still be improved. Allocation of budgets and financial organization, as well as non-financial resources, had created a major challenge to multi-agency working. That said the vast majority believed that integrated centres facilitated multi-agency working in terms of staffing arrangements, teams' expectations and priorities. Staff training was seen to have an important function in developing new ways of working. It was generally highlighted throughout that multi-agency teamworking was strongly promoted and supported by integrated centre leaders.

The next step was to look more forensically at the views and interpretations of challenges as experienced by talking in greater depth to professionals at a number of levels within the organizations concerned, partnership and team members of varying levels of seniority as well as a representative of the lead agency and accountable body. Four areas were examined: knowledge of structures; roles and responsibilities; data protection and information-sharing; and communication.

Knowledge of structures

Discussing the role of leading agencies in ensuring that the financial details outlined in local plans were executed, representatives of the agencies acknowledged a lack of capacity and hence a delay in prioritizing support for integrated centre work. This resulted in members of the finance team being employed on temporary contracts as well as becoming involved in areas outside their remit, such as legal and estate management issues. Partnership board members varied in their level of understanding of the roles and functions of the leading agencies. Team members for their part identified the strategic commitment and financial role and were aware of the absence of permanent staff in the finance department. There was an awareness that as the leading agencies developed, more effective ways of working in partnership, 'things could be achieved more quickly and efficiently', though this was not always apparent at operational level.

Roles and responsibilities

The representatives of the leading agencies emphasized their priorities at a strategic and operational level and recognized that having two leading agencies (representing education and health) added complexity and thus challenge to multi-agency working. This could have a less than positive effect on local integrated centre programmes in terms of time taken to make decisions. Both agreed that integrated centre goals complemented those of their parent agencies. Partnership board members were more mixed in response. Some partnership board members agreed that local programme aims complemented the goals of their parent agency in meeting government targets and this impacted positively on client groups. Others emphasized that working clearly within the terms of reference facilitated local centre leaders, supporting, establishing and developing relationships between families and the local programme. Others were less certain and wondered whether services might be duplicated. Team members of the local programmes expressed a variety of views about the nature of aims of partner agencies and integrated centre work. It was highlighted that the programme offered an innovative approach. One felt that her parent agency was 'very mistrusting of any new initiative' and another declared that her parent agency had little to do with the local integrated centre programmes. Another stressed the impact of external influences such as changing priorities at government level. Yet another indicated the possible tensions between relative emphasis on prevention and intervention that could impact on the parent agency. Some felt confident in managing staff and working at the same time alongside existing programmes and engaging with 'hard to reach' families.

Staffing, resources and work-space

Challenges related to staffing were emphasized by all groups of participants. The leading agencies referred to the challenges posed to staff being employed on temporary contracts and acknowledged lack of office space as a challenge, Partnership board representatives noted the length of time taken to recruit a new programme leader when the previous incumbent had left. Others mentioned problems with recruiting health-related professionals. Yet another mentioned the challenges associated with changing professional practice and integrating professionals from diverse disciplines. With respect to space, reservations were expressed about the desirability of co-locating with another statutory agency. Team members acknowledged the challenge of managing a professionally diverse team, a sense of isolation and a lack of training. Notwithstanding this, staffing arrangements were viewed positively and, despite short-term discomfort and frustration, construction of a new building was generally viewed positively.

Data protection and information-sharing

Representatives of the leading agencies both acknowledged challenges regarding information-sharing between team members and the PCT. Some partnership board members also mentioned ongoing challenges regarding lack of information-sharing of the PCT. It was recognized that different organizations had different arrangements and it was also recognized that the issue was being addressed. Team members also described the PCT as 'taking a controlling role in respect of data protection and information-sharing'. Reluctance of agencies to share information was highlighted. Identifying and accessing client information was regarded as a major challenge by some participants. The need for shared procedures and protocols with a strategy for placing confidential information on shared computer drives was indicated.

Communication

Challenges posed at the strategic level in the authority were identified by representatives of the leading agencies and the impact of constantly changing national policies was also mentioned. It was agreed that centrally held information could be a hindrance to communication and that improved IT networks were needed. At the operational level, it was noted that team members were used to working in different ways. At the level of individual integrated centre programmes, regular meetings of the programme leader with the partnership board and team members were part of an effective communication strategy. In terms of leadership style of the programme managers, it was reported that there was a real willingness and a strong personal commitment to learn, share and 'take the lead'. Partnership board members advocated the use of multiple communication channels, acknowledging the challenge in the face of multiple locations and a sizeable team. Jargon was acknowledged by one member as a barrier to parental engagement, though others indicated that formal partnership board meetings and informal face-to-face communication were successful. Team members felt that formal methods of communications through meetings, telephone contacts, daily transfer of internal post, information chats and social events were successful but that the number of locations, underuse of IT, availability of part-time staff and different ways of working were regarded as a challenge by some.

What emerged strongly from the in-depth discussions with staff from four integrated programmes was a sense of staff from different backgrounds and skills striving towards common goals and shared values, despite barriers to effectiveness and efficiency in the form of shifting national policy. Local authority structures inevitably were too slow in response to financial arrangements and 'contracting in' of services from different professionals. A lack of space, split-site accommodation, challenges to data-storing, information access and sharing, and communication were also barriers. It should be noted at this point that the emphasis has been placed on processes underpinning proficient implementation of multi-agency services, such as partnership functioning, leadership and holistic aspects of implementation such as communications. Rather less emerged that related to what was implemented, service quality and delivery, identification of users and strategies to reach, improve and sustain services over time.

In order to obtain a stronger sense of targets set, preventative strategies employed, perceived effectiveness as well as facilitating factors and barriers from the perspective of specialist services themselves, brief case studies of agency work in the field of social work, speech and language therapy services and special education support were carried out.

8.10 Case studies

Speech and language therapy

All four integrated centre programmes had a speech and language therapist as part of their team, two working at 0.5 of a week, one at 0.7 of a week and one full-time. A detailed personal specification encompassing duties in three key areas was provided: their clinical role, their training role and their team/service role. The speech and language therapists met with their professional leader every three months as a group, and with one another more often to share ideas, new practice and to make visits to other local programmes. There was also collaboration at the strategic level with the whole mainstream speech and language therapy service. All members of the local programme speech and language therapy team worked to achieve agreed targets to increase the proportion of children having normal levels of communication, language and literacy at the end of the early years foundation stage (at age 5 and at the end of the Reception year in school) and to increase the proportion of young children with satisfactory speech and language development at age 2. To achieve these targets, therapists worked in local nurseries providing advice for staff on raising learning and competence in communicating, speaking and listening, being read to and extending early efforts to read and write of individual children and working with identified children to help them develop communication skills, both individually and in a group. They provided training for nurseries, parents and professionals, took part in local programme activities with other members of the team, carried out joint assessment sessions to ascertain children's communication, speaking and listening skills and followed up requests for contact from other personnel such as the health visitor, after the 2-year-old developmental check, nursery staff following the *Every Child a Talker* guidance (DCSF, 2008c), or parents, making home visits and working with individual parents. In line with the *Early Years Foundation Stage* (DfES, 2007), this identified the existing ways babies became effective communicators through responsive interactions with those who care for them in their home and community. It demonstrated how early communication provided a basis for understanding language, vocabulary development and later literacy. Therapists did not have a defined caseload, although some children in the local programme areas received input from mainstream and programme therapists or solely from the local programme therapist.

An initial audit was carried out of speech and language skills of 3-year-old children entering local programme nurseries in 2003 and repeated in 2006. Moreover, annual data from Sure Start Speech and Language Measures (Harris, 2002) were collected on 60 children across projects per year. In terms of achievements, the projects were now experiencing more referrals from both service users and outside agencies such as social services, indicating an increased awareness of the importance of early speech and language communication. This period spanned the time from the introduction of *Birth to Three Matters* (DfES, 2003b) to the *Early Years Foundation Stage* (DfES, 2007) and led to a closer scrutiny of the Early Years Foundation Stage Profile results that by April, 2008 were setting national and local statutory targets. It also ensured that young mothers received key messages that: babies were sociable from birth and used a variety of strategies to gain attention; they made contact through facial expression, movement, gesture and words; they responded to turn-taking patterns of interaction, rhyming games, singing and word play; they enjoyed experimenting and using sounds and words for everyday objects; and soon they used single- and two-word utterances to convey messages that conveyed emotions, experiences and thoughts.

Identified facilitating factors were the supportive integrated centre leader and team, the opportunity to work in new and flexible ways and the availability of increased resources. Identified barriers were difficulties in recruiting suitably trained speech and language therapy assistants in the local programme areas and the lack of suitable premises in which to carry out training. In terms of effectiveness, the speech and language therapy team had been keen throughout to secure evidence for the benefits of an indirect service delivery including the collection of case study data over a three-year period as examples of early intervention, resulting in children not needing a referral to the mainstream speech and language therapy service.

What stood out from the investigation was the clear articulation by therapists of an identified professional knowledge base. This comprised a range of core clinical activities and training responsibilities that distributed this knowledge base as widely as possible to other professionals such as health visitors, midwives, community nurses and parents and that took best account of early intervention in the preventative sense for the majority, as well as recognizing the need for more specialized intervention for a smaller number of children with longer-term additional needs.

Special educational needs service

In respect of a target to increase the number of children who had their special educational needs identified in line with 'early years action' and 'early years action plus' of the *Special Educational Needs Code of Practice* (DfES, 2001) and to have an individual action plan in place, the speech and language therapists had also been involved in city-wide training for parents and new special educational needs (SEN) co-ordinators. Moreover, the original steering committee of one of the local programmes had made a proposal to have a multidisciplinary SEN team attached to the programme in order to address at a very early stage, children's special or additional needs. Accordingly, the programme leader secured the input of an educational psychologist for two days a week, a preschool SEN teacher's input for two and a half days and a parent partnership outreach worker's input for two and a half days. While the *Code of Practice* assigned a statutory role to each of these team members in the statutory assessment of SEN, in the context of their local integrated centre programme role, the team felt that judging their work in terms of caseload might be inappropriate and thus their reported 'case' numbers were quite low. The *Early Years Foundation Stage* (DfES, 2007) was intended to provide a framework for practice for all practitioners, including children with SEN. The notion of a 'unique child' and a commitment to universal development, well-being, safety and inclusion suggested that all early years practitioners should be responsible for promoting positive outcomes for all young children.

Over one exemplar year, for instance, the preschool SEN teacher supported a small number of parents and children; the outreach worker made some home visits and provided caseload co-ordination for a few parents and a larger number of children; and the educational psychologist provided consultation for a relatively small number of parents and children. They felt however, that their effectiveness should be judged in terms of 'quality not quantity'. The opportunity to work more indirectly through family, community and other professionals was relished though it was less clear how this aspect of the work was monitored and evaluated or its impact judged. The criteria in the preschool teacher's service level agreement did however specify the amount of time to be dedicated to working directly with individual children or indirectly by contributing to the development of local integrated centre services and supporting other staff. Terms such as 'prevention' and 'intervention' did not appear to be interpreted in the same manner by all professionals and it was not always clear where work carried out with children and families referred to the traditional 'acute' client group and when, where or how access to different groups with milder difficulties and delays was secured. Indeed, local authority providers have a responsibility to remove or overcome barriers to achievement for all children (DfES, 2004c). While this includes early identification and involving other agencies as appropriate, the emphasis is on adapting the environment to suit the individual child's learning.

In common with the speech and language therapists, the SEN team felt that working with the local multi-agency team was a facilitating factor in their work and 'everything was so much quicker while they were more approachable and accessible'. Identified barriers to SEN work by the team included differences in professional cultures, values and working practices that generated different agendas and resulted in different modes of performance management.

The perceived ethos of the local programme with its emphasis on self-referral could create potential barriers for 'hard to reach' groups, who would then become progressively harder to reach. Their professional leaders noted that in the long term the support services they represented were neither staffed nor resourced to provide an indirect service delivery at the preschool stage. In any case, as a review of Ramey and Ramey (1998) suggested, in order to be effective, early intervention needs to be direct, intensive and sustained. Nevertheless, this early intervention may best be approached through collective rather than specialist responsibility. For her part, the local integrated centre programme leader expressed concern that the annual expenditure on the SEN team amounted to nearly 7 per cent of the annual budget, while staff absences totalling 220 days in one year had had some considerable impact of professional contact.

Social work intervention

Meanwhile, another local integrated centre programme with high rates of child protection cases proposed to employ a social worker to develop preventative strategies. While a common assessment framework (CAF) has been established to create an integrated strategy, for children at risk of abuse the *Children Act* (DoH, 1989) is still a basis for providing children's services. Clear targets were set for local integrated centre programmes at the time to reduce re-registration on the child protection register within the space of 12 months by 20 per cent. In fact, there was no evidence of increase or decrease in child protection rates over the period that the local integrated centre programmes had been in operation. A social work post was thus created in this local programme, specifying 0.5 of the week to develop preventative strategies in the local integrated centre programme area and 0.5 of the week in the local social services office to deal with statutory child protection work for under-5s. The local authority is required to safeguard and promote the welfare of children within their area who are in need, through provision of a range of services to the child and family. While traditionally social workers have provided for children in need, a range of services related to education, health, housing, financial assistance or family support may be offered by different members of a multidisciplinary team.

Within six months, this post broke down and the social worker left. The continuing and developing pressures from the statutory role were perceived by the social worker to 'take precedence' and this she felt hindered what could be achieved in the preventative role. There did seem to be grounds for participants' views that this part-time preventative post, in practice, was not satisfactory but it was also acknowledged that the professional concerned should have been more 'proactive'. The social worker herself felt that 'having a job without a well-defined role was really hard ... very much like a spare part' and that she had really to be given guidance of an agreed and realistic job specification, service level agreement with appropriate supervision and, hence, accountability for work carried out. While joint supervision was reported to be taking place, it appeared that there was some mismatch in expectations with respect to preventative working practices with families between the two managers concerned, as well as perceived lines of accountability for the statutory element of the post. It was acknowledged in this case, as by participants in the other case studies, that having no caseload and the support of a multi-agency team with time and resources should have been regarded as facilitative. Barriers to preventative social work, it was reported by the social worker, included the negative image of social workers and general mistrust of them. She explained that this was a 'big barrier' as people wanted to be 'left alone to get on with their lives'. The role of local integrated centre programmes was 'more voluntary' on the family's side – about wanting services and wanting to join groups as well as wanting help. In this respect, the social worker noted that one had to intervene with a family in order for prevention to occur. This was 'not befriending but somehow more voluntary, less statutory and less punitive'.

In the longer-term, as with the SEN case study, questions were raised by the professional leader about the feasibility of resourcing social work posts that carried no caseload. 'Prevention' was defined here as the promotion of well-being of child, family and community, and thus *all* services had a role and responsibility with a focus on preventing the need for more targeted and specialist services (level 1 or universal services). It was acknowledged, however, that 'too many resources were focused on meeting those needs at level 4 (with a high risk of harm) and level 3 (medium risk requiring a complex multi-agency response), with insufficient resources being available when needs first become apparent (at level 2 or low risk). The result was that 'as though in a vortex children were drawn into expensive interventionist services too quickly'.

8.11 Leadership by the many

The views of participants and the case studies highlighted the complexity of the challenge facing multi-agency integrated centre workers. Co-locating staff from partner organizations to work together when they were still employed by that parent agency with different terms and conditions, working hours, pay scales, holiday allowances and information-sharing strategies, created particular tensions. Though staff clearly had an appetite for the new and 'hybrid' professional that was being thrown up, many of the tensions described here relate to the particular model of multi-agency working in operation. Staff from a particular agency were co-located to work together but were still employed by their own agency, hence, conforming to Øvretveit's (1996) notion of joint management (or leadership). Moreover the challenge of local authority structural constraints, on one hand, and of the shifting and developing internal organization of a children's centre team, on the other, as they 'formed and reformed' multi-agency teams in response to changing requirements both within the organization and outside in a corresponding shifting outside environment may be aptly described as 'knotworking' (Engeström et al., 1999). Within the new children's centre agenda where professionals from different services will continue to work with a hybrid management system, it can be envisaged that existing tensions will not be eradicated. The findings serve to remind us of the investment needed in terms of finance, time and staff resources in order to develop new multi-agency ways of working. It is essential in such a climate that hasty judgements are not made about the impact of local integrated centre programmes, as they seek to acquire new knowledge and skills that are neither stable nor well-defined, and professionals within them learn to work in new ways with corresponding lack of definition and stability.

This chapter has attempted to provide an account of integrated centre programmes as they have moved towards children's centre status. At the level of practice, there is much to be learned by a leader about the challenging process of setting up and establishing a new range of multi-agency services. There was general agreement among the professionals involved that the programmes encouraged and resourced more flexible ways of working, though in the case of the individual social worker this faced her with the additional challenge of defining and developing a new repertoire of skills in terms of service innovation and flexibility, identification of families and 'reach' strategies that from her point of view were insufficiently supported and guided. By contrast, the speech and language therapists, both individually and collectively, with the support of their mainstream service and professional leader were able to develop new and flexible ways of working in order to provide accessible services for other professionals, clear pathways for individual families to follow to access them and strategies for identification of children and families, and shared staff training that were monitored, assessed and fed back into the planning process. The SEN case is a reminder that a large outlay of resource (staff and money) will not compensate for a service that is less well defined overall in terms of service vision, planning, implementation and evaluation of the impact on children and families living in the area and where staff morale, if sickness rates provide any sort of indication, is not high. Moreover, the case studies suggest a relationship between the processes of direct service implementation, impact on children and families, and overall quality (albeit indirect) of leadership provided.

Everything points towards the view that success is highly dependent upon the energy, imagination and expertise of individual professionals or professional groups and their leaders who, despite structural barriers and constraints of performance frameworks, are able to make a difference, whatever the circumstances. This chapter leaves unexamined in any very direct way the effects on and experiences of the families and communities themselves.

Despite the real enthusiasm of the local integrated centre programme members concerned, the survey respondents suggested that effective multi-agency working had not always been easy to achieve. Multi-agency work by its very nature could disrupt existing professional and agency cultures, and conflicts over areas of responsibility could arise. Establishment of common aims within and across agencies was regarded as essential but, in practice, was not always easy to achieve, with new roles and responsibilities needing to be made explicit at all levels and effective communication developed to increase understanding of these. Practices established to protect confidentiality were still creating tensions and information-sharing strategies could still be improved. Allocation of budgets and financial organization, as well as non-financial resources, had created a major challenge to local multi-agency working. That said, the vast majority believed that their local integrated centre programme facilitated multi-agency working in terms of staffing arrangements, teams' expectations and priorities. Staff training was seen to have an important function in developing new ways of working.

It was generally highlighted throughout that multi-agency team working was strongly promoted and supported by local programme leaders. Despite this, what emerged most strongly from the interviews was the impact on the work of integrated centre leaders of line management by the leading agencies who had overall control of financial arrangements and 'contracting-in' of the services of different professionals. Given that control and funding for children's centres is now being handed over gradually to local authorities, these findings underline the growing importance of effectiveness and cost-effectiveness. In fact, staff with different backgrounds and skills strove towards common goals and shared values despite barriers to effectiveness and efficiency, in the form of constantly shifting social, cultural and educational policies, local authority structures, lack of space and split-site challenges to data storing, information-sharing and communication.

This chapter attests to the power of leadership in context by 'the many'. The presence of the local integrated centre leaders is unmistakable but there is a strong sense of the 'many professionals' taking responsibility for creating and sharing knowledge and an unchallenged assumption that it is their task to remove the barriers that hinder this process. It is a reminder that it is the cultivation of leaders at many levels in the local programmes that together must collectively shape the future of their organization in a time of change.

► Models of effective multi-agency working are still to be identified, although facilitating factors have been identified.

Practitioner's views 8.1

The strategic leader of our leaders was keen to review the effectiveness of multi-agency working and, in particular, the influence of different models of such working in improving outcomes for children and families. While the evidence on effective multi-agency practice is scant, we can be more certain about facilitating factors and barriers, where consistent findings emerge.

Facilitators include:

- *clear aims;*
- *roles and responsibilities and timetables that are agreed between partners;*
- *a multi-agency steering group;*
- *commitment at all levels of the organizations involved;*
- *good systems of communication and information-sharing, including IT systems; and*
- *support and training for staff in new ways of working (there is some evidence that interprofessional programmes of continuing education can remove barriers to joint working).*

We now need to find out more about:

- *the relationship of different models of multi-agency working in services for children to outcomes;*
- *the relationship of facilitating factors to outcomes; and*
- *assessment of cost-effectiveness.*

CHAPTER NINE

LEADING IN A TIME OF CHANGE

This chapter explores the role of interprofessional development in a time of great change in policies and initiatives, nationally and internationally. While Chapter 7 focused on mentoring for individuals and groups, this chapter looks at organization of change and development.

9.1 Introduction

The period of time over which we worked with our leaders was one of swift expansion of the integrated children's centres programme with the goal to 'mainstream' it to all children and a government announcement that there would be 3,500 by 2010. At the same time, a number of broader trends and developments began to emerge.

Rapid growth of services

First, the rapid growth in and changes to the structure and organization of English early childhood services, including the ways that control has been exercised through local authorities, has taken place within a short period of around five years. This change has taken place, as noted by Glass (2006: 54) in a sector with 'little or no experience of running major publicly-funded programmes, *let alone* those based on community development principles, involving local parents in the regeneration of their areas'. Community development aims to give people in disadvantaged areas more control over their lives through the creation of sustainable networks, services and activities that are responsive to available outside opportunities, and encourages engagement with agencies that can affect their lives. It also works with professionals to enhance their capacity to engage effectively with communities and to change ways of working that prevent people from participating effectively. Inevitably, few of the leaders appointed possessed this sort of experience and, as seen in the previous chapter, they were leading professionals themselves with little training or experience of working in an integrated multi-agency manner to deliver a wide range of services. Furthermore, while such leaders were working under pressure to reach particular government targets or outcomes, they were also under pressure to spend the money that had been allocated with the attendant risk that less attention would be given to spending wisely. Chapters 2, 3, 4 and 5 have already highlighted the mixed attitude of early childhood leaders in general and the varied expertise in financial and budgetary management. Meanwhile Chapter 8 has shown that there was much to be learned about the processes of multi-agency working as well as impact judged in terms of achieving vision, ability to change and improve, satisfy stakeholders (children, families and the community as well as local authority requirements) and succeed financially.

Reconfiguring services

Second, long-term relationships have changed between early childhood settings (those offering integrated education, health and social care through children's centres, state, private or voluntary provision or extended schooling), central government (responsible for most services for children under the direction of a Minister for Children) and, in local authority areas, a director for children's services and an integrated mechanism for planning and delivering services, a Children's Trust. There is also a common assessment framework, an integrated workforce strategy and a common core of training and an integrated inspection framework (DfES, 2004a).

Changed governance

Third, the balance of power and governance has changed. For integrated centres the considerable degree of autonomy enjoyed in adapting to local circumstances will be placed under greater local government control with a reduction of the power of parents under local authority governance arrangements. Original guidance on governance envisaged governing bodies comprised of up to one-third of parents, one-third statutory agencies and one-third voluntary and community members. It remains to be seen whether reforms to integrated services will lead in practice to closer collaboration between existing early childhood settings, agencies and professional groups. It seems likely that there will be a reduced role for parents and a redefinition of parent involvement.

The need to create new and shared understandings of integrated practice

The reforms open up the possibility of a greater integration between services and professionals, but they also reflect a greater institutionalization of young children and childhood as educare spans the period from birth to 5 years with a potential greater control and surveillance of families, as noted by the young social worker in the previous chapter. As we have argued elsewhere (in Aubrey et al., 2005) this is not necessarily a positive step.

Cohen et al. (2005: 8) have drawn attention to the fact that 'integrate' is a beguiling word that is 'often used in British policy documents but is less often defined'. They suggest a distinction should be made between structural and conceptual dimensions. As shown in previous chapters, there are structural or management dimensions of staffing, funding and regulation, and conceptual dimensions that include principles, values, approaches to practice involving families and community, understanding of care and education, and learning and development of staff and children. Moreover, while there are different understandings, knowledge and traditions about education and social care, 'lifelong learning' and 'a knowledge society' within the sector, the emphasis is placed on efficiency and effectiveness in meeting targets rather than critical analysis of the nature of integrated children's services that could contribute to the creation of new and shared understandings of integrated practice. The need for local discussion and reflection will be re-examined later in this chapter.

Tensions between policy, provision and practice

It may be beyond the scope of this text to speculate upon the wider workings of a neo-liberal welfare system such as we have in England. Whether emphasizing private responsibility for educare services, targeted financial support for families on low incomes, including what is now called 'working tax credit' can transform the workforce by increasing self-sufficiency through paid work, or whether continued reliance on private and voluntary sector provision and parents' fees to fund services merely serves to reinforce existing ways of working remains to be seen. It is clear that changes in thinking about integrated children's centres have been characterized by an increased emphasis on childcare that in turn reflects a desire to get women, particularly, 'lone' parents, back into work as a means of reducing poverty. A danger lies in placing too much responsibility for ameliorating poverty and exclusion on the shoulders of integrated service providers and early childhood professionals, not to mention the parents in the communities concerned. It can divert attention away from structural causes in the very political systems, economic and welfare regimes within which they are located. Milbourne (2005: 690) has suggested that the benefits of effective inter-agency work 'should lead to the development of new practices from common ground, leading to more responsive, less fragmented services for families and a more successful approach to tackling social problems'. The risks are that the short-term nature of interventions allows insufficient time to overcome professional inflexibilities and places an increased burden on individual workers not only for resolving the tensions involved in defining a new repertoire of interventions but constraints in terms of performance outputs required. Families have no control over the initiative, its nature or when it starts or finishes. Many such initiatives established to tackle social problems, by focusing on individual and family intervention, both 'individualize the path to re-entry into mainstream activities and reinforce the individual blame for failing to do so'.

The danger lies in expecting too much from integrated services and the communities that they serve and seeing failure such as the equivocal outcomes from the NESS (Melhuish et al., 2005) in terms of the limitations of the early childhood professionals concerned and the vulnerable families who fail to engage or become 'empowered'. Tensions between policy, provision and practice may be inevitable.

9.2 A need for interprofessional education

Training for an integrated workforce

Even if policy, provision and practice tensions are taken as a given, it is still the case that each arena is pushing forward change. Policy may set the rate of reform but, as shown in the introduction, broader social, technological and economic change will influence provision, practice and public understanding and expectations as well as policy. A learning organization thus initiates as well as responds to change in order to promote educational, health-related and social care and welfare outcomes. This means that developing effective integrated and collaborative practice is a local, regional and national obligation. In fact it is not just a national challenge but an international challenge. A survey by Magrab et al. (1997) for the Organization for Economic Co-operation and Development (OECD) in seven member states found that few childcare professionals were trained to work in an integrated service-delivery system. As in England, France, Italy and the Netherlands had launched national policies to co-ordinate services for children and young people and families at risk that had generated a variety of multidisciplinary training projects, responses to national policies that tended to be local and idiosyncratic. Magrab et al. (1997: 101) advocated a 'key curriculum' for all professions working with at-risk children:

- knowledge of concepts of service integration;
- knowledge of the roles of the diverse professions that serve such children;
- preparation for effective team member functioning; and
- preparation for co-ordinating services for families.

Mapping the qualifications and training developments across the workforce

This notion of a key curriculum suggests that ongoing professional education as a means of developing collaborative practice may need to take place during initial training and afterwards as post-experience training, but not necessarily being carried out in the workplace. In order to do this in a rational manner there needs to be a mapping of qualifications and training developments across the children and young people's workforce to inform the development of an integrated qualifications framework. In fact, the DfES produced a *Children's Workforce Strategy* consultation document (DfES, 2006c) in order to identify the skills all staff within the children and young people's workforce would need in common to provide an effective and integrated service and a vision of approaches by which a skilled workforce could be achieved and sustained. The *Common Core of Skills and Knowledge for the Children's Workforce* (DfES, 2005) outlined the basic skills and knowledge needed by practitioners working regularly with children, young people and their families.

As noted above an integrated service requires an integrated workforce that shares a common vision of high-quality provision, shares knowledge and information and, moreover, shares a common career structures or qualifications framework with horizontal and vertical pathways in order to disseminate best practice. Johnson et al. (2005) of Sheffield Hallam University were commissioned by the DfES to produce a mapping of qualifications and training developments across the children and young people's workforce to inform the development of an integrated qualifications framework. This mapping covered all major occupational groups within the children's workforce, nationally available and approved qualifications from level 1, with basic knowledge and skills and an ability to apply learning with guidance and supervision, through to level 6, with high specialist knowledge of an area of work at honours graduate level, and on to level 7, at master's degree level and level 8, at leading expert or leading practitioner level in a particular field.

A number of key findings are relevant to the discussion of interprofessional education. First, there were continuing difficulties in defining the children and young people's workforce as roles and job names were subject to constant change. Some workers belonged to strong professional communities and had a strong role identity; others did not. Differences in levels of qualification and age specificity were a challenge to achieving compatibility of qualifications between roles and sectors within the workforce.

Second, with respect to qualifications, there was a confusion about levels of qualifications that needed to be addressed as well as a need to support multi-level training. The question of how to represent 'non-levelled' training and whether all training required level assignation was raised. Consistency over nomenclature and level assignment to roles across the different workforce clusters it was recommended would be of assistance. Some roles had mandatory qualification requirements others did not.

Third, there appeared to be a particular need to simplify qualification sets in very many early years qualifications, an area identified in Chapter 2. Notable gaps in the qualifications frameworks within the workforce sectors included management and leadership qualifications for the sector at levels 3, 4 and 5. These were highlighted by conversations with staff in our study and reported in Chapter 3. In terms of workforce progression, there was a growing body of skilled teaching assistants who needed progression routes. Awareness on the ground of the significance of the Common Core of Skills and Knowledge was patchy. There was a perceived conflict between NHS Core Skills and the Common Core of Knowledge and Skills that cross-mapping might clarify. Interestingly, education and training modules were less well mapped to safeguarding and welfare and multi-agency working. These findings offer some explanation for tensions and uncertainties in multi-agency working that Chapter 8 uncovered.

Fourth, in terms of training, there was questioning of a focus on individual qualifications and an interest in more joint-service led forms of training. Training needs were identified in the area of additional skills required for people to work together more closely in integrated service provision. Managers at senior level were found to be concerned that they had responsibility for professional development of colleagues in key posts with whom they had no shared background and hence minimal understanding of training pathways. Training to support them in this work was viewed as urgent and the need for national training programmes and networks to help learn from best practice underlined.

Fifth, wider progression challenges included training and qualifications for enhanced roles within existing professional groups. A specific concern about lack of structure, qualification routes and career progression pathways for new workers in social care and education was expressed. Currently, the possibility of movement across the workforce was limited. Salary scales and structures, different terms and conditions within key professional groups were a hindrance. Appropriate training for middle managers in respect of joint planning and commissioning of services was noted. Suffice to say that the education training needs for an integrated workforce in this review are underlined.

The nature of interprofessional education and training

Barr et al. (2005: 31) carried out a Cochrane systematic review of effective interprofessional education and found no studies meeting its stringent criteria. On the basis of this, they carried out an assessment of the characteristics of the methodologically strongest literature available using as a definition:

Occasions when two or more professions learn side by side for whatever reason.

They noted that learning that informs such collaboration may occur during uniprofessional (one professional group), interprofessional (between professional groups) and multi-professional (many professional groups) education. This suggests that there may be multiple modes of professional training that relate to working together. Furthermore, there will be inevitable differences in meanings and language usage referring to common professional practices that may constitute not only conceptual but operational barriers.

They proceeded to formulate principles for interprofessional learning, indicating that it should be:

- collaborative, rather than competitive;
- egalitarian, and thus minimizing status differences between leader and learner;
- group directed, so that there is collective responsibility;
- experiential, and hence based on interprofessional encounters;
- reflective, in the sense of Schön's (1983; 1987; 1991) reflective practice that distinguishes between reflection-in-action, where professionals have to make quick decisions and reflection-on-action, where professionals have the opportunity to learn from experience; and
- applied, to the extent that it relates the content and experience of interprofessional education to collaborative practice, identifying barriers that may impede it and strategies to overcome them and enhance practice.

They also noted that interprofessional learning should be judged ultimately by whether or not it led to and reinforced interprofessional practice.

Barr et al. (2005) showed that initiatives focusing on individuals tended to report outcomes linked to individual change in learner reaction, attitude or perceptions of change or acquisition of knowledge and skills, while initiatives focusing on service development tended to report organization change to professional practice and/or improvements to client care. The low incidence of initiatives focusing on team or group collaboration was noteworthy but this it was thought might reflect the difficulty in releasing teams from busy practice areas, such as those described in the last chapter. They emphasized, however, that collaborative group or teamwork was a 'missing link' in their three identified focuses of *interprofessional education* that also included: individual preparation; *collaboration* with a group or teamwork; and *improving services* or quality of care between groups. It also serves as a reminder that individual mentoring will form only one of a number of strategies for generating change within and across professional groups. These findings are compatible with those of Johnson et al. (2005).

Approaches to interprofessional education

Approaches to learning and teaching in interprofessional education were also examined and described as interactive in nature, with little place reserved for 'received learning' (or didactic teaching). It was conceded, however, that didactive teaching still had a place, used sparingly. Almost half of the 107 studies they scrutinized employed a single approach to interprofessional education, a fifth combined two approaches and almost a fifth reported three approaches, while the other studies reported four approaches to learning and teaching. Most frequently used was a so-called 'exchange' approach (for example, using seminar and workshop discussions), followed by 'received' lectures or presentations, followed in turn by 'guideline development', that is, quality improvement initiatives (that included initial learner reaction, modification of attitudes or skills, behavioural change, change in organizational practice that led to benefits to the client groups), practice or placement learning. Other approaches included problem-based learning and problem-solving activities, simulations or role plays, observation (work shadowing, or site visits) and e-learning (or 'blended learning'). This gives some indication of the range of professional development initiatives that may be required.

The role of theory

Few studies referred directly to a particular theoretical framework for interprofessional education. Those that did tended to draw on perspectives from adult learning theory. Some incorporated problem-based learning (for example, of Mann et al., 1996). Others incorporated Knowles's (1975; 1990) theory of adult learning or 'andragogy' that is distinguished from child learning or pedagogy; Kolb's theory of experiential learning (Kolb, 1984; Kolb and Fry, 1975); or Schön's (1983; 1987) theory of reflective practice and organizational learning. Also, implicit in other studies were tenets of adult learning theory and organizational development perspectives.

Systems theory and learning organization theory, total quality management theories and activity theory have all provided tools for improving services. Some reference to such theories was made in the introduction to the book. Systems theory (von Bertalanffy, 1971; Engel, 1977) provided a dynamic model within which relationships of interacting professionals and agencies with one another, inside and outside an organization could be understood. The idea of a 'learning organization' that facilitated learning of itself and its members emerged from organizational theory (Argyris and Schön, 1974; 1978; 1996). 'Single loop learning' associated with enhancing an individual person's advancement in relation to others contrasted with 'double loop learning' of a whole team of organization in response to a changing environment.

Whalley et al. (2004) have drawn on Lewin (1952) to identify stages of organizational learning:

- unfreezing (stimulating the motivation to change);
- moving (developing new attitudes, beliefs and behaviour on the basis of new information that leads to cognitive reassessment); and
- refreezing (integrating new values, knowledge and behaviour into the system).

Organizational performance change often draws upon two quality management theories: total quality management (TQM) of Morgan (1997), and continuous quality improvement (CQI) of Wilcock et al. (2003). Both comprise a set of principles and processes that facilitate the improvement of processes and systems within an organization with planning, changing, monitoring and assessing outcomes. A distinctive feature of the CQI is a 'plan-do-study-and-act' cycle used by individual professionals in their daily work to make small changes to their work that are appropriate to their client group. Simple improvements rapidly introduced may lead to bigger ones that demand more complex changes.

While TQM and CQI have been used to generate small changes, activity theory (Engeström et al., 1999) is directed towards change from the micro or individual level through to the macro community or collective level. It is promising in application to leadership in a time of change since the focus is joint activity rather than individual activity within an unstable environment where internal contradiction is seen as the motive for change.

The implication of this review of interprofessional education is that initial professional training and qualifications cannot go far beyond acquisition of fundamental knowledge, skill and attitude, and much will depend upon the application of these in subsequent employment contexts. The continuing need to update and reinforce specific professional knowledge and skills in a fast-changing world remains clear. A parallel need for career-long, work-based multi-professional continuing professional development may be equally clear but is probably less well understood.

The early childhood leader will have a central role in setting the learning agenda and creating a learning organization. The learning organization, however, interacts and co-operates with sister organizations (at the meso level) and, at the same time, is an integral part of a wider local authority system (at the exo level) to draw attention to the operating environments of leadership in terms of ecological theory (Bronfenbrenner, 1979). The learning organization can thus be fully understood only in the context of other sub-systems that, in turn, are part of a wider social system that consists of many factors. A number of factors must thus be considered in the context of change and improvement in one children's centre, for instance.

9.3 Staff resistance to change

Responses to change

It would be wrong, however, to suggest that rapid and persistent change can take place without tension between a perceived current stability and feelings of anxiety about a less certain future. Some of our leaders regarded staff commitment, motivation and reluctance to change as a barrier and for their part, some staff regarded lack of vision, criticism and dictatorial attitudes of leaders as a barrier to *their* work. It is likely that these barriers represent emotional responses to change. Hoyle (2004) has suggested that these reactions can reflect a concern that change in policy may lead to change in staff's normative primary task, that is, their role and what they are expected to do that is intimately connected to the meaning or value that their work has for them (the existential primary task). Throughout the book, it has been shown that a core value for early years staff is developing a quality service and, associated with this, engaging in professional development. Anything that threatens a core value is likely to be met with a whole gamut of responses that range from active and passive opposition through to an apparent acceptance and support. Threats, real or imagined, may include reduced resources, heavier workloads, more limited career opportunities and related strains in personal relationships that result from these setbacks

Ebbeck and Waniganayake (2000) have emphasized the need to distinguish between resistance that arises from personal and organizational sources. Personal sources can range from trivial misunderstanding, through fear, inertia and lack of identification with change, to the inevitable clashes between personal and organizational goals and motivations that arise. Organization sources may result from structural changes or rigidity, existing organizational climate and/or historical rivalries that may be maintained by long-term employed members of staff who fear loss of power and influence. The latter may be particularly resistant to change as they are often sufficiently hidden and covert so that they present a challenge to any leader seeking to address them openly. Sources of resistance may also lie in the community, with parent pressure groups willing to sabotage changes to organizational routines that may inconvenience their busy time-schedules.

This discussion of resistance to change leads naturally to an examination of strategies available to the leader. Moreover, it suggests that a collaborative style of leadership where working practices are regularly reviewed and decisions are shared, may meet with less organizational resistance.

Strategies for leaders

As noted in Chapter 4, it may serve the health of the organization for staff to have the opportunity to review the primary task on a regular basis. By these means, they are allowed both to voice their concerns about likely changes to patterns of work and indeed to contribute to the change process by clarifying the perceived problem, helping to gather facts about it, generating alternative solutions, setting priorities, planning and assisting with an evaluation. As noted above, the more staff are actively involved in reaching towards an agreed solution, the more constructive is their response likely to be.

Huxham and Vangen (2005: 246), however, stress the complexity of collaborative situations and the tensions generated between alternative courses of action. For them, organizational and personal change are areas in which tensions can be identified. In their theory of tensions, managing in order to collaborate consists of four levels of conceptual 'handles':

1. the notion of tension accepts coping with multiple dilemmas of management is a reality and this shifts thinking towards 'good enough' resolutions;
2. the notion of multiple, interacting tensions views management as a process of continually resolving dilemmas by seeking to isolate tensions so that

reflection becomes manageable but nevertheless regards resolutions as ephemeral;
3. the notion of tensions in specific management areas are defined and redefined by management need but focused on predominant concerns so that reflection becomes manageable;
4. the notion of deconstructed tensions, is learning about specific tensions through the process of deconstructing them and using deconstructed tensions to learn about other situations.

In other words, managing to collaborate is as much about learning to recognize and work with tensions as managing to resolve them. The theory is intended as a basis for supporting managerial judgement, taking practical action, providing a structure for sense-making and consideration of alternatives to support reflective practice. While it underlines the need to create a climate for planned change to involve all parties, consider alternative solutions and evaluate the selected implementation, above all, it is also a caution against simple prescriptions and recipe knowledge. To be effective, leadership during change must be empowering so that staff feel ownership and accept responsibility for the change process and its consequences.

9.4 A model for improving the early childhood integrated centre

One way of identifying where improvements are to be made is to create a model that takes account of inputs, that should be equivalent to costs (such as funding, staffing, buildings and resources, support from the local authority children's services); *procedures* that staff engage in (such as publicity, websites, monitoring and organizing training); *processes* that community members take part in when procedures run smoothly (such as consultation, planning, providing support for parents, children and community); *outputs* that should be immediately observable and measurable (caseload dealt with, improved take up of services and growing awareness of parents and community) and, finally, *outcomes*, or desired effects (better educational, health and social outcomes). Each box (see Figure 9.1), in turn can be turned into a question (does this really lead to the intended result?). This means that, if required, outputs can be judged in terms of inputs (or costs).

9.5 Understanding change

As noted throughout this book, relationships in organizations and in society as a whole are changing from apparently stable and predictable patterns to more fluid, unpredictable and uncertain forms. As perceived by our leaders, there may be limited time for reflection as they struggle to make sense of ever more new orders. Offering staff ways of making links between individual, group and organizational interactions may help them to make connections between personal experience and organizational dynamics by developing new methods and techniques in working with them.

Fullan (2001: 34) has suggested a culture of change is 'less about innovation and more about innovativeness. It is less about strategy and more about strategizing'. The purpose is to understand change in order to lead it better. There are no shortcuts:

- The goal is not to innovate the most or most quickly but to learn from learning (reflective practice and feedback are needed).
- It is not enough to have the best ideas, strengths and weaknesses of different leadership approaches – authoritative, democratic, affiliative and coaching styles need to be recognized – and all used (Goleman, 2000).
- Appreciating the implementation dip in performance whether through fear of change or lack of technical knowledge is essential in moving forward (Fullan, 2001).
- Redefining resistance in order to learn from those who disagree.
- 'Reculturing' or transforming the culture means creating a culture of change.
- There can never be a checklist or 'recipe' knowledge but always complexity – leaders may be pushed to provide solutions but 'mobilizing people to tackle tough problems may be better' (Heifetz, 1994: 15).
- Complexities of leadership must be addressed through the recognition that different strategies are needed for different circumstances (coercive actions may be needed at the beginning of a crisis).

The message is that different leadership strategies are needed for different circumstances. On the one hand, this supports the notion of contextual leadership that emerged in Chapter 1 and has been elaborated in the previous section. On the other, it is a caution against generalizing from case studies of short-term success (or failure for that matter) as shown in Chapter 8.

Five components of effective leadership are identified by Fullan (2001) to achieve a culture of change:

- *moral purpose* (making a difference to the lives of children, their families and communities has been a theme running through the early childhood leaders' conversations right from the start);
- *understanding the change process* (this was also acknowledged as a challenge by early childhood leaders and knowledge generation was regarded as a key);
- *relationships* (this was high on the agenda for early childhood leaders and practitioners);
- *knowledge creation and sharing* (seeking ways and means of generating and increasing knowledge inside and outside the organization by leaders and followers has emerged as a reciprocal process); and
- *coherence making* (the challenge to tolerate ambiguity, yet seek for coherence has been implicit yet nevertheless central to the process of individual and organizational change).

Inputs →	Procedures →	Processes →	Outputs →	Outcomes
Funding	Promotional strategies, publicity and websites in place	Programme delivery with elements of support/skill prepared and provided	Caseload managed by staff/services delivered	Programme meets needs of a diverse local community
Staff with relevant professional knowledge and skills	Monitoring system/programme evaluation/use of services in place	Evaluation in place	Evaluation information used to improve services	Parent–child outcomes: sensitivity/reciprocity
Provision of buildings and outdoor areas/capital expenditure	Organization of staff training	Feedback/consultation with client groups, local authority and other stakeholders. Further planning	Preventative strategies operating and effective	Home learning environment; parent/carer awareness of learning, health, care and welfare needs
Recurrent expenditure for materials/resources	Dissemination strategy in place with feedback to relevant use groups	Capacity building in Sure Start children's centres	Children healthy, learning and safe	Child outcomes: learning/achievement/social-emotional/adjustment/health/wealth/well-being
Information technology/library services	Arranging meetings with local authority, statutory, private and voluntary agencies, parents and local schools	Capacity building in parent groups/community	Increased awareness of local service providers, parents and community	
Support links in place with local authority, PCT/health services; partnerships with private and voluntary agencies; links with other Sure Start children's centres				

Figure 9.1 *Judging effective early childhood practice*

Indeed, at a time of uncertainty and change the strong commitment to social justice of early childhood leaders and their staff, whether state, voluntary or private institutions, provides a moral purpose and a passion to their quest for quality provision. Despite the uncertainty of their journey, however, the importance to the role of leadership of creating the conditions for learning at all levels has been affirmed and hence the importance of creating a learning organization.

At this point in the book, it is important to consider in more depth some of the measures that the leaders may wish to consider to create a learning organization, in this case, reflective practice and action learning. This will be the task of the next and penultimate chapter.

▶ Leaders considered what advice they would give to a new early childhood leader coming into post.

Practitioners' views 9.1

What advice they would give to other leaders? The following observations were made.

- We need passionate people working in integrated centres. I think that we have to inspire others. I think that we do have to champion this work.
- It's a fantastic opportunity to be a children's centre leader because you have the chance to shape things.
- Don't do it (in the voluntary sector) unless you are willing to work long hours for low pay. It requires dedication.
- It's fun, it's exciting … the new things that are happening. I bought the nursery purely as an investment but now I can't walk away. I am too involved. I have put my whole heart into it.
- Try to maintain enthusiasm for what you are doing in the face of bureaucracy … it's a trial against adversity in the private sector.
- Believe in yourself and be confident because everyone is an expert – your team, your parents, those in the university.
- It's a confidence thing and, I suppose, that's what I am learning. But everyone is scared, everybody thinks that they are going to get found out. But you have got skills that got you where you are.
- In the foundation stage, first and foremost you have to understand the needs of 3- to 5-year-olds. The educational environment is different from Key Stages 1 and 2.
- Take every opportunity to visit others in different settings.
- Leadership is a lonely place. Although the support networks to be fair are there.
- You can't ask people to do things that you would not do yourself.
- Leaders do need help and support as well.

CHAPTER TEN

REFLECTIVE PRACTICE AND ACTION LEARNING

Chapter 9 stressed the importance of creating a learning organization, accordingly this chapter will take a closer look at ways of engaging leaders in reflective practice and action learning, introduced in Chapter 7. The introduction will link this practice to the broader context of social, economic and technological change that was outlined first in Chapter 1. The main body of the chapter will then explore the 'think-do-review' process of conducting an action research approach to informing leaders' practice that, in turn, influences thinking in a cycle intended to create change and improvement. The chapter will draw upon the experience of three integrated centre leaders who opted to take their NPQICL study further in order to complete their Master's degree.

10.1 Introduction

Reflective learning and reflective practice have been considered at various points in this book and they have been associated with the work of Schön (1983). In a context of very rapid societal change, reflective practice will have a more urgent and important role to play. Social knowledge and practices that were once regarded as stable and unchanging, and hence reproduced in the course of human activity, cannot provide a guide to changing action. New knowledge, skills and techniques are endlessly required as workers have to adapt to new circumstances. Entrepreneurial and business skills learned in the course of leaders' professional practice, explored in Chapter 5, provide one such example of on-the-job work-based learning responsive to new circumstances. Furthermore, National Vocational Qualifications (NVQs) in childcare and education provide an example of work-based learning and assessment that offers a means of formal accreditation. These trends reflect new ways of thinking about learning that are not necessarily associated with formal education contexts. Indeed, reflective learning is an ever-present feature of postmodern life and work.

It is clear that members of learning societies need to learn new information or acquire new knowledge and skills in order to keep up to date with the constant changes in the workplace and, anyway, as Jarvis (2004) noted, the concept of a learning society does not distinguish between education and learning. This means that boundaries between formal and informal learning or learning for work and learning for life are becoming more blurred. It may also mean that even research practice is moving out of the university in order for practitioner researchers to conduct research independently or alongside academics in the workplace. Reflective learning and research activity are thus a part of our everyday world.

Alongside the rapid societal changes that have been taking place, research in the social sciences itself has also been undergoing considerable change (Ball, 2004). Large-scale, quantitative investigations of the social world that attempted to adopt approaches and methods of natural science have come under increasing attack. Moreover, qualitative research has rejected the assumptions of objectivity and scientific rigour in the study of the social world. A social constructivist perspective has become increasingly favoured, in which researchers and participants in the research process are regarded as active social agents in and interpreters of their own and one another's actions and interactions to create an intersubjectivity, underlining yet again the important role of reflexivity.

In turn, it has been recognised by critical theorists that particular minority groups have tended to be socially marginalized in the research process. These minorities include women, racial minorities and disabled groups who have been regarded as 'silenced' and 'oppressed' by society and by research. This has led to 'giving voice', for instance to women in feminist research, and to a recognition that research can have a transformative and emancipatory role.

More recently, but overlapping with critical theory, has been postmodern or post-structural theory that raises a challenge to the whole enterprise of the social sciences, its assumptions, practices and truth claims. Claims to dominance of any one meaning is rejected in favour of the notion of competing meanings since meaning itself is regarded as culturally and historically constituted, and 'truth' is seen to rest upon the operation of power. Society and culture, however, are considered as amenable to discursive or textual reading. Texts and discourse speak through us and we use narrative as linguistic resources to think of ('tell') ourselves and describe our actions till we come to 'be' ourselves. In similar fashion, discourse provides a language for producing and discussing knowledge. Attention is thus drawn to the relationships between knowledge, truth and power, as well as the effect of these on us and on our institutions. Already we are beginning to see that leaders' action research may have as its motive social change and improvement.

10.2 Reflective process of progressive problem-solving

As seen in Chapter 7, action research is a reflective process that leads to progressive problem-solving by individuals, teams and organisations. Action research may (or may not) be guided by academic or professional researchers, with the goal to assist organizations improve their knowledge and understanding of the environment in which they operate and their practices, that is propose a new course of action. Lewin (1946) first coined the term 'action research'. He saw it as research on the conditions and consequences of existing social action, with research leading to further social action. It uses a spiral of planning, taking action and feedback of results that leads to further action planning. In keeping with discussion in the previous section, action research challenges formal knowledge of traditional social science researchers by focusing on continuous theorizing, data collecting and inquiring. Knowledge is thus 'emergent' because it is gained in, through and for action that is well informed.

As observed in Chapter 9, Lewin's own description of the change process involved three stages: a planning stage, or *unfreezing*, in which awareness of an initial problem is recognized; an action stage that is a time of *changing*; and a results stage when new behaviours are tested 'on the job' and if monitoring indicates they work, with or without fine-tuning, they will be adopted and *refreezing* takes place. While his model has been used widely in organizational development, action research has developed in a number of other ways. Reason (1994), for example, expanded the notion of co-operative or collaborative enquiry (see Reason and Bradley, 2007) among a group of co-researchers. This entailed four kinds of knowledge: propositional (or formal) knowledge; practical knowledge that arises from the actions that are proposed; experiential knowledge that is derived from feedback from testing out in the real world; and presentational knowledge where new practices are tried out, developed and refined. Recently, participatory action research (PAR) has become popular, particularly with international development agencies and community development workers operating alongside poor and less privileged groups to address their own areas of local concern. Participatory action research engages in the same process of planning, taking action, observing and evaluating (McNiff and Whitehead, 2006). While it has its origins in the 'critical pedagogy' of Paulo Freire (2006), it follows the same action research principles of identifying a problem in the workplace in order to change and improve it.

10.3 Planning an action research cycle with integrated centre leaders

Action research is stimulated by a genuine desire to change professional practice or improve understanding of how and/or why something is happening in the workplace as a means of gaining greater control over it. Karen, Teresa and Mala had all been awarded the NPQICL and decided to build on this qualification to complete a Master's degree. They each had a strong commitment to improving early childhood services for the communities that they served and were motivated to work together with other members of their group to use critical reflection and social criticism to analyse national and international early childhood care and educational policy in the first module of their study. This stage helped them to begin theorizing about their practice situations. Then in the second module, they worked hard to develop understanding of small-scale research design that was ethically informed, valid and trustworthy. This meant that it had a clear sampling strategy and was combined with data-gathering and analysis methods to develop their skills of observation and analysis of texts (documents, questionnaire and interview transcriptions). During this stage, they carried out a pilot study to trial their methods of data-gathering and test their initial ideas and then reported this. In the third module, they carried out their investigation, gathering and analysing data, drawing conclusions and sharing their ideas with their research group. This meant that they developed a collaborative research process with participants in their own local communities who were fully involved not only in the process of planning, implementing and reviewing but also served as a group of critical friends who were a part of their own local communities. The cycle utilized, mirrored the learning-from-experience cycle introduced in Chapter 7: using experience; reflecting on this; making sense of it; and performing differently. While the several stages of reflecting and acting that, in this case, formed part of and were structured by the requirements of a postgraduate qualification, in general, they conformed closely to the outline of an action research cycle outlined by MacNaughton and Hughes (2009) (Figure 10.1).

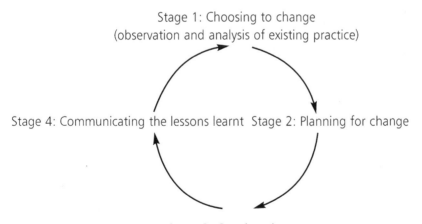

Stage 1: Choosing to change
(observation and analysis of existing practice)

Stage 4: Communicating the lessons learnt   Stage 2: Planning for change

Stage 3: Creating change

Figure 10.1 MacNaughton and Hughes's action research cycle

The implications for this group of leaders of combining action research with postgraduate accreditation were that they engaged in a stage of *Pre-preparation,* when the group developed its own critical thinking about social justice and notions about equity in early childhood care and education that motivated the work that followed, and developed their practical skills as action researchers.

Stage 1 (*Choosing to change*) involved choosing a social practice to change or improve. Stage 2 (*Planning for change*) selected a research focus and generated some research questions to narrow research to manageable proportions. Stage 3 (*Creating change*) concerned the implementation process. Stage 4 (*Communicating the lessons learnt*) entailed sharing with one another and their research supervisor, writing the research report and taking this back to their own research participants as a basis for further reflection and adjustment in practice.

10.4 Doing action research in the early childhood field

Pre-preparation stage

In the pre-preparation stage, our leaders were introduced to core ideas from critical theory that provided some tools to begin the critical examination of early childhood services as they operated in the national and international context, in both OECD countries and in the South. This sensitized them to inequalities that might be operating in their own communities who were living in areas of extreme poverty and comprised minority groups that included recent immigrants to England. Many of these leader groups had led the Labour government's Sure Start programmes that had targeted poor families and young children with the aim to break the cycle of poverty and address inequality. This it was intended was to be achieved initially through encouragement of mothers to improve their children's early learning and development and, hence, life chances. There was an increasing emphasis, however, on the provision of childcare so that these young women would aspire to employment. It was a strategy, as noted by Penn (2007), that avoided structural change and any proper redistribution of taxation that would have been necessary in order to achieve universal childcare and well-being for birth to 5-year-olds, of the Nordic-welfare type. Instead the government settled for minimum state intervention, a childcare credit tax scheme in a marketplace that encouraged development of the private sector (as described in Chapter 5). This policy carried the implicit message that families themselves were to be blamed for their poverty and thus encouraged a change of mind or attitude towards work. As Sure Start programmes evolved into children's centres, the 'core offer' of services included integrated education and childcare; helping parents into work; child and family health services; and 'support' for parenting, as well as access to specialist services for families. It was a small step from this to blaming families for poor parenting skills that were deemed in need of improvement through the proliferation of parenting programmes that have been promoted by government and have at their heart a means of addressing presumed family dysfunction.

Critical social theory provided these leaders with a form of self-reflection that helped them both to understand and explain the unequal political and social systems in which they themselves were implicated. Habermas (see, for instance,

Calhoun, 1993; Finlayson, 2005; Flyvbjerg, 1998), distinguished critical knowledge from the authority of natural and social science knowledge by its orientation to self-reflection and emancipation that increased autonomy and thereby neutralised or reduced political forms of authority and injustice.

Postmodern critical theory thus shifted their focus of attention towards the social problems themselves, situated in particular cultural–historical contexts and modelled in a language that distorted them by authoritative claims to absolute 'truths' about the world. Through analysis of language, concepts and signs, our leaders struggled to 'disrupt' beliefs in scientific progress, political authority and certainty to which they had subscribed, and to replace these ideas with scepticism, uncertainty and ambiguity advocated by a disparate group of post-modern or post-structuralist writers such as Jacques Derrida, Michael Foucault and Gilles Deleuze.

By arguing against existing knowledge systems, and the language concepts and signs (grand narratives) upon which they were based, post-structural thinkers challenged the concept of 'self' as a stable and independent entity and replaced it with a construct that comprised conflicting knowledge claims (related, for instance, to profession, class or race) that played a central part in an individual leader's interpretation of meaning in text. Hence the original author's intended meaning becomes as unstable and subordinate to the reader's meaning. In other words, meanings in texts shift and the reader replaces the author as the primary focus of enquiry. This leaves a space to search for other sources of meaning other than, for example, accepted academic or political authorities, or cultural norms. It allows deconstruction of the assumptions and knowledge systems that give rise to the impression of a single and unchallenged meaning (see Derrida, 1976; 1978). In other words, deconstruction leads to exposure of 'regimes of truth' that promote cultural hegemony, exclusion and oppression and reveal the relationship between meaning, power, social orders and practices (see Foucault, 1980; 1994; 1997; 1998).

Our leaders had been introduced to the application of post-structural ideas to the early childhood field through the writing of MacNaughton (2005) and Dahlberg and Moss (2005). These ideas had provided a tool to question the nature of knowledge and truth that underpinned their early childhood practice and to a broader questioning of the political contexts, social relationships, values, actions and effects on the lives of children and families in their communities, and hence, existing sources of inequality. They became interested in post-colonial scholars such as Cannella and Viruru (2004) who stimulated deconstruction of childcare knowledge, discourses and unequal power relations in the South, perpetuated through powerful Western donors and aid organizations. This revealed for them the continuing effects of colonialism and racialism in the present. It also led to exploration of other post-structural theorists. They marvelled at the way in which powerful official 'truths' about the social world in the guises of 'official' discourses of psychology, sociology and health, served to define and regulate their practice. Reconsidering these knowledge bases as 'regimes of truth', with power to dominate meanings in their professional lives about what was 'normal' or 'healthy' behaviour, expanded their appreciation of the way in which health care, education and social work knowledge was appropriated and sanctioned by government and the professional associations to which they belonged. After an introduction to foundation research methods they were ready to begin their own action research projects.

Stage 1: Observation and analysis of existing practice

The first step of the process was for our leaders to choose a focus for their action research project. It did not cause any problem to them to find a suitable area in their existing practice to change and/or improve. During the pre-preparation period, each one had started to keep a research journal for critical reflections on integrated children's services. The second step was to generate research questions about their chosen focus that would enable them to describe and analysis this more fully from the range of perspectives of people in their local communities that formed the basis for change and development.

Very early in the process, they agreed to allocate a Thursday morning, once a month, in order to create a community of critical friends willing to give and receive feedback and assistance on research practice. Because it was a community of leaders with different professional heritages, this increased richness to the exchange process.

Karen's action research project

Karen's working life had been spent in child and family social work and so she had worked predominantly in child protection, dealing with crisis intervention on a daily basis. She identified as one of the biggest areas of need the provision of family support for complex cases that would enable families to move out of child protection and court arenas, empower them to protect their children and live without state intervention. It helped her to recognize that child protection could be viewed as a social construct related to a particular period of history, a geographical region in the world and developed norms of the society in which she lived. She noticed that her profession was driven by a majority discourse implemented by those with structural power, in this case, the 'safeguarding agenda' of an English neo-liberal government and backed by such institutions as the law and the church, and by society. Nevertheless, she noted that less than 50 years earlier, it had been acceptable for children to be punished physically for what adults defined as unacceptable behaviour.

In today's England, however, the 'safeguarding children' agenda looked not only at child outcomes of staying safe but also of enjoying and achieving, making a positive contribution, being healthy and living free from poverty. Physical punishment was seen as unacceptable and could lead to intervention by the state through social services.

Her aims were to understand how legislation and policy with regard to safeguarding had been translated into local policy and implemented in children's centres; and to identify how risk was managed. The overall research question was:

How do children's centres provide a key safeguarding children role, whilst maintaining early intervention services?

This had a number of sub-questions:

- How has the responsibility for safeguarding been delegated to children's centre leaders?
- Is there a common understanding of safeguarding among children's centre leaders?
- How are safeguarding risks managed in children's centres?

Teresa's research project

Teresa, who had a health background, critically examined the promotion of early sensitive and responsive parenting interactions and positive parent–child relationships, viewed by Labour government policy as fundamental to the optimal development of children's emotional health and well-being (DoH, 2007; 2008). Infant massage programmes had been raised to become a significant element of the health component of children's centres' core offer to support the government position. She noted that the child health promotion programme, purporting to be founded on 'well-tested theory', advocated the use of infant massage as a parenting intervention despite an earlier Cochrane review cautioning against the universal roll-out of infant massage as a stand-alone therapy (Underdown et al., 2006). Nevertheless, 'the use of dyadic therapies such as infant massage to increase maternal sensitivity' was highlighted as a key intervention to 'reduce the risk of insensitive, intrusive or passive parenting' (DoH, 2008: 47).

Her intention was to carry out a detailed exploration of the evidence base to support the concept of interventions in early parenting, including infant massage viewed from various perspectives in child development, as well as examine dominant discourses, values and practices around parenting in terms of their historical, theoretical and political roots. The core questions was:

What is the evidential relationship between infant massage as an early parenting intervention and promotion of parental sensitivity, relationship building and the development of secure attachment?

Sub-questions were as follows:

- How do infant massage training providers and practitioners respond in terms of beliefs, attitudes, understanding and practices (that is, what/how do they teach)?
- How is this interpreted by parents, practitioners and local policy-makers?
- How successful is infant massage judged to be by parents, practitioners and local policy-makers?

Mala's research project

Mala, with a background as an early years practitioner, elected to examine the dangers of accepting 'Western' (European and North American) models of early child development uncritically as 'regimes of truth' that privileged white middle-class and culturally specific child-rearing norms related to infant stimulation. In this way, she came to appreciate better how minority groups could be silenced and marginalized by 'other' early childhood practices.

She noted that the Labour government's emphasis on child-focused play activities in the then current early years pedagogy had been challenged by Cannella and Viruru (2004) who highlighted the influence of caregiver cultural beliefs on children's learning and questioned the universal relevance of play pedagogies. Brooker (2003) had also pointed out that South-east Asian sub-continent communities in England do not regard children's play as a matter for adults. Western ideals of choice, play and individualism in learning might be at odds with cultural norms and collective needs of family and community, respect, listening and the use of memorizing, as tools of learning within South-east Asian communities in Mala's locality. As a children's centre leader, the possibility that the English early years foundation stage might marginalize some children and families from mainstream early education was to be taken seriously. Mala aimed to explore the values and perceptions associated with outdoor learning held by a range of early years professionals and to under-stand how these perceptions impacted on their practice. Her research addressed the following research questions:

- What are the roots of outdoor learning in the early years in England and Europe?
- What are the national and local policy perspectives on outdoor play in the early years?
- What values and perceptions of outdoor learning in the early years are held by local policy-makers and early years professionals?
- How are these values and perceptions reflected in their practice?

The generation of the research questions concluded Stage 1. There was no reason why these should not be regarded as provisional and amended at a later stage. Leaders, at this point moved to Stage 2.

Stage 2: Planning for change

The research literature

The main task for our leaders in Stage 2 was carrying out the literature review and this presented different challenges to different leaders depending upon the particular research focus. Nevertheless there was a common process that all leaders followed to make use of multiple electronic bibliographic databases within education (Educational Research Information), social and political sciences (Applied Social Sciences Index and Abstracts, Psychinfo, Sociological Abstracts and Web of Science) and evidence-based medicine (for example, Medline).

Evidence was derived from primary sources, mostly journal articles, Internet sources, some secondary book sources, mainly following up relevant references cited in the literature that had not been turned up through electronic searching. The research questions provided a framework and determined the kinds of studies that leaders reviewed and thus helped to make explicit key characteristics that the review was able to answer. The characteristics were then set out in a number of statements that were called inclusion and exclusion criteria. Included were: papers that were written within the past 10 years, in English, reporting an empirical study, and focusing on the birth to 5 age range, although papers referring to children birth to 8 were also consulted. Excluded were papers reporting different age groups, where reference to methods was omitted or insubstantial, short reviews and summaries of existing research, papers not subjected to peer review and papers providing only commentary or opinion. Key words were identified: for instance, for Mala they were 'outdoor play', 'outdoor learning' and 'early years'; for Teresa, key words were 'infant', 'baby', 'massage', 'touch', 'infant emotional health', 'parent–infant attachment', 'parent–child interaction', 'parenting' and 'early parenting'.

Ethical considerations

Traditionally, ethics have been seen as a set of principles to be applied in a universal manner but, as noted from the discussion in earlier sections of this chapter, ethical acts are situated in socio-political and cultural contexts that require sensitivity towards the vulnerable groups involved (for instance, young children and mothers) and the nature of the relevant workplace setting. As noted by Teresa, there was a need to be mindful of locating women within dominant moral values of society that pertain to child-rearing and domesticity. Moreover, this raised risks of power imbalance within the research relationship, where children's centre staff might feel obliged to take part and respond in ways it was perceived to be appropriate by their leader to think, act and feel (or 'sanctioned truth'). Simmons and Usher (2000) have called for a situated ethics to address, on the one hand, the challenges posed by contemporary feminist and post-modern thinking and, on the other hand, to address the growing complexity of the social fields in which research is carried out. This means an approach that is sensitive to the local and the specific that gives voice to disadvantaged groups and takes account of the complex and contradictory nature of social experience. It requires an authenticity and honesty on the part of the researcher but also a serious consideration of whether an emancipatory concern for oppressed groups can sit easily with the generation of sound and impartial research knowledge, considering the power base from which it is generated. Simmons and Usher (2000: 10) helpfully remind the reader:

research, whichever paradigm is adopted, is a rhetorical practice, as much about values as it is about methods and outcomes ... in accepting the inseparability of knowledge and power, the emphasis on reflexivity and positioning of the research, the notion of research is itself transformed, with both researcher and researched as active creators of knowledge and where the aim becomes that of exploring what reality could become, rather than simply explaining it.

Practically, ethical practices have to be considered throughout the research process from the planning, literature searching and designing of instruments, through to carrying out fieldwork and analysing data, to report writing and dissemination. The nature of the roles, responsibilities and relationships established throughout that process, particularly with young children demand close attention (see Aubrey et al., 2000). Reflexivity and critical reflection are required throughout. A commitment to document the distinct subjectivities of participants must be balanced by a recognition of the researcher's self and the role of intersubjectivity.

Time frame

Action researchers employ the same methods and approaches as other researchers that may be quantitative or qualitative or more likely mixed, as was the case with our leaders. While this also means that the same sampling strategies apply, purposive or maximum variation sampling may be preferred to random or representative sampling as it increases the range of data to be included. Triangulation is sought through the combination of different participants and different data-gathering methods allow outcomes to be negotiated and agreed and generalization avoided.

The notion of practicalities was raised in the context of ethical considerations but it was equally essential for the leaders that each research question and associated data-gathering method was plotted against a time frame and some thought given to potential risks to the successful completion of the action research project and/or how these might be minimized. Our leaders asked themselves a number of questions. When does analysis of data start and how long will it take? Is there sufficient flexibility within the design to allow for one phase of analysis to feed into the next stage of data gathering and/or incorporate changes to the plan? Overall, is the project feasible?

Trustworthiness

Lincoln and Guba (1985) make a strong case for a set of trustworthiness measures that are approximately equivalent to reliability, validity and objectivity, and seem particularly appropriate to participative action research. They highlighted *prolonged engagement* in the field to allow sufficient time to build trust and instil confidence. It takes time to understand and validly represent experience and voices, particularly marginalized voices. *Persistent observation* is required in order to identify pervasive characteristics of the culture and locality.

Triangulation of evidence from different sources, as indicated in the previous section, was a feature of our leaders' projects. *Peer debriefing* to provide analysis and feedback from critical peers, in this case, was provided by the group of leaders themselves. *Thick description* specifies the elements needed and range of information required to provide the database. *Auditing* the action research process to demonstrate that standards have been maintained was achieved through the storage and potential availability of accounts of processes and products kept. It includes raw data, data reduction and analysis (Miles and Huberman, 1994), process notes that may be kept in the research diary that the leaders used and pilot instruments that have been designed. Coding of data required constant comparison of occurrences that leads to conceptual labels being attached to what may have seemed at first unrelated events or incidents. These concepts then provided the basic unit of grounded theory and the basic analytical procedures by which concepts were generated by asking questions about data, making comparisons to establish common and discrepant concepts. They were then grouped together under a higher-order concept or category. Hence categories and their properties emerged from data in an inductive process, oriented towards uncovering implicit meanings and information that led towards relationships being established among categories, as well as the clear specification of the conditions and consequences under which this conceptual story occurred (Strauss and Corbin, 1990)

Stage 3: Creating change

Preparing for Stage 3

During this stage of the action research project, data are collected and analysed in order to provide evidence for, and to guide, the change action. It is usual to data collect and analyse up to three times, although for the purpose of this chapter just three of our leaders' data collections are outlined. The first collection of data is called *baseline* data. This allows the existing situation to be described and the first change to be made. Further data are gathered in order to gauge the effects of that change and so on. Throughout this stage, the research journal helped the leaders to document the process, carry out critical reflection on this and record possible changes of attitude and/or understanding. The critical group of peers continued to be invaluable throughout this stage and the journal provided a means of capturing initial thoughts, as well as responses to those from other members of the group. Returning to our three leaders introduced above, we trace some of their experiences of creating change.

Karen's data-gathering

As noted above, Karen's particular area of professional interest and expertise was with vulnerable children and families. She recognized the utmost importance of co-operation and co-ordination between services and the need for effective inter-agency working. The Laming Report (Laming, 2003) that revealed the tragic circumstances leading to the death of Victoria Climbié resulted in a government White Paper, *Every Child Matters: Change for Children* (DfES, 2004b) which made recommendations for changes to childcare policy and practice through the common assessment framework (CAF). This attempted to improve partnership work that was related to children and families 'at risk'. This standardized approach to conducting an assessment of a child's additional needs and how they should be met, operated in conjunction with a local authority *windscreen model* that indicated different levels of service required. Level 1 was universal services, leading into level 2 that might require a CAF to be undertaken. Level 3 was the 'heavy end', defining a child as 'in need' and whose family, without support and intervention, might lead to escalation to level 4, where child protection procedures were put in place.

In order to address her research question concerning the key safeguarding children role of children's centres, Karen's baseline data-gathering focused on a large-scale survey of children's centre practice in her authority. She looked at what staff were in place and their qualifications, what policies and procedures were implemented and how they were reviewed. She investigated what family support was in place, using the CAF windscreen model and whether the levels of intervention being employed differed from those required to be delivered by children's centres (levels 1 and 2). She considered how this might impact upon the children's centre and its ability to deliver core functions related to integrated care and education, support for parents, child and family health, and helping parents into work. She also examined whether staff supervision was in place, who were key workers and how they made decisions regarding the support and services offered and, finally, how these were reviewed and evaluated.

Central themes emerged that related to the level of family support that staff were undertaking, their level of training and supervision. She found that children's centres that had previously functioned as Sure Start local programmes seemed to be developing a wider range of services for children and families, in many cases including levels 3 and 4 family support. These findings provided the basis for creating a change in the local authority practice, in this case, identifying development needs of particular children's centres related to refinement of safeguarding policy and procedures, delivery of the core offer and, in particular, delivery of family support. It is beyond the scope of this chapter to detail these actions and their subsequent evaluation or Karen's reflections upon the process. Suffice it to say it illustrates first-step data collection in the action research cycle, what change is required and indicates that the change itself will require monitoring and critical evaluation, in other words, a further data-gathering step. At this point, Karen was in a position to consider whether a further change or improvement to social practice was required or whether new research questions might direct her to another or related social practice and, hence, a new action research cycle. In fact, her next step was to identify and explore in greater depth two children's centres, one that had been previously a Sure Start local programme and one that had emerged more recently from the voluntary sector. This allowed her to carry out an investigation of their safeguarding policies and practices, this time based on document analysis, interview and observation.

Teresa's data-gathering

Teresa's research questions focused on the relationship between infant massage as an early parenting intervention and the promotion of parental sensitivity, relationship-building and development of secure attachment. Focus groups and interviews with trainers and parents in the baseline data-gathering stage revealed that infant massage was regarded as a means of providing parenting support, to reduce parental anxiety and increase confidence and feelings of confidence. Professionals perceived infant massage to provide a form of help that most parents wanted and a 'way in', especially with parents considered difficult to engage. Parents for their part and contrary to the literature (O'Higgins et al., 2008), gave a higher priority to parenting support from friends, books and magazines. In terms of relationships, trainers emphasized cues around attachment and bonding formed in the context of relaxation and 'special time' that *did* correspond with literature. Parents, however, considered cues in the context of infant communication and learning (McGrath et al., 2007). Overall, infant development was viewed by professionals in the light of parental uncertainty and lack of knowledge, thus drawing on a parent-deficit model. Infant massage was perceived as beneficial for infant physiological development and sleep that corresponded with some tentative evidence (Underdown et al., 2006). Meanwhile, parents viewed infant massage as a method to reduce the development of 'colic' and 'wind', despite lack of evidence to support this function.

Teresa's analysis of her findings led her to raise questions regarding the role of infant massage in the perpetuation of dominant discourses that problematized and medicalized normal infant behaviour and development and conveyed society's norms of mothering to parents at vulnerable and emotional stages in their parenting (Fisher and Owen, 2008). In Teresa's case, this phase of data-gathering and analysis led to personal professional change and informed her understanding of national policy assertions, beliefs, attitudes and practices of parents and practitioners and existing research evidence. It led to a further data-gathering phase that compared parental self-report questionnaires, a practitioner focus group and semi-structured interviews with children's centre leaders.

Further data analysis led her to the conclusion that there was an inadequate evidence base to support national and local decision-making regarding public service delivery of infant-massage programmes. She identified a need for greater critical consideration of the social processes that underpin implementation of parenting programmes to disadvantaged parents, with a clear focus on evidence to guarantee high-quality practice and effectiveness. Teresa's action research for professional change and the development of wise practice in her own children's centre contrasts with Karen's action research for strategic social action. Mala's action research lay between these two branches of action research in being both personal action for professional change, yet focused on local authority innovation, and sponsored and supported by the strategic leaders responsible for this social change.

Mala's data-gathering

Mala's action research was built upon a local authority intervention to develop outdoor environments in early education settings that was taken as an opportunity to explore current understanding of outdoor learning and to challenge 'accepted truths'. Her initial baseline data-gathering focused on examining perceptions related to outdoor learning held by practitioners in one such setting that comprised survey, interview and document analysis. She was aware that due to the small-scale nature of this step in the study, the findings could not be regarded as generalizable. In her case, therefore, the analysis of data provided a useful starting point for exploring her areas of interest, testing out the research approach and tools of data-gathering that stimulated deeper reflection and led to greater professional understanding. The findings highlighted a disparity between strongly held values and beliefs of practitioners and their espoused practice. They also indicated that practitioners' values and beliefs were not based on formal knowledge, research evidence or even national or local policy drivers related to health, physical activity or achievement of boys and/or disadvantaged groups but, rather, they represented a romantic construction of childhood.

This first step in data-gathering, analysis and critical reflection led to a second step that comprised a careful design of and further bout of data-gathering that included interviews with the local strategic leader responsible for the programme, a survey of early years practitioners involved in the outdoor environment development programme as well as document analysis, interview and observations in a number of contrasting settings.

Analysis of these data confirmed that thinking and practice were strongly influenced by historical traditions in early years education and romantic constructions of childhood, embedded within philosophies of European pioneers of such work. It was concluded that this called for a reconception of notions of quality, child-centredness and free-play that underpin thinking, policy and practice in relation to the outdoors. More seriously the results pointed to the potential in these practices to be particularly discriminatory towards, and marginalizing of, ethic minority parent and child groups who do not share these Western models and values of child development. Equally concerning was the dearth of empirical research related to outdoor learning. Recommendations made to the local authority highlighted a number of areas for social change and development, including outdoor pedagogy, contexts and practices likely to increase children's physical activity, and a broader consideration of potentially discriminatory play pedagogies that were unquestioning in their assumptions about play, learning and development.

Stage 4: Communicating lessons learned

Stage 3 attempted to produce a summary of conclusions drawn by the three leaders but leaves stage 4 to describe the formal written project report. In the case of these leaders and their peers, they had the formal requirements of a 20,000-word dissertation to meet, well worthy of communicating through an early childhood conference or within peer-reviewed or professional journal system, and in any case forming the basis of a book chapter here. There are challenges to be met in producing a technical report for sponsors who may have less interest in theorizing and background research evidence than our leaders. Nevertheless, the basic format remains the same for any good report:

- title page and contents table;
- summary;
- introduction that addresses the 'why me, why this study, why now?' questions and formally states the research questions;
- systematic review of existing research evidence and its significance to the project;
- methodology that outlines and justifies the research design, methods used and analysis, the ethical considerations and role of the researcher;
- detailed reporting of each stage of data-gathering, analysis, discussion and interpretation of findings;
- overall conclusions drawn and limitations of the study;
- recommendations;
- references;
- appendices.

Meanwhile, in summaries for 'user' groups or stakeholders of such action research, a number of questions can be used to guide the reporting:

- Why did we do this?
- Are the context, aims, purposes and questions clearly stated?
- Are the methods appropriate?
- Are the conclusions of at least limited application?
- If true, would they be likely to alter the way in which we work?

In summary, sponsors and user groups will appreciate accessibility. It means that action researchers will be advised to consider different ways in which findings can be communicated. Thinking through the practical implications of the research findings is enhanced by working alongside practitioners throughout, and leads to the greatest impact. Providing interim evidence at different stages of research will contribute to ongoing discussion and feedback. Finally, if action research is going to have an emancipatory function, it is important that the way society works and forces at play are exposed, for instance, the way poverty is linked to structural inequalities and impacts on young children's health, well-being and development.

10.5 Conclusions

Our leaders' action research projects provided powerful accounts of the way postmodern theories and analyses can serve to stimulate critical reflection about current early childhood policy and practices and how well action research can assist in shifting critical thinking into activity, change (personal, professional and institutional) that leads to a *further* cycle of critical reflection, action and change. The challenge for them and their peers will be to sustain the critical reflection and innovation that action research stimulated and this chapter documents.

▶ The final reflections on their powerful work are left to them.

Karen's conclusions

McCullough (2007) looked at the Labour government's pledge to combat child poverty with the primary goal identified as the need to make services better integrated in order to promote improved communication. This was a recommendation of Lord Laming's report. McCullough went on to note that the government had issued basic guidelines regarding the way children's services should be developed and integrated but allowed each local authority to work out its own interpretation. Giving autonomy can be seen as positive so that services can develop according to local need. However, as demonstrated in this piece of research, policy can be interpreted in vastly different ways and without a requirement of Social Services to become part of integrated services, there may well always be gaps in communication and therefore gaps in safeguarding. Lord Laming suggested that there remained significant problems in the day-to-day reality of working across organization boundaries and cultures, sharing information to protect children and a lack of feedback when professionals raised concerns about a child. Joint working between social workers, youth workers, schools, early years services, policy and health too often depends on the commitment of individual staff, and sometimes this happens despite, rather than because of, the organizational arrangements. This must be addressed by senior management in every service.

I recognize that, due to the small sample of centres that took part in this piece of research, trends identified and conclusions reached cannot be applied more widely. On the one hand, my literature review reveals very little research has been done with regard to managing safeguarding in children's centres. On the other hand, the culture of blame and ongoing media debates about safeguarding, may contribute to a general reluctance to venture views that may be challenged and to discussing personal and professional positions that can be perceived as 'risky' in terms of future work and job security.

Teresa's conclusions

The literature review highlighted a growing need for evidence-based high-fidelity programmes to promote parent–infant interaction, parental sensitivity and infant attachment. However, the study demonstrated a propensity for judgements, adaptations and lack of standardized practice in infant massage in terms of operational technique and social situation of its delivery, as well as ambiguity regarding any assumed benefit that was reflected in research in the area. The literature also determined that there was no conclusive evidence of a beneficial effect of infant massage on infant attachment though there was some evidence of benefit on reducing infant hormonal responses to stress and in supporting warm and less intrusive parent–infant interactions. There was clear agreement within research that early parent interventions should concentrate on nurturing these relationships (Underdown et al., 2010).

These findings revealed incongruities that raised questions regarding the dominant societal discourses regarding parenting, motherhood and the role of fathers on beliefs, attitudes, understandings of parents, practitioners and decision-makers. Discourses conveyed by parenting practitioners within their everyday practice with parents serve as unquestioned truths, positioning parents in power relations with professionals that inform thinking about what constitutes normative parenting. This perpetuates moral discourses that attribute poor outcomes and child poverty to consequences of parental inadequacy (Gillies, 2005).

Mala's conclusions

This study identified that thinking and practice in relation to the outdoors has been strongly influenced by the historic traditions of early years education. The concepts of child-centredness and learning through play were found to be embedded within these traditions and influential in practitioners' beliefs and practices. Both these concepts have been challenged in recent research literature. Concepts of quality and Western models of child development seen to underpin the Early Years Foundation Stage have also been challenged as marginalizing children from poor and minority ethnic backgrounds. The review of literature on outdoor learning identified a lack of empirical evidence focused on children in the early years to support the strong assertions and unquestioned assumptions made about the benefits to children's learning and development. Recent research does suggest, however, that the landscape and context of out-door spaces may have an impact on the development and behaviours they support and highlights that adults have a key role to play in promoting improved learning and health outcomes for children.

Waller (2006) asks whether regular access to the outdoors alone offers an automatic benefit to children or whether particular environments and types of support enhance children's learning and development. The author contends nevertheless that the study and related literature suggest that it is a place, coupled with effective pedagogy, that might offer the greatest benefit to children's learning, health and development.

CHAPTER ELEVEN

REFLECTIONS

This final chapter revisits the initial objectives for our investigation of leadership. It reflects on what leadership means to the practitioners themselves; the nature of the roles; responsibilities and characteristics; the core components of effective leadership; the experience of leadership practices, how they were judged, understood and enacted; and the types of training required. Emerging models of leadership that distribute leadership across the organization are examined and the implications explored.

11.1 Revisiting our initial objectives

In the closing stages of the book, we return to review the objectives that we set for ourselves and reflect on what we have learned about early childhood leadership, creating a culture of organizational learning and sharing knowledge in collaborative ways.

What leadership meant to key participants

First, we aimed to identify, describe and analyse what leadership meant to key participants in the early childhood settings where we worked with practitioners.

In terms of leadership models and informal theories held, across the sector participants described their organizations as hierarchical in structure, hence traditional and positional in leading the way for strategic decision-making processes, yet collaborative in culture and operational functioning. The strong sense of collegiality expressed by staff and the observed pooling of initiative and by teams was suggestive of the possible utility of a distributive model of leadership that emerges from a group or network of individuals working together (Gronn, 2002; Harris, 2005; Spillane et al., 2001). While there may be various styles of leaderships, such as those identified by Goleman (2000), there are also different leadership concepts held by organizations, for example, hierarchical or distributed. Also involved are roles and relationships, the way that staff relate to their leader and the way leaders relate to one another and to the external world. Where a new concept of leadership emerges this allows staff to reflect on their own behaviour as well as the leader's and enables new organizational dynamics to emerge

Roles, responsibilities and characteristics of early childhood leadership

Second, we considered the nature of roles, responsibilities and characteristics of leadership in early childhood settings and noted that a different balance of leadership, management and administration across settings emerged, indicating the existence of multiple leadership roles in diverse domains of an early childhood setting. At one level it was clear that leadership function was contingent upon the context and circumstances of particular early childhood settings as leaders themselves indicated in the review of the video highlights. Interestingly, the survey revealed the high level of agreement that the most important aspect of the role was to deliver a quality service and this was echoed in interviews with leaders and staff. The scale of the organization, that is, the number of children and parents enrolled, the professionals recruited, the agencies involved, as well as the overall staffing levels, appeared from video observation to influence the degree of specialization, delegation and distribution of leadership activity. Moreover, with the flatter organizational structures of the foundation stage units, for instance, there was less role differentiation among staff than in integrated centres.

Of necessity, the extent of team *concerted action* (Gronn, 2002) in foundation stage units was continuous and intense, within the context of wider lines of decision-making and accountability within the school. Moreover, in foundation stage units leaders had a *direct* effect on the educational outcomes of children in their settings, while leaders in the private and voluntary sector and in integrated settings had only an *indirect* effect on outcomes, whether educational, health or social care related (Robinson, 2006). There was evidence in video highlights of a leader in the voluntary sector who was moving towards children's centre status, directly coaching her early childhood practitioners about child observation, gathering evidence and recording for young children's foundation stage profiles in order to have an impact on practice. Also observed to be 'moving staff on' was a private provider shifting towards children's centre status, who was directly provoking change and development through documentation of curriculum planning.

Size of institution and hence overall levels of resourcing also influenced technical functions and responsibilities, with private and voluntary leaders seen to be carrying out their own administrative and management tasks – all suggesting the pragmatic nature of leadership approaches adopted. Interestingly, at this point, in respect of resourcing levels, it will be remembered that adopting an entrepreneurial approach that was mindful of competition with others in the sector was not ranked highly in the survey, obtained an ambivalent response in interview and yet, in practice, was seen to have a huge impact on the leader's role.

Video highlights showed integrated centre leaders working in large organizations demanding specialized knowledge, functions and activities structurally dispersed within a single site or across multiple sites and creating different boundaries in leadership. As noted above and to be emphasized here again, there is a strong case for adoption of a different form of leadership as a means of distributing multiple services and complex responsibilities, and achieving greater clarity in professional roles. However, there may still be structural and attitudinal constraints on early childhood leadership, both internal and related, for instance, to staffing levels and resourcing, or external and related to governmental or local authority regulations. The form of leadership that emerged was one that recognized and indeed depended upon the specialist knowledge of others, whether related to community development, child and family need, staff or centre administration. This engendered empowerment of others through sharing of knowledge and complex responsibilities by collaborative means to sustain and promote organization learning in a long-term perspective. In integrated centres, for instance, there appeared to be an openness of leaders to widen the boundaries of leadership. While there were reported constraints from a directive 'top-down' local authority hierarchy in which these early childhood centres operated, there was a participative internal culture and team dynamic exerting its own 'bottom-up' influence on practice.

'Leadership at all levels', however, seemed to be operating with horizontal networks among foundation stage teachers, teaching assistants and other professionals; cross-functional team-building in integrated centres, for example, in the field of social care and welfare and strategic alliances with other leaders in the private sector and among integrated centre leaders.

Core components of effective leadership

Third, we investigated core components and characteristics of effective strategic and operational leadership. Here the principal components analysis of the survey contrasted those participants who attributed relatively high importance to one group of variables with those who attributed relatively high importance to another group. This may account for the differential emphasis placed on different elements of leadership that was consistent with interview and video recordings; for example, older respondents attached more importance to being proactive, empowering and visionary and relatively less importance to being authoritative. Those who had more experience in early childhood settings attached less importance to being authoritative and were warm and sympathetic. Those with postgraduate qualifications, for example, those with a teaching qualification and/or a Master's degree, tended to the first pole of principal component 1 (see Table 2.17) favouring warmth, rationality, knowledgeability, assertiveness, goal orientation, coaching, mentoring and guidance (hence, valuing *leaders as guides*). Those with 'other' qualifications, some with different professional heritages, leaned towards the second pole, favouring systematic planning, risk-taking, influence, proactivity, vision and empowerment (favouring *leaders as strategists*). Those with NVQ qualifications, in some cases to be found in the private and voluntary sector, tended towards the first pole of principal component 3, favouring vision, warmth, professional confidence, systematic planning, proactivity and empowerment (*leaders as motivators*), while postgraduates leaned towards the second, valuing influence, authority, economic competitiveness, business awareness and risk-taking (*leaders as business oriented*).

Exploration of leadership practice

Fourth, an exploration of how leadership practice was judged, understood and enacted was achieved largely through video-recording, reduction and review. Leaders acknowledged in their final review meeting a difficulty in standing back from and reflecting upon their own practice and called upon the view of researchers who recognized and fed back to them that an essential aspect of leadership was ongoing, moment-by-moment thinking and decision-making, inaccessible unless leaders themselves 'talked aloud' as they engaged in professional practice. This suggests a need to develop effective early childhood practitioners' own reflective and strategic skills to increase self-understanding, thinking about complex problems and looking for alternative routes to problem-solving. This has been stressed throughout the book.

Types of leadership development programmes

It also leads, fifthly, to an exploration of the types of leadership development programmes or preparation required to maximize the effectiveness of early childhood leaders. What the interview data suggested most strongly is a need to extend the opportunity for early childhood staff in general to have access to leadership programmes and thus to opportunities for leadership development. If distributed leadership is to be understood as an important property within relationships, there may be a need for the development of understanding of conjoint leadership. If teamwork skills are to be regarded as prerequisite, then early childhood staff were already observed to be strong in two-way interactive teamwork. Given the current rate of social and cultural change in the early childhood sector overall, the stimulus for further professional development is strong and the argument for examination of distributed leadership compelling.

This, however, as the previous chapter has shown, is just one strand of an overall programme of continuing interprofessional education and training that is required to enhance learning between the professional groups involved in early childhood settings and extend the collaborative activity being practised.

In the final review meeting, leaders reported that intensification and pressure of work left little time for reflection. Based on the evidence collected by this project, it has been found in practice that exemplar leadership video highlights and professional development materials are serving to stimulate discussion and analysis of leadership in different early childhood organizational contexts and to facilitate organizational analysis. Opportunities for sharing experiences of other leadership situations could provide a foundation for more focused consideration, not just of distributed leadership but a learning organization that draws upon group development theory, team learning, organization theory and organization change theory, to identify just a few promising perspectives. The challenge is now to exploit theory not only as an aid to reflection but also to serve as an agency for change.

11.2 Conclusions

A narrow view of leadership?

Our own initial review of the literature pertaining to leadership in early childhood settings indicated a narrow view of the leadership role, a reluctance to engage with leadership theory, a gender bias in the workforce and a relative absence of leadership development. Theorizing, where it did happen, was limited and did not connect to key concepts in educational, public sector or business leadership. This may be because of sector differences or the complexity of the field, characterized by a great diversity of institutions, state, private and voluntary. International comparative studies, as noted in the introduction are stimulating exchange of theory, practice and development in the field. In the English context, the increasingly multi-professional nature of early childhood settings is generating a need to draw upon a broader theory, knowledge, evidence and practice base.

A need for new models of leadership

Ebbeck and Waniganayake (2003: 28) concluded that definitions of early childhood leadership work lacked clarity, coherence and comprehensiveness due to 'failure to take into account changing circumstances and the consequent evolution of appropriate roles and responsibilities'. They argued for a paradigm shift and a reconceptualization of early childhood leadership within what they described as the 'distributive leadership model'. Findings from this study certainly suggest that while early childhood leadership carried core functions related to leadership, management and administration, these could take many forms. In this respect, the concept of distributed leadership model, presented an interesting theoretical framework that could be applied more widely to the early childhood leadership field (Bennett et al., 2003). Bennett et al. put forward three distinctive elements of distributed leadership that resonate with early childhood practice. First, it is an emergent property of a group or network of interacting individuals that contrasts with leadership as a phenomenon arising from the individual. Second, it widens the boundaries of leadership to consider which individuals and groups might be brought in and contribute to leadership. Third, it acknowledges that capabilities and expertise are distributed across many in the organization and that, if brought together within a trusting and supportive culture, can lead to concertive action (Gronn, 2002).

Taking a distributed perspective on leadership makes social context and the interrelationships therein an integral part of the leadership activity (Spillane et al., 2001: 28). It focuses upon interaction and the exploration of complex social processes that align very closely with the findings from the research study. From the distributed perspective, leadership is best understood as 'practice distributed over leaders, followers and their situation and incorporates the activities of multiple groups of individuals' (Spillane et al., 2001: 28). It implies a social distribution of leadership where the leadership function is 'stretched over the work of a number of individuals and the primary tasks are accomplished through the interaction of multiple leaders' (Spillane et al., 2001: 28). It also implies that interdependency rather than dependency embracing the way in which leaders of various kinds and in various roles share responsibility. Within early childhood settings there is evidence that leadership is being 'stretched' and that the emphasis is primarily upon engendering collaborative ways of working. While early childhood leadership takes different forms and is embedded in different structures, there is also evidence from the study of a core vision, collegial ways of working and a climate of trust and openness. If leadership is distributed among many, it must also be integrated, hence in line with the spirit of integrated centre practice. Moreover, distributed leadership brings together the characteristics of a learning community with leadership – a theme that threads throughout this book.

Limitations to the concept of distributed leadership

At the same time there are limitations to the concept of distributed leadership. Locke (2003), for example, identifies eight key tasks of top leaders (vision, core values, structuring the organization, motivating employees, selection and training, communicating, team-building and promoting change) and queried what role the top leader plays as new leadership models emerge. Other questions about the nature of responsibility that accompanies a devolved model are raised. Along with responsibility goes accountability and the need for increased monitoring and feedback from those to whom leadership is distributed.

As noted by Fullan (2001) in times of crises and uncertainty, more coercive leadership roles may be called for that sit uneasily with the increased uncertainty and ambiguity about roles likely to be generated by devolved practice. Another model of distributed leadership that might emerge from the integrated context is one where leaders negotiate joint responsibility for performance of primary tasks, for example, in the meeting of education, health-related or social care and welfare targets. One wonders whether the social worker in our Chapter 7 multi-agency case study would have left if the integrated centre leader and professional social work leader had taken the development of her role as a collaborative project that had led to real partnership. The example also serves to highlight the potential loss of self-worth and confidence that can be engendered in an individual worker expected to work in new and as yet untested ways and the personal risks attached to renegotiating roles and accountabilities by his or her leader.

Clearly there are constraints in the term of non-negotiable and hierarchical lines of accountability both within and outside the organization. At the same time the rate of external social and cultural change does provide a stimulus for radically rethinking early childhood leadership. The concept of distributed leadership with its emphasis on increased capacity through shared leadership seems particularly pertinent therefore to early childhood settings (Harris, 2004; 2005).

The future

In their recent review of the research evidence about educational leadership, Leithwood and Levin (2004: 45) recommend that future research work needs to 'measure a more comprehensive set of leadership practices than have been included in most research to date'. They suggest that these measures should explicitly be based on 'coherent images of desirable leadership practice' and that such research 'is likely to produce larger estimates of leadership effects than has been provided to date'. This links to Robinson's (2006) call to examine the extent to which existing research and theory provides high-quality information about how to increase the impact of leaders on a range of outcomes. Although this analysis is based on school leadership research, it has a particular relevance to a sector that has lacked case studies of effective leaders or quantitative analyses of characteristics set against effectiveness measures. This situation has been exacerbated by the level of rapid change and uncertainty in the English context that has been accompanied by fundamental changes in a sector traditionally underresourced and with poor training. The particular challenges of integrated centre leadership, with little experience of managing major publicly funded projects and multi-agency teams, engaging with community development or sharing governance with parents and statutory bodies, has been well elaborated.

As more coherent images of practice emerge there will be a requirement for a broader notion of what constitutes effective leadership practice and generation of a more sophisticated set of analytical and conceptual tools to assess its impact. Already national standards for leaders of integrated centres for children and families have been identified that closely align with *Every Child Matters* outcomes and charge leaders with the responsibility to translate the aims of the *Every Child Matters* (ECM) agenda into effective and creative services that improve the lives of children and their families (DfES, 2006e).

Within the early childhood setting, as the study has shown, there is evidence of broad-based distributed leadership practice and therefore much more to be explored about the actual leadership processes within early childhood settings. The growth in co-location of schools with children's centres is creating a new stimulus for reorganizing leadership and management structures that reflect the provision of services and signposting for parents that lead to collaborative advantage (Huxham and Vangen, 2000).

This raises implications not only for leadership preparation but also for the continuing professional development of all those working in early childhood settings. Indeed, the findings from this study suggest a gap in education and training between the most highly qualified leaders in integrated centres and early childhood staff in general who have not had access to opportunities for leadership development. Everything points towards the need for continuing professional and interprofessional education and development as an effective means to create leaders and learning communities that are responsive to the needs of co-workers and professional teams as well as the needs of the communities, families and young children they serve.

▶ Our investigation of early childhood leadership provided an account of current practice in a variety of settings across the sector.

Key findings 11.1

- The role of early childhood leaders has become more challenging due to the raft of new interrelated policies and initiatives associated with the ECM agenda.
- The range and complexity of tasks required of them has increased the need for increased expertise in finance, large-scale building projects as well as human resource management.
- It is likely that models of good multi-agency practice will emerge from this sector, given the experience of collaboration and networking that is being accrued across the early childhood sector.
- The scale and range of children and communities, professionals and agencies and hence, degree of specialization, delegation and distribution of responsibility within settings varies very considerably across the sector.
- Among foundation stage leaders, teaching is still the most dominant activity to place them in a position to have a greater impact on children's learning, care and welfare than those leaders only in indirect contact with children.
- Administrative and organizational activities take a substantial amount of the working day, particularly in the private and voluntary sector, with relatively less time being taken to engage in future-oriented planning tasks.

- Levels of funding constitute a significant challenge and will increase as ring-fenced funds for children's centres are phased out.
- There is a clear need for early childhood leaders to develop and 'bring staff on', that is, distribute leadership through the setting. This depends upon there being an appropriately trained and experienced workforce that leaders find is not always available.
- In general, while leaders still tend to be line-managed in traditionally organized local authority hierarchies, the work they carry out is pulling them in new directions. These demand different models of leadership, taking account of their partnerships with other agencies and operation in leadership teams that create flatter organizational structures and collaborative cultures.
- There is an urgent need to have a better understanding of the relationship between different models of multi-agency working and positive outcomes for children.
- The relationship between factors that facilitate multi-agency working and positive outcomes for children needs to be investigated.
- It is unlikely that one model or a single approach can be appropriate for such a diverse sector.
- There is an urgent need for more early childhood leadership training.

POSTSCRIPT

Our quest for a grounded theory model of early childhood leadership began and ended with a group of experienced early childhood leaders who were working in a field where no such model had hitherto existed. The challenge was to attempt to specify it in terms of the conditions that gave rise to it, the context in which it was embedded, the actions and interactions by which it was handled, managed or carried out, and the consequences of these strategies, in other words, explicating the 'story line' or clear analytical story (Strauss and Corbin, 1990). Our investigation took place in the English context, in conditions of great national change to services for young children. We felt, however, that it served as an exemplar for early childhood leadership in a wider world of intense political, economic, social and technological change and complexity that was globally unsettling, if not destabilizing traditional family configurations, work and school life, and inevitably provision made for early childhood care and education. Moreover, such global trends and influences were increasing uncertainty and challenging traditional forms of leadership by favouring new kinds of decentralized alliances between leaders and followers and encouraging collaboration and teamwork, responsive to fast-changing circumstances and very compatible with our leaders' preferred ways of working.

First, it was essential that the way we conceived, planned, implemented and analysed practice was in full collaboration with a group of experienced early childhood leaders working in a diverse range of early years settings, from children's centres, through private and voluntary provision to foundation stage units in primary schools. Thus we attempted to capture early childhood leadership at a time of profound national and international change through surveying the views of the leaders themselves and those whom they led, through conversations with leaders and their staff, through video and diary records of the 'day in the life' of each leader. It was 'cutting edge' in the sense that it linked early childhood leadership practice to a wider context of leadership theory in changing times and examined the distinctive challenges of multiple types of leadership, providing multiple perspectives on the multiple contexts within which they worked.

By these means we documented the processes of early childhood leadership in a variety of settings and the way it was promoted in the context of different internal and external opportunities and constraints. We examined journeys into leadership from novice, through competent leader to 'master' leader and identified a need for the creation of group and individual mentoring systems in order to generate new professional understandings, learning and development that was being created by the new circumstances they experienced.

What emerged was that there was no single style of leadership that seemed to suit all types of early childhood provision in the foundation stage (for children of 3 to 5 years). To start with, we revealed that although the workforce was predominantly female and leaders were typically aged between 30 and 49 years of age, these practitioners had different qualifications and professional heritages and worked in very different kinds of settings. In terms of their overall roles and responsibilities, providing a quality service was regarded as being of the highest importance, while entrepreneurial skills were thought of as being of less importance. Offering a quality service was associated with continuing professional development but, while the least well-qualified childcare workers appeared to have opportunities for 'on-the-job' training, most training received by early childhood professionals was in the form of short courses and in-service training, little of which focused on leadership. More early childhood leadership training opportunities are required. Progress has been made but there is still some way to go.

Those early childhood professionals with postgraduate qualifications, such as teachers, tended to favour leadership qualities such as warmth, rationality, knowledgeability, assertiveness, goal orientation, offering coaching, mentoring and guiding (*leaders as guides*) and those with qualifications from related professions such as children's library services, social work, health or community development tended to favour systematic planning, risk-taking, influence, proactivity, vision and empowerment (*leaders as strategists*). Those early years practitioners with vocational qualifications (NVQs) tended towards favouring vision, warmth, professional confidence, systematic planning, proactivity and empowerment in leaders (*leaders as motivators*). However, postgraduates also favoured leadership by influence, authority, economic competitiveness, business awareness and risk-taking (*leaders as entrepreneurial and business oriented*).

Those with postgraduate qualifications may thus value the role of coaching, mentoring and guiding or 'moving staff on', while those with vocational qualifications may prefer an empowering and motivating role. This contrasts with those with other types of professional qualifications, who emphasized the leader's strategic role in a fast-changing context. Up until this point our participants had *not* emphasized business and entrepreneurial skills but those with postgraduate qualifications here acknowledged the value of such competence.

Questioned about who made the decisions in their institutions, all practitioners rated all groups (including governors/trustees, senior and middle management, all staff, parents and community and children themselves) as being involved in decision-making at least some of the time, though 'children' was reported as having slightly less input. This suggested shared decision-making.

However, differences emerged again. There was some evidence that professionals from children's centres, integrating care, welfare, health and education were more likely to say that parents made decisions all of the time and were less likely to say that they never made decisions. Given the emphasis in the early integrated centre programmes on children's services being locally-driven and responsive to the needs of families, this finding was not surprising. Those practitioners from day nurseries and 'other' professional settings were more likely to say decisions were never delegated to appropriate individuals. Since these respondents included different professional groups from health, social care and welfare that had different value bases, ethical codes, regulatory bodies, traditional roles and boundaries, this finding was unremarkable. Nevertheless, given the current international emphasis on accessing and understanding children's perspectives on their own lives, a stronger emphasis on children's role in decision-making might have been anticipated.

What was particularly interesting overall, was the evidence that people with different professional heritages, following different routes into the early childhood sector, hold different views about early childhood leadership and different attitudes towards aspects of their role. The mixed response towards organizational decision-making that emerged may reflect value differences, but there was at least some support for the view that commitment to parental participation and involvement, as well as to children's right to participation, varied across the types of settings and that this might reflect the very different aims, purposes and origins of different early childhood services, as well as the differing needs of the client groups they served.

We were beginning to uncover what early childhood leadership meant to this group of leaders and practitioners and to examine the roles, responsibilities and characteristics of leaders. Further in-depth conversations with leaders and their staff were needed to illuminate areas already exposed; so, for example, although availability, affordability and sustainability were acknowledged to be linked, unease was expressed about profit-making in a sector where childcare workers were still very poorly paid.

Further discussion about decision-making indicated that early childhood settings were observed to be hierarchically organized, yet collaborative in culture. This changing culture in organizations reflected wider national and international changes that were presenting new challenges to leadership and leading to the creation of new leadership forms. These changes were associated with changed expectations as well as new requirements in the workplace. As organizational boundaries, both inside and outside the organization became less rigid and clearly defined, conventional organizational structures seemed to be breaking down and roles were becoming less certain. In a very real sense, staff were articulating what they saw as important for leadership in terms of direction and commitment for the management of change. Indeed, in a changed world, in which traditional roles and boundaries are dissolving, it may be a real strength that early childhood leaders are predominantly women who tend to favour collaboration, power sharing, caring and relationships, in a context where leadership, authority from work roles, organization and change are being redefined.

The scale and range of children and communities, professionals and agencies involved and hence the degree of specialization, delegation and distribution of responsibility required within early childhood settings, was seen to vary. When we followed leaders into their workplaces in order to capture a day in their lives, among foundation stage leaders in primary schools, teaching was still the most dominant activity. That placed them in a position of having a greater impact on children's learning, care and welfare than those leaders with only indirect contact with children. Administrative and organizational activities took up a substantial amount of the working day, particularly so in the case of private and voluntary sector leaders who lacked administrative support. This left them with relatively less time for engagement in future-oriented, strategic planning tasks. Where leaders did not have administrative support they were inevitably engaged in a broader range of administrative tasks and more traditional management roles.

At the same time, it is likely that new models of effective multi-agency practice will emerge from the early childhood sector, given the current experience of collaboration and networking that is being accrued across professional groups in the early childhood sector in response to policy and service development at national and local levels. Moreover, the range and complexity of tasks required of leaders has increased the need for greater expertise in finance, large-scale building projects, as well as human resource management in a sector that traditionally has lacked these skills. Levels of funding, however, constituted a significant challenge to leaders and are set to increase as early childhood provision competes with a range of other services for families, children and youth.

There was an observed need for early childhood leaders to develop and 'bring staff on', that is 'distribute' leadership through the setting to meet the challenge of recruiting and training a workforce fit for future early childhood services. Indeed, these services depend upon there being the appropriately trained and experienced workforce that leaders found was not always available. In general, while leaders themselves still tended to be line-managed in traditionally organized local authority hierarchies, the work they carried out was pulling them in new directions. Thus different models of leadership were demanded in order to take account of the partnerships with other agencies and operation within leadership teams that created flatter organizational structures and collaborative cultures.

In conclusion, the role of early childhood leaders has become ever more challenging due to a raft of new interrelated policies associated with collaboration between professionals within the national context and a broader international agenda associated with workforce reform and improvement of quality in care of health, social welfare and education. In this climate, there is an urgent need to have a better understanding of the relationship between different models of multi-agency working and positive outcomes for children. It is unlikely however that any one model or a single leadership approach can be appropriate for such a diverse sector; in other words, flexible leadership is key.

APPENDIX 1 GATHERING INITIAL VIEWS ON EARLY CHILDHOOD LEADERSHIP

In order to identify what early childhood practitioners already think and believe about leadership you may wish to invite them to consider these five key questions:

- What does leadership mean in your setting?
- What factors contribute to the effectiveness of this role?
- What factors hinder the effective fulfilment of this role?
- What are your staff training needs?
- How can we build knowledge, skills and capacity in the field?

What does this tell you about how early childhood leadership is experienced by leaders and staff and what are their ongoing interprofessional development needs (at the individual, team and organizational level)?

APPENDIX 2 SURVEYING LEADERSHIP

You may find the following questions useful in exploring what early childhood leadership means to staff within your setting. It may of course be more helpful to focus on specific questions in order to consider staff's view on ranking and rating particular items.

Early Childhood Leadership Survey

We are conducting research that is exploring early childhood leadership in a range of settings. We are interested in what is meant by leadership from a range of perspectives and on the range of roles and responsibilities that leaders actually have in a particular setting. The questionnaire will take about 20 minutes to complete.

Where appropriate, please tick the box ❑ that best matches your response

SECTION 1: BACKGROUND INFORMATION

Q1. Can you describe the title of your present position?

Owner	❑ 1
Principal	❑ 2
Head of Centre	❑ 3
Programme Manager	❑ 4
Foundation Stage Leader	❑ 5
Nursery Manager	❑ 6
Deputy Nursery Manager	❑ 7
Team Leader (please specify responsibilities)	❑ 8
Other (please state)	❑ 9

Q2. State previous posts held, if any

Q3.   In what type of early childhood setting do you work ?

Integrated centre (Sure Start/Early Excellence Centre)	☐ 1
Day nursery (private)	☐ 2
Day nursery (voluntary)	☐ 3
Day nursery (state)	☐ 4
Foundation unit (attached to primary school)	☐ 5
Foundation unit (attached to infant school)	☐ 6
Other (please state)	☐ 7

_____

Q4.   Are you:

Male? ☐ 1   Female? ☐ 2

Q5.   What is your age?

Less than	20 years	☐ 1
Between	20–29 years	☐ 2
Between	30–39 years	☐ 3
Between	40–49 years	☐ 4
Between	50–59 years	☐ 5
Over	59 years	☐ 6

Q6.   What length of time have you worked in the early childhood field, in general?

0–2 years	☐ 1
3–5 years	☐ 2
6–10 years	☐ 3
11–15 years	☐ 4
16–20 years	☐ 5
Over 20 years	☐ 6

Q7.   How long have you been in your current post?

0–2 years	☐ 1
3–5 years	☐ 2
6–10 years	☐ 3
11–15 years	☐ 4
16–20 years	☐ 5
Over 20 years	☐ 6

Q8. **What was your original qualification?**

Q9. **What age group was your initial training for?**

Birth to 5 years	☐ 1
Birth to 8 years	☐ 2
3 to 7 or 8 years	☐ 3
5 to 7 or 8 years	☐ 4
3 to 11 years	☐ 5
5 to 11 years	☐ 6
7 to 11 years	☐ 7
Secondary	☐ 8
Other (please state)	☐ 9

_____

Q10a. **Since your original qualifications, have you had any (other) training for working in early childhood or not?**

Yes   ☐ 1   No   ☐ 2

Q10b. **If yes, can you say what additional training/qualifications you have received (include short courses, in-service training, degree/certificate/diploma courses) and say what area, for example, courses related specifically to leadership/management.**

	a completed	b working on
a) In-service training	☐ 1	☐ 2
b) Short courses	☐ 1	☐ 2
c) Advanced Certificate	☐ 1	☐ 2
d) Advanced Diploma	☐ 1	☐ 2
e) MA (Master's degree)	☐ 1	☐ 2
f) Further professional qualification such as NNEB, DPP, NVQ2 or 3, City & Guilds (please state)	☐ 1	☐ 2

Area _____

g) Other (please state)	☐ 1	☐ 2

_____

SECTION 2: LEADERSHIP ROLES AND RESPONSIBILITIES

Q11. **Which aspects of the early childhood leader's main roles, responsibilities and functions do you regard as most important?**

Rank the *top five* aspects in order of importance, with 1 as most important

a) To describe and articulate a philosophy, values and vision ☐ 1

b) To deliver a quality service ☐ 2

c) To engage in ongoing professional development and to encourage it in all staff ☐ 3

d) To be accountable to and act as an advocate for children, parents, staff, the profession and the general community ☐ 4

e) To engage in a collaborative and partnership style of leadership ☐ 5

f) To be sensitive and responsive to the need for change and manage change effectively ☐ 6

g) To adopt an entrepreneurial approach that is mindful of competition with others in the sector ☐ 7

h) Other (please state) ☐ 8

_____

Q12. **What indicators of leadership potential would you identify as important in early childhood professionals at the start of their career?**

Rank the *top five* aspects in order of importance, with 1 as most important

a) Dedication ☐ 1

b) Willingness to work with others ☐ 2

c) Attitude of lifelong learning ☐ 3

d) A variety of teaching experiences ☐ 4

e) Constantly questions own practice ☐ 5

f) Guides and mentors during professional experience ☐ 6

g) Critically evaluates and tries new ideas and ways of working ☐ 7

h) Other (please state) ☐ 8

_____

Q13. In your experience, what <u>personal characteristics</u> (if any) do you consider to be integral to being an effective leader in an early childhood setting?

Very important 1; important 2; moderately important 3; low importance 4; very low importance 5

	1	2	3	4	5
Authoritative	☐	☐	☐	☐	☐
Calculated risk-taker	☐	☐	☐	☐	☐
Influential	☐	☐	☐	☐	☐
Proactive	☐	☐	☐	☐	☐
Empowering	☐	☐	☐	☐	☐
Visionary	☐	☐	☐	☐	☐
Professionally confident	☐	☐	☐	☐	☐
Systematic planner	☐	☐	☐	☐	☐
Goal oriented	☐	☐	☐	☐	☐
Assertive	☐	☐	☐	☐	☐
Mentor and guide	☐	☐	☐	☐	☐
Professionally confident	☐	☐	☐	☐	☐
Kind, warm, friendly, nurturing, sympathetic	☐	☐	☐	☐	☐
Knowledgeable	☐	☐	☐	☐	☐
Rational, logical, analytical	☐	☐	☐	☐	☐
Coach	☐	☐	☐	☐	☐
Economically competitive	☐	☐	☐	☐	☐
Business oriented	☐	☐	☐	☐	☐
Other (please state)	☐	☐	☐	☐	☐

Q14. What aspects of the early childhood leadership role would you say contribute most to the sustainability of provision in your institution?

Contribution: very high 1; high 2; moderate 3; low 4; very low 5

a) **Community leadership**
(understanding and responding to local realities) ☐ 1 ☐ 2 ☐ 3 ☐ 4 ☐ 5

b) **Pedagogical leadership**
(bridging research and practice) ☐ 1 ☐ 2 ☐ 3 ☐ 4 ☐ 5

c) **Administrative leadership**
(focusing on administrative and financial management) ☐ 1 ☐ 2 ☐ 3 ☐ 4 ☐ 5

d) **Entrepreneurial leadership**
(vision, forward thinking, planning, taking risks) ☐ 1 ☐ 2 ☐ 3 ☐ 4 ☐ 5

e) **Conceptual leadership**
(vision to change in context of broader social policy shifts) ☐ 1 ☐ 2 ☐ 3 ☐ 4 ☐ 5

f) **Career development leadership**
(enabling practitioners to see progressive and fulfilling career paths) ☐ 1 ☐ 2 ☐ 3 ☐ 4 ☐ 5

g) **Advocacy leadership**
(represents, brings to public attention and seeks to improve) ☐ 1 ☐ 2 ☐ 3 ☐ 4 ☐ 5

h) **Performance-led leadership**
(emphasizes efficiency, performance and technicist practice) ☐ 1 ☐ 2 ☐ 3 ☐ 4 ☐ 5

i) **Other** (please state) ☐ 1 ☐ 2 ☐ 3 ☐ 4 ☐ 5

_____

Q15. How would you say that leadership in the early childhood sector was different from leadership in other phases, for instance, primary or secondary?

Q16. How are early childhood leaders selected in your institution?

SECTION 3: LEADERSHIP IN THE CURRENT CONTEXT

Q17.   Can you say how, if at all, you think the early childhood leadership role has changed over the last five years?

Q18.   Rate the impact of external requirements such as OFSTED inspections, competition, national standards, performance-related appraisal or changing policy on the role of the early childhood leader?

Contribution: very helpful 1; no impact 2; unhelpful 3

		1	2	3
a)	OFSTED inspections	☐ 1	☐ 2	☐ 3
b)	Competition for places with other settings	☐ 1	☐ 2	☐ 3
c)	Performance-related appraisal	☐ 1	☐ 2	☐ 3
d)	Changing policy	☐ 1	☐ 2	☐ 3
e)	Scarcity of suitably-qualified staff	☐ 1	☐ 2	☐ 3
f)	Other (please state)	☐ 1	☐ 2	☐ 3

_____

Q19.   Who makes the decisions in _your_ institution?

All the time 1, some of the time 2, none of the time 3

		1	2	3
a)	Governors/trustees	☐ 1	☐ 2	☐ 3
b)	Senior management	☐ 1	☐ 2	☐ 3
c)	Middle management	☐ 1	☐ 2	☐ 3
d)	Decision distributed to individuals according to task	☐ 1	☐ 2	☐ 3
e)	All staff collectively	☐ 1	☐ 2	☐ 3
f)	Parents and community	☐ 1	☐ 2	☐ 3
g)	Children	☐ 1	☐ 2	☐ 3
h)	Other (please state)	☐ 1	☐ 2	☐ 3

_____

Q20. **What do you see as your current/future leadership development and training needs?**

Q21. **Do you have anything further to add?**

APPENDIX 3A THE EARLY CHILDHOOD LEADER'S UNDERSTANDING OF LEADERSHIP

You may wish to talk in more depth to early childhood leaders in different contexts about their experience and understanding of leadership. For follow-up leads that emerged from the survey.

Date:		Time:	
Name and address of setting:			
Participant:			
Position:			

We are interested in exploring your perspectives, on what you think leadership in your setting (and in general) means to you, your approaches to leadership, and so on. In our discussion with you today, we will be asking questions which cover 9 broad areas relating to:

- **First, (and very quickly) some background information**
- **How you define and what your perceptions of leadership are**
- **Your roles, responsibilities and functions**
- **Internal and external influences**
- **Decision-making**
- **Support**
- **Training and professional development**
- **The culture of the organization, and**
- **Any words of advice or comments you might have.**

This conversation will last 30 minutes to an hour and will depend on the extent of your answers and our ensuing conversation. We would like you to be as honest and as open as you feel comfortable being, and reassure you that we will make every effort to keep these as confidential as possible.

BACKGROUND

1. What is the title of your current post (confirm above)?
2. Describe what your typical day looks like.
3. How long have you been in this post?
4. What was your previous post (very briefly) – role, responsibilities, place of work/setting.

DEFINITION AND PERCEPTIONS OF LEADERSHIP

5. What does leadership mean to you in this setting? Where did you get this idea of leadership from?

6. What would you say is the difference between leadership and management?

7. Do you see leadership in an early childhood setting as being any different from other settings/sectors? If so, what do you believe are the differences? (Probe: How do you know this?)

8. What characteristics do you think a good role model in terms of an EY leader should have?

   • Essential professional

   • Personal characteristics

ROLES, RESPONSIBILITIES AND FUNCTIONS

9. What aspects of your roles, responsibilities and functions as an EY leader do you regard as most important? (Check this covers all three dimensions of leadership: pedagogical, organizational and distributive.)

   Prompts:
   • Understanding the local community?

   • How important is raising children's achievement?

   • What does performance-led management mean in your setting?

   • Do you think that business/entrepreneurial skills are important? Why?

INSIDE/OUTSIDE INFLUENCES

10. What helps to facilitate your leadership role?
    • **Internal** (e.g. operational management, annual training plan, line management, part of teacher team, supervision, are they encouraged to network beyond organization?).

    • **External** (e.g. Early Years Development and Childcare Partnership [EYDCP], clinical supervision, how does the owner support if managed by someone else, regional management?).

    • How have these helped?

11. What are the barriers to fulfilling your role as a leader?
    - **Internal** (e.g. time, staff shortages, plus coverage – in more depth – to thinking about: own skill set, level of confidence).

    - **External** (e.g. organizational culture – does it encourage leadership?).

    - How have these hindered?

12. How did you overcome possible obstacles/challenges without forms of support?

DECISION-MAKING

13. How are decisions made in the organization? (processes)

14. To what extent are decisions communicated?

15. What is your role and what is the extent of your involvement in decision-making at various levels in the organization?

SUPPORT

16. What support would have helped when you first started as a leader?
    - Did you have a role model/mentor?

    - Did you have a choice in deciding who this should be?

TRAINING/PROFESSIONAL DEVELOPMENT

17. What forms of professional development in terms of leadership have you had/experienced, if any?
    - Which, if any, would you say have been most useful?

    - Which, if any, would you say have been less useful?

18. How are decisions made about the priorities for professional development?
    - First, by yourself. Could you please give a couple of examples.

    - Second, by others in the setting. Again a couple of examples.

19. As a leader, what you do think your responsibility for your own leadership is? (personal drive, response to learn more)

CULTURE OF ORGANIZATION

20. How would you describe the culture of this organization (i.e. is it collegial [not hierarchical]/collaborative? Does this relate to decision-making? Do you work as a team, i.e. are all staff members equally valued and respected, are all voices heard, do you share a common vision for development?).

21. How would you describe your setting's/unit's/institution's relationship with other organizations such as the local authority, other schools, other similar EY organizations, interested parties and individuals and your role within this (networking, general indication of outward lookingness, formal and informal)?

CLOSURE

22. What advice would you give to other EY leaders?

23. Any other comments?

APPENDIX 3B THE EARLY CHILDHOOD PRACTITIONER'S UNDERSTANDING OF LEADERSHIP

You may wish to explore more about what other staff in the setting think about early childhood leadership.

Date:		Time:	
Name and address of setting:			
Participant:			
Position:			

The focus of this group conversation is on understanding leadership in a range of early years settings. We are interested in exploring perspectives of a range of staff in the early years – on what you think leadership in early years means, how you perceive the approaches of leaders in this phase.

The questions we will be focusing on are around:

- **your previous knowledge and experience of leadership (if any)**
- **how you perceive leadership, i.e. what you understand by it**
- **possible inside/outside influences**
- **your own personal and professional assessment of the roles, responsibilities and functions of EY leaders**
- **your thoughts on decision-making, and**
- **the culture of the organization.**

A focus group, unlike an interview, is an informal discussion, and will be directed by questions around the areas just mentioned. The purpose of having more than one participant in the group is to invite stimulating discussion and debate and constructive dialogue. Feel free to support each other as well as disagree, but do answer as honestly and as openly as you feel comfortable doing.

BRIEF BACKGROUND/INTRODUCTIONS

In a sentence or two, as a way of introduction, could you please tell us a little bit about yourself?

- Name, who you are, i.e. what your current post/post title is and your role in this setting (fill table above)?

- How long have you been in this post?
- Where did you work previously and for how long, and what was your role there?

PREVIOUS KNOWLEDGE AND EXPERIENCE OF LEADERSHIP

1. What forms of leadership professional development have you had/experienced?

   - Which would you say have been wonderful/beneficial? OR which, if any, would you say have been most useful?

   - Which would you say have been bad/unhelpful? OR which, if any, would you say have been less useful?

DEFINITION AND PERCEPTIONS OF LEADERSHIP

2. What does leadership mean to you? Where did you get this idea of leadership from?

3. What would you say is the difference between leadership and management?

4. Do you see leadership in an early childhood setting as being any different from other settings/sectors?

   - If so, what do you believe are the differences?

   - How do you know this?

5. Has your perception of leadership in Early Years changed at all since you first started working at this setting? Elaborate.

   - If so, what have been some of the influences?

INSIDE/OUTSIDE INFLUENCES (support and barriers)

Think about a leader (not necessarily your own) in an early years setting the same as or similar to yours ...

6. What do you think helps to facilitate/support a leader's role within a setting like yours?

   - From the inside? Briefly elaborate.

   - From the outside? Briefly elaborate.

7. What do you think hinders your leader's role in a setting like yours? What may some of the barriers/challenges be?

  - From the inside? Briefly elaborate.

  - From the outside? Briefly elaborate.

  - In your opinion, how do you think these barriers could be overcome or addressed?

8. Do you see staff in an EY team, like yourself, having any influence on the role of the leader? Explain.

9. Do you see staff in an EY team, like yourself, taking any responsibility for the leadership in this setting?

ROLES, RESPONSIBILITIES AND FUNCTIONS

Again, think about a leader (not necessarily your own) in an early years setting the same as or similar to yours ...

10. What aspects of an EY leader's approach to leadership do you regard as most important? Elaborate.

  Other aspects (very briefly, how important and why for each one) Prompts:

  - understanding the local community?

  - raising children's achievement?

  - business/entrepreneurial skills?

  - emphasis on performance among children?

  - emphasis on staff performance?

11. What aspects of leadership do you regard as negative, i.e. those that perhaps hinder work within an early years setting?

DECISION-MAKING

12. How are decisions made in the organization? (processes)

  - How are decisions about future development in your institution made?

13. To what extent are decisions communicated?

14. How are decisions made about the priorities for your own professional development?

- First, by yourself. Could you please give a couple of examples.

- Second, by others in the setting. Again a couple of examples.

15. What is the role of your leader and the extent of his/her involvement in decision-making at various levels in the organization?

16. What is *your* role and the extent of your involvement in decision-making at various levels in the organization?

CULTURE OF ORGANIZATION

17. How would you describe the culture of this organization (i.e. is it collegial/not hierarchical/collaborative?) – do you work as a team, are all staff members equally valued and respected, are all voices heard, do you share a common vision for development?

18. How would you describe your setting's/unit's/institution's relationship with other organizations such as the local authority, other schools, other similar EY organizations, interested parties and individuals and *your role* within this (networking, general indication of outward looking, formal and informal)?

CLOSURE

19. Is there anything you might like to add to enable us to better understand leaders and leadership in EY?

APPENDIX 4 THE LEADER'S DIARY FOR 'A DAY-IN-THE LIFE ... '

Ask an early childhood leader to keep a diary for a day and then to reflect on 'critical moments' or incidents. Critical incidents (Flanagan, 1954) relate to incidents that have special significance and involve behaviour that was especially helpful in accomplishing an assigned mission, in this case, leadership. Collecting critical incidents is a way of helping to identify requirements for successful leadership.

Instructions: we ask you to keep a running record of the day against a time line and, later, to consider particular critical moments, incidents or activities that strike you. If, on reflection, you are aware of using particular leadership knowledge or skills at particular points, we should be very grateful if you can identify these, too.

What happened? (date, day, time, location, ongoing activities and those involved)	Leadership knowledge and skills that you are aware of using (*Think about experience and professional training*)	Any other comments?

Re-examine the critical incidents in the light of leadership strengths and weaknesses, as well as opportunities and threats in the context.

APPENDIX 5 AN AUDIT OF THE EFFECTS OF MARKET FORCES IN THE CHILDCARE MARKET (SUMSION, 2006: 115–16)

Market operation and effects

- What do corporate childcare providers offer that cannot be provided by the not-for-profit sector and small for-profit owner-operators? What are they unable to offer? Does this matter?
- How do corporate services benefit from economies of scale? What are the limitations of economies of scale and how can these limitations be minimized?
- What are the effects of an emphasis on efficiency and the promotion of a highly-visible brand?

Goals and obligations

- Are there 'new clusters of goals, obligations and dispositions' (Cribb and Ball, 2005: 125) associated with corporatized childcare? If so, are they compatible with or in opposition to the goals, obligations and dispositions traditionally associated with not-for-profit childcare?
- What tensions do corporate providers experience between goals and obligations? How do these tensions play out and how are they reconciled?
- Do corporate services contribute to the development of the social fabric of the communities they serve? If so, how are their contributions similar to/different from those of not-for-profit services?

Quality

- What conceptions of quality underpin corporate childcare provision?
- What convincing evidence is there that corporate services offer high-quality care?
- What 'new inflections' (Singh et al., 2005: 4) of quality provision might corporatized childcare make possible?
- Can potentially negative effects of corporatization be addressed adequately through the childcare accreditation process?

Staffing practices and professionalism

- How do staffing profiles and practices of corporate childcare providers differ from those of other providers? What is the impact on employees, children and families?
- What constructs of professionalism are enabled, constrained and silenced by corporatization?

Ethical behaviour

- Are there 'contrasting cultural and ethical dispositions' (Osgood, 2004: 9) between corporate and not-for-profit providers?
- How well do corporate childcare providers do 'if judged against (i) the full set of norms/values they espouse, or (ii) sets of norms/values very widely held by those around them?' (Cribb and Ball, 2005: 124).
- What, if any, practices do corporate providers aim to conceal or refrain from publicizing 'because they know them to be incompatible with the standards they would subscribe to in public?' (Cribb and Ball, 2005: 124).

APPENDIX 6 JOURNEYS INTO LEADERSHIP

Mary Catherine Bateson (1990) noticed a continuous thread and links between different situations and events in life. She also recognized interruptions that forced a change in direction. She asked the question: How does one survive this kind of interruption? One way to respond was to call into play existing skills and adaptive patterns that could be transferred to the new situation, that is, to stress continuity. Another way to respond was to feel that life had ended and that there was a need to start from zero, or stress discontinuity. The choice people made about how to interpret continuities and discontinuities in their lives she found had implications for the way they approached the future.

She identified three meanings for 'composing a life'. First, an artist would take a set of disparate elements to make a visual composition of form and colour in order to create balance. Second, a musical composer would create something through various transitions over time. The first approach characterizes simultaneous and multiple demands from multiple directions that at any one time are handled and incorporated, and the second characterizes the changes, discontinuities and transitions that take place over a lifetime. The third meaning refers to the stories that people make about their lives for themselves and for others in order to interpret experience as it occurs. She advocated playing with and composing multiple versions of a life. It is easy to edit out the discontinuities, to reshape our histories without the zigzags. Adjusting to change, however, has much to do with discovering threads of continuity. It is difficult to adjust to change and transfer learning unless you can recognize some analogy between your old situation and your new one. Those who stay the course, she concluded, are those who are able to ride the changes and to adapt.

Answer the following questions as honestly as you can and consider the implications of your answers for the continuing education and development of early childhood leaders.

Paula Jorde Bloom (1997: 32) described early childhood directors' careers and professional development in terms of 'navigating the rapids'. She described the beginnings of leadership in terms of survival.

i) **Beginning leaders**

What age were you when you first achieved a leadership position?
How did you react to and feel about your first leadership position?
How did you deal with the amount of paperwork, the multiple demands that you faced from staff, parents and children, the multiple interactions, activities and interruptions?
Did you feel in control or out of control, calm or anxious?
How adequate did you feel?

Did you feel that staff liked and appreciated you?

Did anyone say that you were doing a good job?

What did you think about the quality of the service that your organization was providing?

Where did you get support, guidance or specialized training?

Do the answers to these questions tell you anything about professional development needs of beginning leaders?

Bloom suggested that somewhere between one and four years early childhood leaders gained competence.

ii) **Competence leaders**

How long was it before you felt you shifted from muddling to juggling in order to build a repertoire of competence?

How would you say that you achieved a better balance between your professional and private lives, between people and paperwork, individuals and the whole organization?

Are you now confident that you know what you have to do, how to do it and how to manage the demands of the job?

Can you prioritize and attend to big issues?

Are you flexible and tolerant?

Are you comfortable about not always being noticed, liked, and not always being right?

Is your vision-building realistic or idealistic?

Overall, do you feel confident that you are able to meet internal and external expectations?

How could leaders be helped to develop competence?

According to Bloom, some early childhood leaders reach a higher level of reflection and competence to become 'master' leaders.

iii) **Master leaders**

Is the focus of your leadership on organizational change and improvement and your own long-term goals?

Are you confident that you can handle any change?

Are you a role model, mentor and advocate for the field of early childhood?

Can you stand back and think how well you are doing, while you are doing it?

Do you have a deep level of self-understanding and awareness of your own strengths and weaknesses?

Are you confident in your style/s of leadership?

Can you achieve emotional neutrality and objectivity in conflict situations?

Do you feel that you can still find new ways to solve old problems?

How well do you delegate?

Are you satisfied with outcomes achieved by your organization for children, parents and community?

Do you feel a responsibility to change the public perception of the (low) status of work with early years children and families?

Do you embrace your role in creating contexts that encourage and support less experienced staff?

Do individuals, teams and the whole organization have distinct development and improvement needs? How can these needs be balanced?

When you have answered these questions you may be interested to consider the extent to which you think that Bloom's stages of early childhood leadership are compatible with the 'conscious competence' learning model. Here the learner or trainee always begins at stage 1 or 'unconscious incompetence' and ends at stage 4 or 'unconscious competence', having passed through stage 2 or 'conscious incompetence' and stage 3 or 'conscious competence'. It is often assumed that trainees will be at stage 2 and training is focused towards achieving stage 3, when often trainees are actually still at stage 1. This suggests the need for an ability to recognize and develop consciousness of competence in others. (The origins of the conscious competence model are not altogether clear and have been attributed to various authors, including Gregory Bateson (1973), father of Mary Catherine Bateson.)

APPENDIX 7 GUIDELINES FOR SETTING UP A MENTORING SCHEME

In setting up a mentoring scheme, guidelines may be helpful to ensure:

- voluntary participation (mentors and mentees must want to take part in this process);
- clear purpose (mentors and mentees must understand their respective roles and responsibilities);
- mentor training must be provided in order for mentors to develop effective skills in the context of an effective mentoring relationship;
- choice of mentor (mentees should be allowed within reason to state their preference from an identified group of mentors);
- practical matters, such as availability of the mentor are important, as the expectation is that there will be regular mentoring meetings (this means that any one mentor should not take on too many mentees);
- ground rules will need to be established that ensure confidentiality, that specify the purpose of mentoring, that enable either party to withdraw from the relationship without being required to offer a detailed explanation, that build-in a review process that considers learning that has taken place or progress that has been made and may involve refocusing or considering future direction;
- overall monitoring of the effectiveness of the mentoring process; and
- continual quality improvement.

A simple and inexpensive alternative to a formal mentoring scheme is peer mentoring, where two people meet regularly and agree to share time mentoring and being mentored. This will involve sharing the planning, monitoring and reviewing of any action plans put in place. What are the key tasks of the mentor during this process?

Stage 1: confirming the action plan

- The responsibility for the action plan lies with the mentee (a mentor may provide guidance, access to information and serve as a 'sounding board' but is not responsible for the mentee's performance).
- The mentor's role is to identify and anticipate the mentee's likely needs in reaching their chosen goal.
- The mentor will use open questioning in order to encourage self-awareness and honest self-evaluation.
- The mentor can check goals meet SMART criteria (that they are specific, measurable, achieveable, relevant and timescaled).

Stage 2: encouraging self-management

- The mentor may need to ask probing questions that stimulate the mentee to organize administrative aspects of implementing the action plan.
- The mentee can also indicate the range of available support options.
- The mentor should remain objective and impartial but not tell the mentee how to proceed.

Stage 3: support during the implementation phase

- The mentor needs to agree an appropriate schedule of meetings.
- The mentor will need to achieve a balance of support and information with suggestions, when requested.
- The mentor should be willing to consider alternative strategies and offer help in evaluating appropriate ways forward.
- The mentee should be allowed to make errors and experience setbacks that may constitute valuable learning experiences.
- The goal of the mentor is to increase self-confidence in the mentee, a positive attitude and the motivation to complete the action plan.

Stage 4: evaluating the success of the action plan

- Formal evaluations at the end of the process should be encouraged.
- The mentor has a role to play in assisting in evaluating the performance.
- The mentor can stimulate the process of reflection on facilitators and barriers to progress and learning as well as benefits to the mentee and the organization.
- The mentor will be responsible for celebrating success, benefits gained and in agreeing to maintain contact for the future when the relationship comes to an end.

And as a final check, do you:

- really understand the role?
- really want to do it?
- really feel able to draw on your own and other resources to support the mentee?
- really have time?
- really feel confident enough to help create a realistic action plan?
- really feel comfortable acting as 'sounding board' but letting the mentee figure out the solutions?
- really think you can give constructive feedback, build confidence and capacity in the mentee?
- really know when to end the relationship after reviewing achievements and finish on an upbeat note?

APPENDIX 8 VALUES UNDERPINNING MULTI-AGENCY WORKING

How do we achieve a common value base given that different values may be held by different professional groups and that these will influence their attitudes and behaviour in the course of collaborative work? Consider the multiple sources of conflicting attitudes.

- What are informal knowledge and beliefs of professionals, client groups and the public that underpin the existing professional practice of the different agencies working together?
- What traditions, customs and mores are practitioners from different agencies socialized into, in the course of their professional training?
- How (if at all) do you think that these contribute to professionals' own sense of professional identity and self-worth?
- How have these values been reinforced and rewarded by the profession concerned and internalized by new entrants to the profession (through professional standards, peer pressure or public expectations)?
- Do differences in the academic disciplines and traditions within which different professionals have trained influence their attitudes (or ours towards them) and their work?
- Do professions grounded in the natural sciences (such as medicine or health-related fields) enjoy a higher prestige than professions or agencies located within the social science field (such as social work or community development)?
- To what extent do perceived differences in status, salary levels, conditions of work and career progression contribute to the attitudes of professionals (and our attitudes towards them)?
- Does a predominance of women in the profession (such as early childhood) or men have any bearing on public attitudes towards the role?
- To what extent do differences in initial professional education and training contribute to perceived status and prestige in the workplace?
- Does the relative power and autonomy of the professional association concerned make a difference?
- Are there differences in values, customs and culture between types of organization (offering education, health, social care and welfare or all of these)?
- Are differences in ethical codes of practice a source of difference in attitude (or perceived attitude)?
- To what extent does conduct related to information-sharing and confidentiality create professional differences (real or perceived)?
- Does respect for a client's privacy and dignity play a role?
- How far do these differences contribute to professional stereotypes and prejudices that may be held?
- Do we now need a new set of multi-agency or interprofessional values that may contribute to the effectiveness of such work?

- Finally, in this context how can different professions and agencies learn to substitute value differences for value plurality that is underpinned by collaboration, inclusion and equality?

APPENDIX 9 BUILDING EFFECTIVE LEARNING COMMUNITIES

Just as the mentor–mentee working together will prepare, take action and review, Taylor (1979) of the Coverdale Organization argues for a similar approach for teams and organizations. The strength of the approach lies in the structure it provides for carrying out a group task, measuring of success and reviewing learning.

Preparation will include aims and planning

Aims

- What is the purpose of the task?
- What is the desired end product?
- How will we recognize success?

Planning

- Gathering information.
- Deciding what has to be done.
- Making detailed plans.

Action

- Carrying out the plans.
- Modifying as necessary.

Review

- What did we achieve (did we achieve what we set out to do and how could it be improved)?
- How did we achieve it (what went well that we can use next time and what were the difficulties and how can we avoid them next time)?

APPENDIX 10 QUESTIONS TO ASK WHEN PREPARING FOR THE ACTION RESEARCH CYCLE

Phase 1: observation and analysis of existing practice

1. What is your research focus?
2. What are your research questions?

Phase 2: planning for change

1. What is the existing literature in the field?
2. What are the ethical considerations?
3. What is the time frame?
4. How will trustworthiness be ensured?

Phase 3: creating change

1. What baseline data will be collected and how will it be analysed?
2. What change will be implemented to improve professional or social practice?
3. How will it be monitored and judged for effectiveness?
4. What further data will be collected and how will this be analysed?
5. What further change will be implemented to improve practice ... and so on?

Phase 4: communicating the findings

1. What formal research report will be written?
2. What form of report will sponsors (or potential users) want?
3. How will accessibility be ensured?

REFERENCES

Alban-Metcalfe, J. and Alimo-Metcalfe, B. (2000) 'The convergent and discriminant validity of the Transformational Leadership Questionnaire', *International Journal of Selection and Assessment*, 8: 158–75.

Argyris, C. and Schön, D. (1974) *Theory in Practice: Increasing Professional Effectiveness*. San Francisco, CA: Jossey-Bass.

Argyris, C. and Schön, D. (1978) *Organizational Learning: A Theory of Action Perspective*. Reading, MA: Addison Wesley.

Argyris, C. and Schön, D. (1996) *Organizational Learning II: Theory, Method and Practice*. Reading, MA: Addison Wesley.

Atkinson, M., Doherty, P. and Kinder, K. (2005) 'Multi-agency working: models, challenges and key factors for success', *Journal of Early Childhood Research*, 3(1): 7–17.

Atkinson, M., Wilkin, A., Scott, A. and Kinder K. (2002a) *Multi-Agency Working: An Audit of Activity*. Slough: NFER.

Atkinson, M., Wilkin, A., Scott, A., Doherty, P. and Kinder, K. (2002b) *Multi-Agency Working: A Detailed Study*. Slough: NFER.

Aubrey, C., Dahl, S. and Clarke, L. (2005) *Multi-Agency Working in Sure Start Projects: Successes and Challenges*. Warwick: University of Warwick.

Aubrey, C., David, T., Godfrey, R. and Thompson, L. (2000) *Early Childhood Educational Research. Issues in Methodology and Ethics*. London: RoutledgeFalmer.

Aubrey, C., Godfrey, R., Harris, A. and Dahl, S. (2006) 'How do they manage? An Investigation of Early Childhood Leadership', symposium at British Educational Research Association Conference, University of Warwick, 9 September.

Ball, S.J. (2007) *Education plc: Understanding Private Sector Participation in Public Sector Education*. London: Routledge.

Ball, S.J. (ed.) (2004) *The RoutledgeFalmer Reader in Sociology of Education*. London: RoutledgeFalmer.

Barr, H., Koppel, I., Reeves, S., Hammick, M. and Freeth, D. (2005) *Effective Interpersonal Education: Argument, Assumption and Evidence.* Oxford: Blackwell.

Bateson, G. (1973) *Steps to an Ecology of Mind: Collected Essays in Anthropology, Psychiatry, Evolution and Epistemology.* Boulder, CO: Paladin Books.

Bateson, M.C. (1989) *Composing a Life.* New York: Plume Books.

Bell, L., Bolam, R. and Cubillo, L. (2003) *A Systemic Review of the Impact of School Headteachers and Principals on Student Outcomes.* London: EPPI-Centre, Social Science Research Unit, Institute of Education, University of London.

Bennett, J. (2003) 'Starting strong: the persistent division between care and education', *Journal of Early Childhood Research,* 1(1): 21–48.

Bennett, J. and Taylor, M. (2006) *Starting Strong II: Early Childhood Education and Care.* Paris: Organisation for Economic Co-operation and Development.

Bennett, N., Wise, C. and Woods, P. (2003) *Distributed Leadership. A Review of the Literature.* Nottingham: National College of School Leadership.

Bennis, W. (1999) 'The end of leadership: exemplary leadership is impossible without full inclusion, initiatives and co-operation of followers', *Organisational Dynamics,* 28(1): 71–9.

Berger, P. and Luckman, T. (1966) *The Social Construction of Reality: A Treatise in the Sociology of Knowledge.* London: Allen Lane.

Blackmore, J. (1989) 'Educational leadership: a feminist critique and reconstruction', in J. Smyth (ed.), *Critical Perspectives on Educational Leadership.* London: Falmer Press.

Bloom, P.J. (1997) 'Navigating the rapids: directors reflect on their career and professional development', *Young Children,* 52(7): 32–8.

Bloom, P.J. (2000) 'How do we define director competence?', *Child Care Information Exchange,* 138: 13–18.

Bloom, P.J. and Sheerer, M. (1992) 'The effect of leadership training on child care program quality', *Early Childhood Research Quarterly,* 7: 579–94.

Bloom, P.J., Sheerer, M. and Britz, J. (1991) *Blueprint for Action.* Mt Rainier, MD: Gryphon House.

Bricker, D. (2000) *Interdisciplinary Early Intervention/Early Childhood Special Education Leadership Program: Final Report.* Eugene, OR: Oregon University, Eugene College of Education.

Bronfenbrenner, U. (1979) *The Ecology of Cognitive Development.* Cambridge, MA: Harvard University Press.

Brooker, L. (2003) 'Learning how to learn: parental ethnotheories and young children's preparation for school', *International Journal of Early Years Education,* 11(2): 117–28.

Calhoun, J. (ed.) (1993) *Habermas and the Public Sphere.* Cambridge, MA.: The MIT Press.

Cameron, A., Lart, R., Harrison, L., MacDonald, G. and Smith, R. (2000) *Factors Promoting and Obstacles Hindering Joint Working: A Systematic Review.* Bristol: School for Policy Studies, University of Bristol.

Cannella, G.S. and Viruru, R. (2004) *Childhood and Postcolonization.* London: RoutledgeFalmer.

Carter, M. (2000) 'What do teachers need from their directors?', *Child Care Information Exchange,* 136: 98–101.

Caruso, J. (1991) 'Supervisors in early childhood programs: an emerging profile', *Young Children,* 46(4): 20–6.

Caruso, J.J. and Fawcett, T.M. (1986) *Supervision in Early Childhood Education: A Developmental Perspective.* New York: Teachers College Press.

Cherniss, C. (1995) *Beyond Burnout.* New York: Routledge.

Cohen, B., Moss, P., Petrie, P. and Wallace, J. (2005) *A New Deal for Children? Re-forming Education and Care in England, Scotland and Sweden.* London: Policy Press.

Coleman, M. (2001) *Women as Headteachers: Striking the Balance.* London: Trentham Books.

Council of Europe (1996) *European Convention on the Exercise of Children's Rights.* Strasbourg: Council of Europe.

Cribb, A. and Ball, S. (2005) 'Towards an ethical audit of the privatization of education', *British Journal of Educational Studies,* 53, pp. 115–28.

Croll, P. (ed.) (1993) *Teachers, Pupils and Primary Schooling.* London: Cassell.

Court, M. (1994) *Women Transforming Leadership.* Palmerston North, NZ: ERDC Press.

Culkin, M. (1997) 'Administrative leadership', in S. Kagan and B. Bowman (eds), *Leadership in Early Care and Education.* Washington, DC: National Association for the Education of Young Children.

Dahl, S. and Aubrey, C. (2005) *Multi-Agency Working in Sure Start Projects: Successes and Challenges.* Coventry: University of Warwick.

Dahlberg, G. and Moss, P. (2005) *Ethics and Politics in Early Childhood Education.* London: RoutledgeFalmer.

Department for Children, Schools and Families (DCSF) (2007a) *Children's Workforce Strategy March Update.* London: DCSF.

Department for Children, Schools and Families (DCSF) (2007b) *The Children's Plan: Building Brighter Futures.* London: DCSF.

Department for Children, Schools and Families (DCSF) (2007c) *National Standards for Leaders of Sure Start Children's Centres.* London: DCSF.

Department for Children, Schools and Families (DCSF) (2008a) *Building Brighter Futures: Next Steps for the Children's Workforce.* London: DCSF.

Department for Children, Schools and Families (DCSF) (2008b) *Childcare and Early Years Providers Survey 2007. DCSF-RR047.* London: DCSF.

Department for Children, Schools and Families (DCSF) (2008c) *Every Child a Talker. Guidance for Early Language.* London: DCSF.

Department for Education and Employment (DfEE) (1998) *Meeting the Childcare Challenge.* London: Her Majesty's Stationery Office.

Department for Education and Skills (DfES) (2001) *Special Educational Needs Code of Practice.* London, DfES.

Department for Education and Skills (DfES) (2002) *Special Educational Needs: Removing Barriers to Achievement.* London: DfES.

Department for Education and Skills (DfES) (2003a) Every *Child Matters.* Green Paper. London: The Stationery Office.

Department for Education and Skills (DfES) (2003b) *Birth to Three Matters – a Framework to Support Children in their Earliest Years.* London: DfES.

Department for Education and Skills (DfES) (2003c) *National Standards for Under-Eights Day Care and Childminding.* London, DfES.

Department for Education and Skills (DfES) (2004a) *Children Act.* London: DfES.

Department for Education and Skills (DfES) (2004b) *Every Child Matters: Change for Children.* London: DfES.

Department of Education and Skills (DfES) (2004c) *Every Child Matters: Next Steps.* London: DfES.

Department for Education and Skills (DfES) (2005) *Common Core of Skills and Knowledge for the Children's Workforce.* London: DfES.

Department for Education and Skills (DfES) (2006) *Childcare Act.* London: DfES.

Department for Education and Skills (DfES) (2007) *Early Years Foundation Stage.* Nottingham: DfES.

Department for Education and Skills (DfES) (2006c) *Children's Workforce Strategy: A Strategy to Build a World-Class Workforce for Children and Young People.* Consultation Paper. London: DfES.

Department for Education and Skills (DfES) (2006d) *Children's Workforce: Building an Integrated Qualifications Framework.* London: DfES.

Department for Education and Skills (DfES) (2006e) *Children and Adoption Act.* London: DfES.

Department of Health (DoH) (1989) *Children Act.* London: HMSO.

Department of Health (DoH) (2004) *National Service Framework for Children, Young People and Maternity Services.* London: DoH.

Department of Health (DoH) (2007) *Delivering Health Services through Sure Start Children's Centres.* London: DoH.

Department of Health (DoH) (2008) *The Child Health Promotion Programme.* London: DoH.

Derrida, J. (1976) *Of Grammatology.* Baltimore, MD: Johns Hopkins University Press.

Derrida, J. (1978) *Writing and Difference.* Chicago, IL: University of Chicago Press.

Doyle, J. (2000) *New Community or New Slavery? The Emotional Division of Labour.* London: The Works Foundation.

Ebbeck, M. and Waniganayake, M. (2003) *Early Childhood Professionals: Leading Today and Tomorrow.* Marrickville, NSW: Elsevier.

Eisenberg, E. and Rafanello, D. (1998) 'Accreditation facilitation: a study of one project's success', *Young Children,* 53(5): 44–8.

Engel, G.I. (1977) 'The need for a new medical model: a challenge for biomedicine', *Science,* 196(4286): 129–36.

Engeström, Y. (1999) 'Expansive visibilization of work: an activity-theoretical perspective', *Computer Supported Co-operative Work,* 8: 63–93.

Engeström, Y., Engestrñm, R. and Vahaaho, T. (1999) 'When the centre does not hold: the importance of knotworking', in S. Chaklin, M. Hedegaard and U.J. Jensen (eds) *Activity Theory and Social Practice.* Aarhus: Aarhus University Press.

Engle, P., Black, M.M., Behrman, J.R., Cabral de Mello, M., Gertler, P.J., Kapiri, L., Martorell, R. and Young, M.E. (2007) 'Strategies to avoid the loss of developmental potential in more than 200 million children in the developing world', *The Lancet,* 369, 229–42.

European Convention (2000) *Explanation by the Convention. The Charter of Fundamental Rights of the European Union* (2000/C 364/01). Available at: www.europarl.eu.int/charter.

Evans, L., Packwood, A., Neill, S.R.St.J. and Campbell R.J. (1994) *The Meaning of Infant Teachers' Work.* London: Routledge.

Evetts, J. (1994) 'The new headteacher: the changing work culture of secondary headship', *School Organisation,* 14(1): 37–47.

Finlayson, J.G. (2005) *Habermas: A Very Short Introduction.* Oxford: Oxford University Press.

Firestone, W.A. and Riehl, C. (eds) (2005) *A New Agenda: Directions for Research on Educational Leadership.* New York: Teachers College Press.

Fisher, P. and Owen, J. (2008) 'Empowering interventions in health and social care: Recognition through ecologies of practice', *Social Science and Medicine,* 67: 2063–71.

Flanagan, J.C. (1954) 'The critical incident technique', Psychological Bulletin, 51(4): 327–58.

Flyvbjerg, B. (1998) 'Habermas and Foucault: thinkers for civil society?', *British Journal of Sociology,* 29(2): 210–33.

Foucault, M. (1980) *Power/Knowledge: Selected Interviews and Other Writings 1972–1977*. New York: Pantheon.

Foucault, M. (1994) 'Truth and power', in J.D. Faubion (ed.), *Power: Essential Works of Foucault: 1954–1984* . London: Penguin. pp. 111–33.

Foucault, M. (1997) *Ethics: Essential Works of Foucault 1954–1984*. Vol. 1. Ed. P. Rabinow. Harmondsworth: Penguin.

Foucault, M. (1998) *Aesthetics, Method and Epistemology: Essential Works of Foucault 1954–1984*. Vol. 2. Ed. P. Rabinow. Harmondsworth: Penguin.

Freeman, N.K. and Brown, M.H. (2000) 'Evaluating the child care director: the collaborative professional assessment process', *Young Children*, 55(5): 20–6.

Freire, P. (2006) *Pedagogy of the Oppressed*. 30th anniversity edition. Trans M.B. Ramos. London: Continuum .

Fullan, M. (2001) *Leading in a Culture of Change*. San Francisco, CA: Jossey-Bass.

Gallwey, T. (1974) *The Inner Game of Tennis*. San Francisco, CA: Jossey-Bass.

Gardner, H. (1995) *Leading Minds. An Anatomy of Leadership*. London: HarperCollins.

Giddens, A. (1984) *The Constitution of Society*. Cambridge: Polity Press.

Giddens, A. (1990) *The Consequences of Modernity*. Cambridge: Polity Press.

Giddens, A. (1991) *Modernity and Self-Identity*. Cambridge: Polity Press.

Gillies, G. (2005) 'Meeting parents' needs? Discourses of support and inclusion in family policy', *Critical Social Policy*, 25(70): 70–90.

Gilligan, C. (1982) *In a Different Voice: Psychological Theory and Women's Development*. Cambridge, MA: Harvard University Press.

Glass, N. (2006) 'Sure Start: where did it come from; where is it going?', *Journal of Children's Services*, 1(1): 51–7.

Goleman, D. (2000) 'Leadership that gets results', *Harvard Business Review*, March: 63–70.

Gronn, P.C. (1993) 'Psychobiography on the couch: character, biography and the comparative study of leaders', *Journal of Applied Behavioural Science*, 29(3): 343–58.

Gronn, P.C. (1994) 'Educational administration's Weber', *Educational Management and Administration*, 22(4): 224–31.

Gronn, P.C. (2000) 'A realistic view of leadership', *The Practising Administrator*, 22(1): 24–7.

Gronn, P.C. (2002) 'Distributed leadership', in K. Leithwood, P. Hallinger, K. Seashore-Louis, G. Furman-Brown, P. Gronn, W. Mulford and K. Riley (eds), *Second International Handbook of Educational Leadership and Administration*. Dordrecht: Kluwer.

Gronn, P.C. and Ribbins, P. (1996) 'Leaders in context: postpositivist approaches to understanding educational leadership', *Educational Administration Quarterly*, 32(3): 452–73.

Hall, V. (1996) *Dancing on the Ceiling: A Study of Women Managers in Education*. London: Paul Chapman Publishing.

Hallinger, P. and Heck, R. H. (1998) 'Exploring the principal's contribution to school effectiveness: 1980–1995', *School Effectiveness and School Improvement*, 9: 157–91.

Handy, C. (1999) *Understanding Organizations. Fourth Edition*. London: Penguin.

Hargreaves, A. (1994) *Changing Teachers, Changing Times*. London: Cassell.

Harris, A. (2004) 'Leading or misleading? Distributed leadership and school improvement', *Journal of Curriculum Studies*, 37(3): 255–65.

Harris, A. (2005) *Crossing Boundaries and Breaking Boundaries: Distributing Leadership in Schools*. Pamphlet published by the Specialist Schools Trust. Available at: www.sst-inet.net.

Harris, A., Day, C., Hadfield, M., Hopkins, D., Hargreaves, A. and Chapman, C. (2002)

Effective Leadership for School Improvement. London: Routledge.

Harris, F. (2002) *The First Implementation of the Sure Start Language Measure*. London: Department of Language and Communication Science, City University.

Hatherley, A. and Lee, W. (2003) 'Voices of early childhood leadership', *New Zealand Journal of Educational Leadership*, 18: 91–100.

Hayden, J. (1996) *Management in Early Childhood Services*. Wentworth Falls, NSW: Social Sciences Press.

Hayden, J. (1997) 'Directors of early childhood services: experience, preparedness and selection', *Australian Research in Early Childhood*, 8(1): 49–67.

Heifetz, R. (1994) *Leadership without Easy Answers*. Cambridge, MA: Harvard University Press.

Her Majesty's Treasury (HMT) (2004) *Choice for Parents, the Best Start for Children: A Ten-Year Strategy for Childcare*. London: The Stationery Office.

Hoyle, L. (2004) 'From sycophant to saboteur – responses to organisational change', in C. Huffington, D. Armstrong, W. Halton, L. Hoyle and J. Pooley (eds), *Working Below the Surface: The Emotional Life of Contemporary Organizations*. London: Karnac. pp. 87–106.

Huffington, C. (2004a) Introduction, in C. Huffington, D. Armstrong, W. Halton, L. Hoyle and J. Pooley (eds) *Working Below the Surface. The Emotional Life of Organizations*. London: Karnac.

Huffington, C. (2004b) 'What women leaders can tell us', in C. Huffington, D. Armstrong, W. Halton, L. Hoyle and J. Pooley (eds), *Working Below the Surface: The Emotional Life of Contemporary Organizations*. London: Karnac. pp. 49–66.

Hujala, E. and Puroila, A.-M. (eds) (1998) *Towards Understanding Leadership in Early Childhood Context: Cross-cultural Perspectives*. Oulu, Finland: Oulu University Press.

Hunter, M. and Egan, K. (1995) *Narrative in Teaching, Learning and Research*. New York: Teachers College Press, Columbia University.

Huxham, C. and Vangen, S. (2000) 'Leadership in the shaping and implementation of collaborative agendas: how things happen in a (not quite) joined up world', *Academy of Management Journal*, 6: 1159–75.

Huxham, C. and Vangen, S. (2005) *Managing to Collaborate. The Theory and Practice of Collaborative Advantage*. London: Routledge.

Jarvis, P. (2004) 'Globalisation, the learning society and comparative education', in S.J. Ball (ed.), *The RoutledgeFalmer Reader in Sociology of Education*. London: RoutledgeFalmer.

Johnson, S., Dunn, K. and Coldron, J. (2005) *Mapping Qualifications and Training for the Children and Young People's Workforce. Short Report 6*. Research Report. Sheffield: Sheffield Hallam University.

Jones, C. and Pound, L. (2008) *Leadership and Management in the Early Years*. Maidenhead: Open University Press.

Kagan, S. and Bowman, B. (1997) 'Leadership in early care and education: issues and challenges', in S. Kagan and B. Bowman (eds), *Leadership in Early Care and Education*. Washington, DC: National Association for the Education of Young Children. pp. 3–8.

Kagan, S.L. and Hallmark, L.G. (2001) 'Cultivating leadership in early care and education', *Child Care Information Exchange*, 140: 7–11.

Kincheloe, J.L. and McLauren, P. (2005) 'Rethinking critical theory and qualitative research', in N.K. Denzin and Y.S. Lincoln (eds), *The Sage Handbook of Qualitative Research*. 3rd edn. Thousand Oaks, CA, London and New Delhi: Sage. pp. 303–42.

Kirkpatrick, D.L. (1967) 'Evaluation of training', in R. Craig and L. Bittel (eds), *Training and Development Handbook*. New York: McGraw-Hill. pp. 87–112.

Knowles, M.S. (1975) *Self-Directed Learning: A Guide for Learners and Teachers.* Chicago, IL: Follett.

Knowles, M.S. (1990) *The Adult Learner: A Neglected Species.* Houston, TX: Gulf.

Kolb, D.A. (1984) *Experiential Learning.* Englewood Cliffs, NJ: Prentice-Hall.

Kolb, D.A. and Fry, R. (1975) 'Towards an applied theory of experiential learning', in C. Cooper (ed.), *Theories of Group Processes.* London: John Wiley.

Kontos, S. and Fiene, R. (1989) 'Child care quality: compliance with regulations and children's development: the Pennsylvania study', in D. Philips (ed.), *Quality in Child Care: What Does Research Tell Us?* Washington, DC: National Association for the Education of Young Children.

Kunesh, L.G. and Farley, J. (1993) *Collaboration: The Prerequisite for School Readiness and Success.* 356906. Arlington, VA: ERIC.

Laing and Buisson (2010) *Children's Nurseries UK Market Report 2010.* London: Laing and Buisson.

Laming, Lord (2003) *The Victoria Climbié Inquiry Report.* (The Laming Report.) London: Her Majesty's Stationery Office.

Lawrence, W.G. and Robinson, P. (1975) 'An innovation and its implementation: issues of evaluation', Tavistock Institute of Human Relations: document no. CASR 1069 (unpublished). Cited in Miller, E. (1993) *From Dependency to Autonomy: Studies in Organization and Change.* London: Free Association Books.

Leithwood, K. and Jantzi, D. (2005) 'A review of transformational school leadership research 1996–2005', *Leadership and Policy in Schools,* 4(3): 177–99.

Leithwood, K. and Levin, B. (2004) *Approaches to the Evaluation of Leadership Programmes and Leadership Effects.* London: Department for Education and Skills.

Leithwood, K. and Louis, K.S. (eds) (1998) *Organizational Learning in Schools.* Lisse: Swets and Zeitlinger.

Leithwood, K., Seashore-Louis, L., Anderson, S. and Wahlstrom K. (2004) *How Leadership Influences Student Learning.* New York: Wallace Foundation.

Lewin, K. (1946) 'Action research and minority problems', *Journal of Social Issues,* 2: 34–46.

Lewin, K. (1952) *Field Theory in Social Science.* London: Tavistock Publications.

Liabo, K., Newman, T., Stephens, J. and Lowe, K. (2001) *A Review of Key Worker Systems for Disabled Children and the Development of Information Guides for Parents, Children and Professionals.* Cardiff: Wales Office of R and D for Health and Social Work.

Lincoln, Y.S. and Guba, E.G. (1985) *Naturalistic Inquiry.* Thousand Oaks, CA: Sage.

Locke, M. (2003) 'Leadership: starting at the top', in C. Pearce and J. Conger (eds), *Shared Leadership: Reframing the Hows and Whys of Leadership.* Thousand Oaks, CA: Sage. pp. 271–84.

MacNaughton, G. (2005) *Doing Foucault in Early Childhood Studies. Applying Poststructural Ideas.* London: Routledge.

MacNaughton, G. and Hughes, P. (2009) *Doing Action Research in Early Childhood Studies. A Step by Step Guide.* Maidenhead: Open University Press.

Magrab, P., Evans, P. and Hurrell, P. (1997) 'Integrated services for children and youth at risk: an international study of multidisciplinary training', *Journal of Interprofessional Care,* 11(1): 99–108.

Mann, K.V., Viscount, P.W., Cogdon, A., Davidson, K., Langille, D.B. and Maccara, M.E. (1996) 'Multidisciplinary learning in continuing professional education: the Heart Health Nova Scotia experience', *Journal of Continuing Education in the Health Profession,* 16: 50–60.

Mant, A. (1997) *Intelligent Leadership.* St Leonards, NSW: Allen & Unwin.

Marzano, R.J., Waters, T. and McNulty, B. (2005) *School Leadership that Works: From Research to Results.* Aurora, CO: ASCD and McREL.

McCullogh, M. (2007) 'Integrating children's services: the case for child protection', in I. Siraj-Blatchford, K. Clarke and M. Needham (eds), *The Team Around the Child: Multi-Agency Working in the Early Years.* Stoke-on-Trent: Trentham Books.

McGrath, J. Thillet, M. and Van Cleave, L. (2007) 'Parent delivered infant massage: are we truly ready for implementation?', *Newborn and Nursing Infant Reviews,* 7(1): 39–46.

McNiff, J. and Whitehead, J. (2006) *All You Need to Know About Action Research.* London: Sage.

Melhuish, E., Belsky, J. and Leyland, A. (2005) *Variation in Sure Start Local Programmes' Effectiveness: Early Preliminary Findings. Report of the National Evaluation of Sure Start (NESS) Programme Variability* Study. London: DfES, HMSO.

Milbourne, L. (2005) 'Children, families and inter-agency work: experiences of partnership work in primary education settings', *British Educational Research Journal,* 31(6): 675–96.

Miles, M. and Hubernan, A. (1994) *Qualitative Data Analysis.* London: Sage.

Miller, E.J. and Rice, A.K. (1967) *Systems of Organization: Task and Sentient Systems and their Boundary Control.* London: Tavistock Publications.

Mitchell, A. (1989) 'Kindergarten groups that are good for children and for parents', *Principal,* 68(5): 17–19.

Mitchell, A. and Serranen, P. (2000) *Leadership for Change in the Primary Grades to Improve Student Achievement: A Report on the Success for All Children.* Principals' Academy, Clayton, MO: Danforth Foundation.

Morgan, G. (1997) *Images or Organisation,* 2nd edn. London: Sage.

Moriarty, V. (2002) 'Early years professionals and parents: challenging the dominant discourse?', in V. Nivala and E. Hujala (eds), *Leadership in Early Childhood Education.* Oulu, Finland: University of Oulu.

Moyles, J. (2006) *Effective Leadership and Management in the Early Years.* Maidenhead: Open University Press.

Muijs, D., Aubrey, C., Harris, A., Briggs, M. (2004) 'How do they manage? Research on leadership in early childhood', *Journal of Early Childhood Research,* 2(2): 157–69.

Nivala, V. (2002) 'Leadership in general, leadership in theory', in V. Nivala. and E. Hujala (eds), *Leadership in Early Childhood Education: Cross-cultural Perspectives.* Oulu, Finland: Oulu University Press. pp. 13–24.

O'Higgins, M., St James Roberts, I. and Glover, V. (2008) 'Postnatal depression and mother and infant outcomes after infant massage', *Journal of Affective Disorders,* 109, 189–92.

Oberhuemer, P., Schreyer, I. and Neuman, M.J. (eds) (2010) *Professionals in Early Childhood Education and Care Systems. European Profiles and Perspectives.* Opladen and Farmington Hill, MI: Barbara Budrich.

Obholzer, A. with Miller, S. (2004) 'Leadership, followership and facilitating the creative workplace', in C. Huffington, D. Armstrong, W. Halton, L. Hoyle and J. Pooley (eds), *Working Below the Surface: The Emotional Life of Contemporary Organizations.* London: Karnac. pp. 33–48.

Office for Standards in Education (OFSTED) (2009) *The Annual Report of HM Chief Inspector 2008–9 Quality and Standards in Care, Early Education, Schools, Colleges, Adult Learning and Skills, and Children's Services.* London: Ofsted.

Organisation for Economic Co-operation and Development (OECD) (2006) *Starting Strong II. Early Childhood Education and Care.* Paris: OECD.

Osgood, J. (2004) 'Time to get down to business? The response of early years practitioners to entrepreneurial approaches to professionalism', *Journal of Early Childhood Research*, 2(1): 5–24.

Owen, S. and Haynes, G. (2010) 'Training and workforce issues in the early years', in G. Pugh and B. Duffy, (eds), *Contemporary Issues in the Early Years*. 5th edn. London: Sage. pp.195–208.

Øvretveit, J. (1990) *Co-operation in Primary Health Care*. Uxbridge: Brunel Institute of Organization and Social Studies.

Øvretveit, J. (1996) 'Five ways to describe a multidisciplinary team', *Journal of Interprofessional Care*, 10(2): 163–72.

Øvretveit, J., Mathias, P. and Thompson, T. (1997) *Interprofessional Working for Health and Social Care*. London: Macmillan.

Penn, H. (2007) 'Childcare market management: how the United Kingdom government has reshaped its role in developing early childhood education and care', *Contemporary Issues in Early Childhood*, 8(3): 192–207.

Philips, D., Scar, P. and McCartney, K. (1987) 'Child care quality and children's social development', *Developmental Psychology*, 23: 537–43.

Pietroni, P.C. (1992) 'Towards reflective practice – languages of health and social care', *Journal of Interprofessional Care*, 6(1): 7–16.

Poster, M. and Neugebauer, R. (1998) 'How experienced directors have developed their skills', *Child Care Information Exchange*, 121: 91–3.

PricewaterhouseCoopers (2006) *Government and Public Sector DfES Children's Services: The Childcare Market*. London: PricewaterhouseCoopers.

Qualifications and Curriculum Authority (QCA) (2000) *Curriculum Guidance for the Foundation Stage*. London: QCA.

Qualifications and Curriculum Authority (QCA) (2001) *National Framework of Qualifications*. London: QCA.

Ramey, C.T. and Ramey, S.L. (1998) 'Early intervention and early experience', *American Psychologist*, 53(2): 109–20.

Ramey, S.L., Ramey, C.T., Philips, M.M., Lanzi, R.G., Brezausek, C., Katholi, C.R., Snyders, S. and Lawrence, F.L. (2000) *Head Start Children's Entry into Public School: A Report on the National Head Start/Public School Early Childhood Transition Demonstration Study*. Birmingham, AL: Curtan International Research Centre.

Reason, P. (1994) *Participation in Human Inquiry*. London: Sage.

Reason, P. and Bradley, H. (2007) *Handbook of Action Research* 2nd edn. London: Sage.

Reay, D. and Ball, S. (2000) 'Essentials of female management: women's ways of working in the education market place', *Educational Management and Administration*, 28(2): 145–59.

Rice, A.K. (1958) *Productivity and Social Organisation*. New York and London: Garland.

Richardson, L. (2002) 'Writing: a method of inquiry', in N.K. Denzin and Y.S. Lincoln (eds), *Handbook of Qualitative Research*. 2nd edn. Thousand Oaks, CA: Sage. pp. 923–48.

Robinson, V.M. (2006) 'Putting education back into educational leadership', *Leading and Managing*, 12(1): 62–75.

Rodd, J. (1996) 'Towards a typology of leadership for the early childhood professional of the 21st century', *Early Childhood Development and Care*, 120: 119–26.

Rodd, J. (1997) 'Learning to be leaders: perceptions of early childhood professionals about leadership roles and responsibilities', *Early Years*, 18(1): 40–6.

Rodd, J. (1999) *Leadership in Early Childhood*. Buckingham: Open University Press.

Rodd, J. (2006) *Leadership in Early Childhood: The Pathway to Professionalism*. Buckingham: Open University Press.

Rogoff, B. (1984) 'Introduction: thinking in social context', in B. Rogoff and J. Lave (eds), *Everyday Cognition: Its Development in Social Context*. Cambridge, MA: Harvard University Press. pp. 1–8.

Rost, J.C. (1991) *Leadership in the Twenty-First Century*. New York: Praeger.

Rost, J.C. (1993) 'Leadership development in the new millennium', *The Journal of Leadership Studies*, 1(1): 92–110.

Sanders, B. (2004) 'Inter-agency and multidisciplinary working', in T. Maynard and N. Thomas (eds), *An Introduction to Early Childhood Studies*. London: Sage.

Schön, D. (1971) *Beyond the Stable State*. New York: Random House.

Schön, D. (1983) *The Reflective Practitioner: How Professionals Think in Action*. New York: Basic Books.

Schön, D. (1987) *Educating the Reflective Practitioner*. San Francisco, CA: Jossey-Bass.

Schön, D. (ed.) (1991) *The Reflective Turn: Case Studies in and on Educational Practice*. New York: Teachers College Press.

Schweinhart, L.J. (2005) 'The High/Scope Preschool Study at Age 40'. Available at: www.highscope.org/Research/PerryProject/perrymain.htm.

Scrivens, C. (2002) 'Constructions of leadership: does gender make a difference? Perspectives from an English-speaking country', in V. Nivala and E. Hujala (eds), *Leadership in Early Childhood Education: Cross-cultural Perspectives*. Oulu, Finland: Oulu University Press.

Shakeshaft, C. (1989) *Women in Educational Admini*stration. Beverly Hills, CA: Sage.

Silins, H. and Mulford, B. (2002) 'Leadership and school results', in K. Leithwood (ed.), *The Second International Handbook of Educational Leadership and Administration*. Norwell, MA: Kluwer Academic. pp. 561–612.

Simmons, H. and Usher, R. (eds) (2000) *Situated Ethics in Educational Research*. London: RoutledgeFalmer.

Singh, M., Kenway, J. and Apple, M. (2005) Globalizing education: Perspectives from above and below', in M.W. Apple, J. Kenway and M. Singh (eds), *Globalizing Education: Policies: Pedagogies and Politics*. New York: Peter Lang. pp. 1–29.

Siraj-Blatchford, I. and Manni, L. (2006) *Effective Leadership in the Early Years Sector (ELEYS) Study*. London: General Teaching Council for England.

Sloper, P. (2004) 'Facilitators and barriers for co-ordinated multi-agency services', *Child: Care, Health and Development*, 30(6): 571–80.

Social Exclusion Unit (SEU) (1998) *Truancy and School Exclusion*. London: Cabinet Office.

Social Exclusion Unit (SEU) (2001a) *Preventing Social Exclusion*. London: Cabinet Office.

Social Exclusion Unit (SEU) (2001b) *A New Commitment to Neighbourhood Renewal*. London: Cabinet office.

Spillane, J., Halverson, R. and Diamond, J.B. (2001) 'Investigating school leadership practice: a distributed perspective', *Educational Researcher*, 30(3): 23–8.

Stipek, D. and Ogana, T. (2000) *Early Childhood Education*. Los Angeles, CA: UCLA, Centre for Healthier Children, Families and Communities.

Strauss, A. and Corbin, J. (1990) *Basics of Qualitative Research. Grounded Theory, Procedures and Techniques*. London: Sage.

Sumsion, J. (2006) 'The corporatization of Australian childcare: towards an ethical audit and research agenda', *Journal of Early Childhood Research*, 4(2): 99–120.

Sylva, K., Melhuish, E. and Sammons, P., Siraj-Blatchford, I. and Taggart, B. (2004) *The Effective Provision of Pre-school Education (EPPE): Technical Paper 12 – The Final Report: Effective Pre-school Education*. London: DfES and Institute of Education, University of London.

Taylor, M. (1979) *Coverdale on Management*. London: Heinemann.

Teddlie, C. and Reynolds, D. (2000) 'School effectiveness processes', in C. Teddlie and D. Reynolds (eds), *The International Handbook of School Effectiveness Research*. London: Routledge. pp. 14–28.

Thomson, B. (2006) *Growing People. Learning and Developing from Day to Day Experience*. Oxford: Chandos.

Tomlinson, K. (2003) *Effective Interagency Working: A Review of the Literature and Examples for Practice*. Slough: NFER.

Underdown, A., Barlow, J. and Stewart-Brown, S. (2010) 'Tactile stimulation in physically healthy infants: results of a systematic review', *Journal of Reproductive and Infant Psychology*, 11: 11–29.

Underdown, A. Barlow, J., Chung V. and Stewart-Brown, S. (2006) 'Massage intervention for promoting mental and physical health in infants aged under six months', *Cochrane Database of Systematic Reviews*, issue 4.

United Nations General Assembly (1989) *Adoption of a Convention on the Rights of a Child* (UN Doc. A/Res/44/25). New York: UN General Assembly.

Van Velzen, W., Miles, M., Elholm, M., Hameyer, U. and Robin, D. (1985) *Making School Improvement Work*. Leuven: ACCO.

Vincent, C. (1996) *Parents and Teachers: Power and Participation*. London: Falmer Press.

Von Bertalanffy, L. (1971) *General Systems Theory*. London: Penguin.

Waller, T. (2006) '"Don't come too close to my octopus tree": recording and evaluating young children's perspectives of outdoor learning', *Children, Youth and Environments*, 16(2): 75–104.

Waniganayake, M. (2000) 'Leadership in the early years: new directions in research', keynote presentation to professional development conference, Melbourne, January.

Waniganayake, M. and Hujala, E. (2001) 'Leadership for a new century: what do early childhood leaders do?' Critical reflections from Australia and Finland, paper presented to Association for Childhood Education International Annual Conference, Toronto, Canada, April.

Waniganayake, M., Morda, R. and Kapsalakis, A. (2000) 'Leadership in childcare: is it just another job?', *Australian Journal of Early Childhood*, 25(1): 3–19.

Watson, D., Townsley, R. and Abbott, D. (2002) 'Exploring multi-agency working in services to disabled children with complex healthcare needs and their families', *Journal of Clinical Nursing*, 11: 367–75.

Watson, D., Townsley, R., Abbott, D. and Latham, P. (2000) *Working Together? Multi-Agency Working in Services for Disabled Children with Complex Health Care Needs and their Families: A Literature Review*. Birmingham: The Handsel Trust.

Whalley, M., Whitaker, P., Fletcher, C., Thorpe, S., John, K. and Leisten, R. (2004) *Programme Leaders' Guide: National Professional Qualification in Integrated Centre Leadership*. Nottingham: National College of School Leadership.

Whelan, S. (1993) 'Involving Staff', *Child Care Information Exchange*, 135: pp.8–10.

Whitty, G. (1997) 'Marketization, the state and the re-formation of the teaching profession', in A.H. Halsey, H. Lauder, P. Brown and A.S. Wells (eds), *Education, Cultures, Economy and Society*. Oxford: Oxford University Press.

Wilcock, P., Campion-Smith, C. and Elston, S. (2003) *Practice Professional Development Planning: A Guide for Primary Care*. Abingdon: Radcliffe Medical.

INDEX